Love, Lust, and Rebellion

Reinhold Grimm

Love, Lust, and Rebellion

New Approaches to Georg Büchner

The University of Wisconsin Press

Published 1985

The University of Wisconsin Press
114 North Murray Street
Madison, Wisconsin 53715

The University of Wisconsin Press, Ltd.
1 Gower Street
London WC1E 6HA, England

First printing

Printed in the United States of America

For LC CIP information see the colophon

ISBN 0-299-09860-5

To Annelie

Contents

Abbreviations ix

Acknowledgments xi

Introduction: Georg Büchner, Contemporary 3

Part 1

1 Büchner's Paradox: The Modern Concept
   of Revolt 35

2 "Cœur" and "Carreau": Love in the Life and Works
   of Büchner 79

Part 2

3 Culmination, Conclusions, and a New Beginning:
   The Present State of Büchner Reception and
   Research 115

Part 3

4 *Danton's Death*: A "Counterconception" to Goethe's
   Egmont? 139

5 A Dirge That Is a Paean: Paradox Once More 176

Postface 201

Notes 203

Index 261

Abbreviations

Benn   Maurice B. Benn, *The Drama of Revolt: A Critical Study of Georg Büchner* (Cambridge: Cambridge University Press, 1976).

CCW   Georg Büchner, *The Complete Collected Works*, translations and commentary by Henry J. Schmidt (New York: Avon Books, 1977).

GB I/II *Georg Büchner I/II*, edited by Heinz Ludwig Arnold (München: Edition Text + Kritik, 1979).

GB III   *Georg Büchner III*, edited by Heinz Ludwig Arnold (München: Edition Text + Kritik, 1981).

HA   Georg Büchner, *Sämtliche Werke und Briefe*. Historisch-kritische Ausgabe mit Kommentar, edited by Werner R. Lehmann (Hamburg: Christian Wegner Verlag [and, subsequently, München: Carl Hanser Verlag], 1967–).

Martens *Georg Büchner*, edited by Wolfgang Martens (Darmstadt: Wissenschaftliche Buchgesellschaft, 1965).

Y/T   *Yale/Theatre* 3/3 (Winter 1972) (Georg Büchner issue).

Acknowledgments

The present study has occupied me, with lengthy and numerous interruptions, for about a decade. Sizable portions of it have been given as talks, in changing form and on different occasions, both in this country and abroad; earlier versions of its main chapters have appeared, in English and/or in German, in two European journals, in the newly founded yearbook devoted to Büchner, and in a volume by various hands published in commemoration of a friend and colleague. To wit: "Georg Büchner and the Modern Concept of Revolt," *Studi tedeschi* (Napoli), 21/2 (1978 [*recte* 1979]): 7–66, also in a revised German version, "Georg Büchner und der moderne Begriff der Revolte," *Georg Büchner Jahrbuch* 1 (1981 [*recte* 1982]): 22–67; "Cœur und Carreau: Über die Liebe bei Georg Büchner," in *Georg Büchner I/II*, edited by Heinz Ludwig Arnold (Text + Kritik: München, 1979; 2d ed. 1982), pp. 299–326; "Abschluß und Neubeginn: Vorläufiges zur Büchner-Rezeption und zur Büchner-Forschung heute," *Georg Büchner Jahrbuch* 2 (1982 [*recte* 1983]): 21–40; "*Dantons Tod*—Ein Gegenentwurf zu Goethes *Egmont?*," *Germanisch-Romanische Monatsschrift*, n.f. 33 (1983 [*recte* 1984]): 424–57; "Fragments of a Dirge: On Georg Büchner, Gottfried Benn, and Others," in *Erkennen und Deuten: Essays zur Literatur und Literaturtheorie Edgar Lohner in memoriam*, edited by Martha Woodmansee and Walter F. W. Lohnes in cooperation with many specialists (Erich Schmidt: Berlin, 1983), pp. 143–71. My thanks for granting permission to rework and reprint these texts are due to the publisher of Erich Schmidt Verlag, Dr. Ellinor Kahleyss (Berlin), as well as to the editors, especially Heinz Ludwig Arnold (Munich), Dr. Thomas Michael Mayer (Marburg), Prof. Dr. Conrad Wiedemann (Gießen), and Prof. Dr. Luciano Zagari (Naples). Unless otherwise indicated, all translations are mine. All English quotations from Büchner's works and letters are from Georg Büchner, *The Complete Collected Works,* translated and edited by Henry J. Schmidt (Avon Books, New York) with only occasional minor adjustments. Permission to use them is gratefully acknowledged. I also wish to thank my research assistant, Yuki Matsuyoshi, for preparing the index; my editors, Betty Steinberg and Jack Kirshbaum, for many excellent suggestions; and, in particular, my former student and collaborator who now is himself a teacher in the field and a Büchner scholar, Dr. Bruce Armstrong, for providing the basic renditions of those of my essays which were originally written in German.

Love, Lust, and Rebellion

Introduction

Georg Büchner, Contemporary

> *I can think of no greater loss to world*
> *drama, indeed to world literature,*
> *than that untimely decease.*
> —John Simon

1

Germany, 1835. A student of philosophy, medicine, and science, twenty-one years of age, founder of a conspiratorial society that has recently been denounced to the authorities and co-author of a revolutionary pamphlet several of whose distributors have already been arrested, is hiding in his parental home in the city of Darmstadt, the capital of the Grand Duchy of Hesse. A warrant has been issued against him; at any moment, the police may knock at the door, search the house, and arrest him, too. He has been served with a summons—though he was, as it turned out, merely asked to testify.

The outlaw is not idle. He spends almost all day and night upstairs in the laboratory of his father, a physician and a law-abiding, if liberal, state official. But, though all kinds of instruments can be observed in the room, as well as a heavy tome sitting on the dissecting table, the young medical man and scientist-to-be is neither conducting experiments nor cramming up on his anatomy; rather, he is working, in feverish haste and excitement, on the draft of a play on revolution. That learned scientific volume has been placed there so handily and conspicuously for a very different, very unprofessional, purpose: to cover up the manuscript of the play whenever the father, with whom the son is decidedly at odds, appears. Less conspicuous though equally handy are a few other items: among them a ladder outside the

3

window, leaning, as if by accident, against the wall, but convenient enough to enable the student to escape through the backyard and the adjacent orchards should the ducal henchmen finally approach. His younger brother, whom he has taken into his confidence, is on permanent guard, watching the street and the front entrance; he will try to sound a warning in due time.

It was under such circumstances that Georg Büchner—with the Hessian police force as his Muse, as he jested in retrospect[1]—composed his "magnificent" revolutionary drama, *Dantons Tod (Danton's Death)*.[2] When, after about five weeks of frantic scribbling, it was completed, he had created what has been called "the most amazing first play ever written."[3] Since he was in dire need of cash for his intended flight across the French border, he sent off the manuscript immediately, submitting it to one of the progressive German intellectuals of the period, the author, critic, and editor, Karl Gutzkow. But "submitting" is perhaps not the right term. Gutzkow was virtually held up at gunpoint, as it were; this, and nothing else, is the meaning of Büchner's famous phrase in his accompanying letter: "You will . . . not be astonished, therefore, when I throw open your door, step into your room, point a manuscript at your chest, and demand alms from you." Büchner went on to "beseech" Gutzkow to read the text "as quickly as possible" and to recommend it, if his conscience as a critic should permit, to the Frankfurt bookseller and publisher, Sauerländer, "and to answer at once."[4]

The literary holdup at manuscript-point ("la bourse ou la vie!")[5] proved to be successful. Gutzkow read the play on the spot, praised it enthusiastically, and promised to see to its publication; and *Danton's Death*, albeit in a bowdlerized version, came out the very same year, both in Sauerländer's journal, *Phönix*, and as a book . . .

France, 1836. The young writer and revolutionary is pursuing his studies in safety, if in exile, at the University of Strasbourg. From the reports of friends and acquaintances there, he learns of the fate of the hapless poet and playwright Jakob Michael Reinhold Lenz, who had gone to a remote valley of the Vosges— the mountainous region southwest of the old Alsatian town—in January 1778, to stay with the village pastor, Jean-Frédéric Oberlin, and to be treated for an incipient mental disorder. Along with Goethe and, later on, Schiller, Lenz (1751–92) was without doubt the most gifted and innovative dramatist of the Storm and Stress movement, the first outgrowth of European Romanticism on German soil; indeed, he had been an eager companion and even rival of Goethe's during the 1770s. Toward the end of the decade, however, after many disappointments and hardships, he had begun to show signs of insanity, and was persuaded to seek the help of Oberlin. That renowned healer, unfortunately, could not prevent the ultimate assault of the illness; he failed to cure his patient, but he did record Lenz's behavior in a diary.

These diary entries are made available to the author of *Danton's Death*. Of course, Büchner is already familiar with at least some of his fellow dramatist's writings, especially Lenz's seminal plays, *Der Hofmeister* (*The Private Tutor*) and *Die Soldaten* (*The Soldiers*), as well as with Lenz's theoretical tract, "Anmerkungen übers Theater" ("Notes on the Theater"); also, Büchner knows "every peak and every valley" in the Vosges mountains, which he loves "like a mother," as he reports in his letters.[6] Small wonder that he is both moved and fascinated by the material entrusted to him. His scientific interests no less than his poetic fancy are roused by the triple impact of a kindred spirit's work, the disintegration of a congenial mind, and the majesty of a landscape so dear to him. And straightaway, taking up his pen, the refugee produces a second masterpiece: his sole novella, *Lenz*. Among other things, this amazing tale of barely twenty-odd pages intimately evokes the stages of the deterioration of a troubled psyche amid the grandiose and gloomy, or beautiful and tender, scenes of a nature either confirming or contradicting them. Gutzkow (again the first to bring out the text, though after the author's death) was surely justified in exclaiming: "Welche Naturschilderungen; welche Seelenmalerei!"[7]

Indeed, what depictions of nature, what a portrayal of a soul! Here is Büchner's Lenz on his way through the wintry mountains:

> The peaks and high slopes covered with snow, gray rock down into the valleys, green fields, boulders, and pine trees. It was cold and damp, water trickled down the rocks and leaped over the path. Pine branches hung down heav-

ily in the moist air. Gray clouds moved across the sky, but everything so dense, and then the fog steamed up, oppressive and damp, trailing through the bushes, so sluggish, so shapeless. He went on indifferently, the path did not matter to him, up or down. He felt no fatigue, but at times he was irritated that he could not walk on his head. At first he felt tension in his chest when stones jumped away, when the gray forest shivered beneath him, when at times the fog enveloped these shapes or partly revealed the powerful branches; he felt an urge, he searched for something, as though for lost dreams, but he found nothing. Everything seemed so small to him, so close, so wet, he would have liked to set the earth behind the stove, he could not understand why he needed so much time to climb down a steep slope, to reach a distant point; he felt he should be able to cover any distance in a few steps. Only at times when the storm hurled the clouds into the valley, and they steamed up through the forest, and voices awakened on the rocks, often like thunder echoing in the distance and then raging up violently, as if they wanted to celebrate the earth in their wild rejoicing, and the clouds galloped along like wild neighing horses, and sunshine pierced through them and emerged and drew its flashing sword along the snowy slopes, so that a bright, blinding light cut across the peaks down into the valleys; or when the storm forced the clouds downward and tore a light blue sea into them, and then the wind died down, humming up like a lullaby and chiming bells from deep within the ravines, from the tops of the pine trees, and when a soft red glow arose against the deep blue, and tiny clouds fled by on silver wings, and all the mountain peaks, sharp and firm, gleamed and flashed far across the countryside: then pain tore through his chest, he stood panting, his body bent forward, eyes and mouth wide open, he thought he must draw the storm into himself, contain all within him, he stretched out and lay over the earth, he burrowed into the cosmos, it was a pleasure that hurt him; or he stood still and rested his head on the moss and half-closed his eyes, and then it all moved far away from him, the earth receded below him, it became small like a wandering star and plunged into a rushing river flowing limpidly beneath him.[8]

This is the opening passage of Büchner's narrative. The conclusion runs as follows:

In cold resignation he sat in the coach as they rode out of the valley toward the west. He did not care where they were taking him; several times when the coach was endangered by the bad road he remained sitting quite calmly; he was totally indifferent. In this state he traveled through the mountains. Toward evening they were in the Rhine valley. Gradually they left the mountains behind, which now rose up like a deep blue crystal wave into the sunset, and on its warm flood the red rays of evening played; above the plain at the foot of the mountains lay a shimmering, bluish web. It grew darker as they approached Strasbourg; a high full moon, all distant objects in the dark, only the mountain nearby formed a sharp line, the earth was like a golden bowl from which the foaming golden waves of the moon overflowed. Lenz stared out quietly, no perception, no impulse; only a dull fear grew in him the more things became lost in the darkness. They had to stop for the night; again he made several attempts on his life but he was too closely watched. Next morning he arrived in Strasbourg in dreary, rainy weather. He seemed quite rational, spoke with people; he acted like everyone else, yet there was a terrible void inside him, he no longer felt any fear, any desire; his existence was a necessary burden.—So he lived on.[9]

Even if nothing were extant of Büchner's novella but these two passages, one would be able to recognize his genius. Yet what is most striking is that *Lenz*, as well as being a moving portrayal of an afflicted soul and a masterly poetic depiction of dynamic or tranquil land- and skyscapes, also constitutes a detached, nearly dispassionate—though, paradoxically, quite fascinating and powerful—psychological case study. Its anticipation of basic insights of modern psychiatry has been well established; its penetrating analysis of madness corresponds exactly to what was to be defined, more than half a century later, as "schizophrenia." Indeed, it has been argued that the most advanced specialist of today would be hard put to provide a better, more thorough, depiction of psychic pathogenesis.[10] (Oberlin's notes, needless to say, served merely as raw material for Büchner; the uncanny precocity was, as any comparison will demonstrate,[11] entirely his.) Whether the story is really a fragment—a view advocated long ago and shared by a large number of critics and scholars—is still being disputed . . .

Switzerland, 1837. Not only has the twenty-three-year-old been awarded his doctorate by the newly founded University of Zurich, but he has also almost simultaneously been granted the *venia legendi*, the equivalent of a professorship. That distinction was conferred after his delivery of a public *Probevorlesung*, "Über Schädelnerven" ("On Cranial Nerves"). Both this "probatory lecture" and, from its very beginning, the course he is teaching on Vergleichende Anatomie der Fische und Amphibien (Comparative Anatomy of the Fish and the Amphibians) have greatly impressed, indeed stunned, the experts. Further, they all admire his treatise, written and published in French, on the nervous system of the barbel: it is a piece of painstaking research which, apart from earning him his degree, has won international acclaim, even inducing an academy, the Société d'histoire naturelle de Strasbourg, to name him its corresponding member. The author of *Mémoire sur le système nerveux du barbeau (Cyprinus barbus L.)* is, moreover, prepared to give a course on the development of philosophy since Descartes and Spinoza, has translated two dramas by the then leading playwright in France, Victor Hugo, and has himself composed, incredible though it may sound, two more, perhaps three, remarkable plays—among them what is now regarded by many as his finest work and most outstanding contribution to avant-gardism, *Woyzeck.*

But Georg Büchner, "the proletarian of intellectual labor," is also "its victim."[12] He has contracted typhoid fever; no efforts to save his life have been of any avail; the malignant disease, rapidly consuming him, will cause his death shortly. His friends, gathered around his sickbed, look on in silence and helpless despair. In his delirious ravings, he is haunted by hallucinations of being arrested and extradited to his homeland; he is obsessed with the ghastly lot of his fellow conspirators imprisoned there, such as Friedrich Ludwig Weidig, the co-author of that subversive pamphlet, *Der Hessische Landbote* (*The Hessian Messenger*), which brought about Büchner's flight from his native country and Weidig's close confinement in a dungeon. In point of fact, this Lutheran minister and upright democrat, having been tortured for two years, both physically and mentally, will die in Hesse (murdered, as some maintain, or, in any case, systematically driven to suicide) only four days after the political refugee expires in Swiss exile. Yet, strangely enough, it is Büchner, the radical revolutionary and, as is commonly held, atheist and nihilist, who on his deathbed utters words about the necessity of suffering that have a distinctly Christian, near pietistic ring, much to the surprise and consternation of those attending to him.

One of them was Wilhelm Schulz, who afterwards claimed that Büchner must be hailed as "der Proletarier der geistigen Arbeit und das Opfer derselben," adding that the young scientist and playwright, philosopher and translator—to repeat but his latter-day activities—"hatte sich lächelnd zu Tode gearbeitet" ("had worked himself smilingly to death").[13] Schulz and his wife, Caroline, cared for their friend during his fatal sickness, as they were dwelling wall to wall with him in an old house in Zurich. It was Caroline Schulz who jotted down, and transmitted to us, his strange "last words."

There are other things worthy of note, however, not only with respect to the place where Büchner died, but also in regard to Schulz, whose role and significance have long been neglected. For Schulz (1797–1860)[14] was, like Weidig (1791–1837),[15] a militant Hessian democrat who had been thrown into jail, but had managed to break out. Like Büchner, he had found refuge in Switzerland and been granted a teaching position at the new university. In later years, he investigated the maltreatment and death of Weidig and, with the accusatory documents he either compiled and edited himself, or assisted in collecting and publishing, was instrumental in the abolition of secret criminal proceedings in Germany; in addition, he wrote a monograph titled *Die Bewegung der Produktion* (*The Movement of Production*) that inspired one of the most momentous thinkers in modern times: namely, the author of *Das Kapital*. And as to that location in downtown Zurich—a memorable coincidence in literary history, if ever there was one—both Schulz, the "man who gave Marx ideas,"[16] and his doomed friend (who has, indeed, been recently labeled an "early communist")[17] had rented rooms in the Spiegelgasse, which is the same small street where, almost three generations thereafter, the exiled Lenin lived, working incessantly, before he set out to lead the Russian Revolution to victory, and to change the world for good. Also, the Spiegelgasse was the location of the Cabaret Voltaire, the germ of what was to become Dadaism, the most radical movement in modern art and literature.

2

How, then, are we to approach "that scarcely accountable genius"[18] who was "all in one person,"[19] that stupendous youth of whose untimely death in nineteenth-century Switzerland a contemporary American critic ventures to state that he cannot think of a greater loss to world drama, indeed to world literature at large?[20] What is the proper way of dealing with that slim and, apparently, plain and straightforward oeuvre consisting, for the most part, of a story that may well be a fragment, plus a mere triad of plays (for there exists only a comedy, *Leonce und Lena* [*Leonce and Lena*], in addition to the two dramatic pieces already mentioned, one of which is definitely fragmentary)? What are, in sum, the meaning and the importance of Georg Büchner and his writings? In the five chapters that follow, I shall attempt an answer to these questions; at least, I shall try to open up novel avenues that may lead to an adequate understanding of Büchner's rich and manifold legacy. But first, let us briefly situate his life and work in their historical context, and supply whatever seems necessary to complement the preceding biographical vignettes!

Clearly, Büchner must be seen against the background of his own time, as well as in relation to ours. The twenty-three years he was allotted concur, more or less, with the heyday of that era of widespread restoration in Europe which lasted from 1815 to 1848, succeeding not only the eruption of the French Revolution and its shattering repercussions, but also the quiet though equally repercussive triumph of Enlightenment in German thought. On either side of the Rhine, the hallmarks of modernism in its broadest sense had manifested themselves. Or as Heinrich Heine (whom Büchner read) put it in the early 1830s: In France, the monarchy, the keystone of the old social order, had collapsed; in Germany, the same thing had happened to deism, the keystone of the old intellectual order.[21] But the forces of the past—call them conservative or reactionary—having long since rebounded to form a Holy Alliance that was, as a matter of fact, precious unholy, were desperately trying to set up again what had broken down, and to do away with what had been achieved. The whole era was one of constant repression of civil liberties and liberalism in general. It was one of ruthless exploitation and oppression as well, and hence of social no less than political unrest. Not just the Congress of Vienna, nor the notorious Karlsbad Decrees and the persecution of the Young Germans (a loose group of democratic authors comprising, among others, Heine and Gutzkow), but also the July Revolution in Paris, the storming of the guardhouses in Frankfurt, and a number of peasants' or workers' revolts, such as the insurrection of the weavers of Lyons—all occurred during Büchner's short span of life. And it can safely be said, considering what we know of him, that there were few who felt the overall backlash—especially the misery of the poor, which was particularly prevalent in Hesse—more keenly and deeply, and had more resolutely set their minds on fighting it, than this young student and son of a bourgeois family.

When he was born in Goddelau, a small Hessian market town, on October 17, 1813, his father was still a country doctor (*Distriktsarzt*). But Ernst Karl Büchner, with his wife, Karoline Louise née Reuß, and their first two children, soon moved to Darmstadt, where he eventually became a high-ranking medical official (*Großherzoglicher Medizinalrat*) and where, between 1818 and 1828, five more children were born to the couple. (The mother, incidentally, was herself a physician's daughter.)[22] Both the date and the year of Georg Büchner's birth, as well as the lives of some of his brothers and sisters, deserve comment, if only in passing.

Most significantly, from October 16 to 19, 1813, the Battle of Leipzig was raging. It was the so-called *Völkerschlacht* ("Battle of the Nations") or, as Schulz phrased it poetically, "the day when freedom was slaughtered":[23] it marked the beginning of Napoleon's fall, leading to the debacle at Waterloo, and, by the same token, gave rise to that stifling restoration which, under the dominance of Austrian Chancellor Metternich, was to extend over more than three decades. Doubtless, the date of Büchner's birth is as fraught with symbolic weight as is the place of Büchner's death. In the realm of German letters, on the other hand, the same year turned out to be a veritable *Geniejahrgang*, or "vintage of geniuses"; for not only Richard Wagner (an essayist and dramatist in his own right, apart from being a composer) but two lesser luminaries, Friedrich Hebbel and Otto Ludwig, also were born in 1813. (Wagner lived until 1883; the other two died in 1863 and 1865, respectively.) Like Büchner, Hebbel and Ludwig are remembered chiefly as playwrights; the latter, hardly known outside Germany, is of somewhat limited importance in our context, but the former is normally placed side by side with the prescient Hessian, as well as with another avant-gardist, Christian Dietrich Grabbe (1801–36). It should further be noted that, aside from Gutzkow, Hebbel appears to have been the only German writer among Büchner's contemporaries who realized the greatness, indeed "magnificence," of *Danton's Death*.[24] In his diary of 1839, he readily attested to the "power" of "creation" exuding from it, as opposed to the mere creative "pattern" or "urge" evinced by the plays of Grabbe.[25]

Büchner's family also seems to have been aware of his genius fairly early. This may be unusual for a bourgeois home, but is not so surprising in his case. Parents and offspring alike were themselves remarkably bold and talented individuals. For example, Büchner's sister Luise, herself an author, was a leading German feminist of the nineteenth century, while his brother Ludwig— the first to edit the writings of the deceased Georg, albeit without *Woyzeck*—was a physician and made a name for himself as one of the foremost philosophical materialists and atheists of the time. In 1855, each of them published a major book: Ludwig, his influential *Kraft und Stoff* (*Power and Matter*), Luise, her emancipationist *Die Frauen und ihr Beruf* (*Women and Their Profession*). Two other members of the Büchner family, less brilliant yet noteworthy all the same, were involved either in political journalism or in parliamentary politics. Alexander, a lawyer by profession, worked for a while as co-editor of the radical newspaper, *Der jüngste Tag* (*Doomsday*), before emigrating to France where he was appointed Professor of Foreign Literatures—a comparatist *avant la lettre*, so to speak—by the city of Caen in Normandy; Wilhelm, a scientist and industrialist who had founded a chemical factory, served for years as a democratic deputy, first, to the regional Landtag of Hesse-Darmstadt, then to the central Reichstag in Berlin. (The one exception to this formidable crew was the eldest sister, "lazy Mathilde"; a fourth brother, Karl, had died as an infant.)

Schooling went quite smoothly for Georg Büchner. Initially, he was taught by his mother; then, in 1822, he was sent to a private school until, in 1825, he entered the Darmstadt *Gymnasium* (a traditional German high school emphasizing the humanities), which he attended until his graduation in 1831. As might be expected, the boy, though far from being a model youth, proved to be an excellent and even diligent pupil, and developed swiftly; still, if there is anything we can single out as particularly precocious in his life, it is his inclination toward revolutionary thought. Indeed, not only did Büchner dream of a universal republic and the establishment of a commonwealth which, alas, has remained utopian to this very day—namely, the United States of Europe—but he also adopted as his favorite greeting, which he exchanged with a classmate who would join him in conspiring just a few years afterwards, the subversive shibboleth from beyond the Rhine, "Bonjours, citoyen!"

Equally smooth at least on the surface, and certainly no less expeditious, was Büchner's progress as a university student. He embarked on his academic career in the fall of 1831. With a special dispensation his father had obtained for him from the Hessian authorities, Büchner was allowed to enroll at the Alsatian University of Strasbourg, an institution doubly "foreign"—because both French and liberal—in the eyes of the domestic censors, and to pursue there his combined studies of philosophy, medicine, and the sciences. All in all, save for the long summer vacation he spent with his parents, Büchner stayed in Strasbourg nearly two years. They comprised probably the happiest weeks and months he ever spent. He breathed freely in the urbane and relatively unrepressed atmosphere of the erstwhile Imperial City, with its rows of high-gabled buildings and that towering minster which had already enchanted Goethe some sixty years earlier; he explored, and greatly enjoyed, the surrounding countryside, from its lovely plains and foothills up to those vast and shimmery mountains which so charmed him. He took a liking to the Alsatian people as well, and an interest in their folklore, especially the simple and touching songs and legends then still alive in the area. And it was during the same peaceful and carefree time—or, to be precise, at the beginning thereof—that Büchner met his future fiancée, Wilhelmine (Minna) Jaeglé, the daughter of a widowed Protestant minister in whose house in Strasbourg he had found lodgings.

Thus, when his dispensation ran out in August 1833, he left Alsatia rather unwillingly, in order to report back to Hesse, and to continue his studies at the local, almost rural, University of Gießen, which any subject of the Grand Duchy who aimed at a position licensed by the state, such as a medical one, had to attend. That the young man, after the love and freedom he had tasted in Strasbourg, should now suffer all the more profoundly, not only from the loneliness which now beset him but also from the oppressive brutality pervading his country, is understandable enough. With wrath and indignation, with gloom and a growing bitterness of heart, Büchner watched what was going on around him. At last, his depression reached so intense and unbearable a degree that he actually fell ill with meningitis, and had to return to his parental home in Darmstadt. "The political conditions could drive me insane," he cried out in a letter written to a friend in December 1833, while he was recovering from this illness. "The poor people [*Volk*] patiently pull the cart on which the princes and the liberals"—note Büchner's determined radicalism—"perform their ludicrous comedy [*Affenkomödie*]. Every night, I pray to the hangman's rope and to the lamp posts."[26] (The lamp posts were those employed by the Parisians in lynching sundry aristocrats and, as Büchner seems to intimate, some of the rich as well; in any event, a scene in his *Danton's Death* [I/2] makes effective use of this motif, however ambiguously.)[27]

Yet there is no need to record all the ups and downs of the young student's rapid development. Suffice it to say that in 1834 he began to steep himself in the history of the French Revolution, but by no means uninterruptedly, and that, in early March of that year, he sent Minna Jaeglé what has come to be referred to as his "fatalism letter."[28] Constituting, in fact, one of the most widely debated texts in German literature, this contradictory utterance of Büchner's, parts of which recur nearly verbatim in the mouth of his Danton, amounts to nothing short of an avowal of boundless distress and desperation, indeed of a sudden abandonment of the very values—historical, social, political—otherwise held in highest esteem by him. Hence, how can it be reconciled with his previous and, even more, his subsequent attitudes and actions? For he revealed himself, almost immediately thereafter, as an unflagging rebel again, indeed a truly indefatigable agitator and conspirator. Having resumed his studies at the university, Büchner prepared the founding of his Gesellschaft der Menschenrechte in Gießen, his secret "Society for Human Rights," modeled after the Société des Droits de l'homme et du citoyen, a group formed in Paris in 1832. Simultaneously, he started working on his revolutionary pamphlet, *The Hessian Messenger*, and established yet another section of his conspiratorial society in his hometown, Darmstadt, when he was passing through on his way back from Strasbourg, where he had visited his fiancée for a couple of weeks. And all this was done by the same frail student who had just recovered his health, and by the same untiring scientist and budding scholar who had just confessed that any "control" of the "iron law" of history, thus of mankind in its entirety, was "impossible"!

Clearly, Büchner's singular letter and various activities will occupy us repeatedly in the pages to follow. For the time being, we shall do well to clarify the role of the co-author of *The Hessian Messenger*, Pastor Weidig, and to relate the events surrounding the printing of that pamphlet and its, for the most part, abortive dissemination. Although it is true that the title of the pamphlet, *Der Hessische Landbote*, was in effect coined by the pastor, the remainder of his collaboration was confined, in general, to toning down Büchner's radical language, and to imbuing it with a more Biblical wording instead. Büchner protested, but he was outvoted in the ensuing discussions, both by his own faction and by the followers and associates of Weidig, and he accepted the compromise, if reluctantly, for the sake of the common cause. Moreover, he was one of the two members of the joint conspiracy who, making a nocturnal journey on foot, delivered the manuscript to the printer—a fairly hazardous undertaking, it should be recognized, for they had to cross two borders in the then multiply divided Germany. They did succeed, though, arriving and returning safely.

But the whole endeavor was doomed from the very beginning.

No sooner had the pamphlet been printed, by the end of July 1834, than the inevitable traitor, a certain Kuhl, went about his sinister business, planting carefully calculated denunciations. The first of a growing number of conspirators to be arrested was Büchner's Francophile classmate from highschool days, Karl Minnigerode; he carried a total of 139 copies, sewn into his coat and boots, of *The Hessian Messenger*. When Büchner learned what had happened to his friend, he at once set out to warn the others, spending, as he had done before, all night traveling. In the meantime, the Hessian Ministry of the Interior and of Justice took further measures. A warrant of apprehension was issued against Büchner, and the official in charge of the investigation, University Judge Georgi, a notorious alcoholic prone to fits of delirium tremens and a sadist destined to become Weidig's torturer, searched the dauntless student's room and had it sealed. Yet nothing to incriminate Büchner could be discovered; thus, when he braved the judge, rather than fleeing, and demanded satisfaction, Georgi, baffled by this show of audacity, dared not arrest him. Büchner was in fact permitted to leave Gießen, and to join his parents in Darmstadt—or, at any rate, he was not hindered from doing so. Unabashed, though under secret surveillance, he started trying to reorganize the local branch of his conspiratorial society. Indeed, not only did Büchner and the others still at large plan to continue their rebellious work, but they also intended to buy a printing press of their own, and even plotted to rescue Minnigerode (they had weapons as well as ammunition).

None of this ever came to pass (although, to be sure, copies of the pamphlet were successfully distributed in Upper Hesse, and an affiliated organization in the city of Marburg was able to produce and disseminate a second edition).[29] The denunciatory acts persisted; the Hessian police, as time went by, kept closing in upon the members of the conspiracy. Yet, while those political plots and counterplots were in progress, Büchner, for all his endangerment and his ardent commitment to the revolutionary cause, did not forsake his literary pursuits, however incipient and inconspicuous they were then. On the contrary, he now began steadfastly to intensify and broaden them. After October 1834, we find him steeped again in the history of the French Revolution. He was studying it along with seventeenth- and eighteenth-century philosophy; he made and collected excerpts for his *Danton's Death*, the play he would compose during the first two months of the following year, writing it down in one creative outburst. . . .

This is the scene we started with, and only a few additional data remain to be appended.

3

By early March 1835, so penetrating a mind as Büchner's could no longer deceive itself with any illusions. Nor could the young writer wait for the publication of his drama, or for any advance payment he might obtain. (As it appears, an adequate amount of money was by then at his disposal, anyhow.) So Büchner decided to escape from German soil: on March 9, having crossed the French border near Weißenburg, he reemerged in his beloved Alsatia. Subsequently, more and more Hessian conspirators were apprehended and thrown into jail, but *Danton's Death*, after its first printing in the Frankfurt journal *Phönix*, did come out as a book in July, albeit with the misleading subtitle, *Dramatische Bilder aus Frankreichs Schreckensherrschaft* ("Dramatic Scenes from the Reign of Terror in France"). Still, the persecutions in Germany, not only of radical democrats but of moderate dissenters and critics as well, spread and grew as the year was drawing to its close; they reached their culmination with the sweeping measures taken against the entire "school," or "movement," of bourgeois intellectuals lumped together under the name of the Young Germans. One of its foremost representatives was Karl Gutzkow, Büchner's enthusiastic promoter, at whose request he had translated Hugo's plays *Lucrèce Borgia* and *Marie Tudor*, both of which were published in October 1835. In November, Gutzkow was arrested and jailed; the other members of Young Germany were proscribed, and their writings, including those of the exiled Heine, prohibited.

All this time Büchner's own literary pursuits went on unabated. After the completion of *Lenz*, he wrote his comedy, *Leonce and Lena*, submitting it to the prize committee of the prestigious Tübingen publishing house, Cotta; unfortunately, he failed to meet the deadline. Likewise in 1835–36, he started the groundwork for his course (full of trenchant observations) on recent philosophy, as well as a series of detailed and extensive studies for his zoological treatise on the barbel; at the same time, he may also have attempted to intervene, anonymously, on behalf of his friends and fellow conspirators in prison. Büchner's life and career became almost precipitous during the two years following the creative explosion that resulted in *Danton's Death*. Thus, even after his remarkable academic successes, he nonetheless continued working to the point of exhaustion: on his first drafts of *Woyzeck*; on a Renaissance drama—irretrievably lost, so it seems—devoted to Pietro Aretino; and, once more, on philosophy, now ancient as well as modern. In addition, he had to prepare the talk he was expected to give at the University of Zurich as a prerequisite for his admission to its faculty. Tired but elated, Büchner left Strasbourg on October 18, 1836, the morning after his twenty-third birthday. On November 5, he delivered his lecture in Zurich; upon its favorable reception (which might indeed be called an enthusiastic acclamation), he began right away to teach his course on Comparative Anatomy of the Fish and the Amphibians and, despite certain premonitions, announced his plans for the future, specifically a comprehensive course he would offer in the summer on Vergleichende Anatomie der Wirbelthiere (Comparative Anatomy of the Vertebrates). However, Büchner's time had run out. He died in Zurich on February 19, 1837.

At his funeral on February 21 several hundred people were present, among them the two mayors of the city, plus many other dignitaries. Thirteen years afterwards, when his brother Ludwig brought out what must be considered the earliest, if incomplete and defective, collection of Georg Büchner's works,[30] nobody cared a straw about it.[31] Büchner's fame was all but extinguished, first by the brazen and unconcealed oppressiveness of the restoration era, then by the more subtly stifling aftermath—political, literary, and otherwise—of the German revolution of 1848–49, the scattered uprisings of which were so thoroughly quelled. To sum it up in one pithy sentence: The dominance of Austria and her Chancellor Metternich were supplanted by the dominance of Prussia and her Chancellor Bismarck. After the middle of the century, Germany was heading (by way of three victorious Prussian wars) for her Second Empire, and a man and writer like our indomitable Hessian was as "untimely" as Nietzsche termed his own "meditations," those scathing diatribes launched in the 1870s, soon after the new Reich had been proclaimed. Only with the appearance of a critical edition of his complete oeuvre in 1879[32] were Büchner's greatness and importance realized.[33] He was acknowledged little by little, and finally praised and admired—although still, it has to be stressed, by the select few, the avant-gardists of Naturalism and, in later decades, Expressionism. But his writings were being read at least by some, no longer dismissed or ignored altogether, nor libeled and labeled "dirt" (*Schmutz*), "plague-spots of impudence" (*Pestbeulen der Frechheit*), and "blasphemies of the holiest things" (*Lästerungen des Heiligsten*), as had been the case in an anonymous review of his *Danton's Death*.[34] (This attack of 1835 was, incidentally, the most fulsome review published during Büchner's lifetime, as well as for years to come.) Still, while in fact *Leonce and Lena* was produced as early as 1885, and *Lenz* can be shown to have influenced storytellers since the late 1880s,[35] another generation passed on before *Danton's Death* was staged in Berlin in 1902, and *Woyzeck*—a whole century after the playwright's birth—in Munich in 1913.

Then, however, things did change drastically. The impact exerted by the various productions of *Woyzeck*, whether in Munich or elsewhere, was both immediate and enormous, indeed totally overwhelming: as witness, above all, the reactions of Rainer Maria Rilke and Bertolt Brecht, who, moreover, could hardly have been more divergent in their views.[36] Rilke's testimony (in a letter to his benefactress, Princess Marie von Thurn und Taxis-Hohenlohe, of July 9, 1915) is particularly revealing, for not only do his words bespeak the profundity of the experience for him: they also betray the vagueness and paucity of information that prevailed in regard to the text and author of *Woyzeck*. The play is said to take place "around 1848, roughly," although Rilke—who actually deemed it necessary to insert: "G. Büchner was the . . . brother of the better-known Ludwig B."—rightly observes that the work was written "more than eighty years ago"; and *Woyzeck* is listed side by side with August Strindberg's "truly unheard-of" *Ghost Sonata*, and called simply "the most definite event" in recent theater. "Stupendously," Rilke goes on to explain, Büchner's drama demonstrates that "[even] around the lowliest being," a creature like this poor and downtrodden soldier, there "stands all the grandeur of existence; he cannot help that here and there, before, behind, beside his gloomy soul, the horizons tear apart into violence, into monstrousness, into endlessness. It is a drama without compare how this misused being stands in the cosmos wearing his worker's jacket, *malgré lui*, in the endless order of the stars."[37] Ecstatically, Rilke concludes: "This is theater, this is what theater could be. . . ."[38]

Theater at its greatest! Such was, quite evidently, also the opinion of Brecht. Throughout his life, the performance he had seen of *Woyzeck*, the immediate revelation and its subsequent repercussions, remained one of the most memorable experiences for him. His words, it is true, are characterized by brevity, sobriety, and matter-of-factness, as opposed to the mysticism lurking in Rilke's; yet they are, in their way, no less suggestive and, clearly, far weightier. His reaction to Büchner is derived not from an isolated statement but rather from an entire array of testimonies extending over decades. Indeed they are, in all likelihood, not yet all known to us, for more documents have been coming to light continually. For instance, in a volume entitled *Brecht in Context*, published in 1984, John Willett has included some scrawly notes he once jotted down when visiting Brecht in 1956, only weeks before the latter died. A faithful reproduction of Willett's scribbling as transcribed and emended by him reads thus: "Shakes[peare] via Büchner Woz[zeck]—first perf. by Steinrück after '18/'19 rev[olutio]n. Made [Brecht] read Shakes."[39] Doubtless, this Shakespearean context, if highly laconic, is most telling; it scarcely needs any commentary. And Steinrück, by the way, became a theatrical celebrity precisely through his portrayal of Woyzeck.

Steinrück did not have the stature of the legendary Max Reinhardt, the most influential practitioner in early twentieth-century German theater. Twice, that famous director, who was also a leading Büchnerian, assured none other than Brecht that he believed *Woyzeck* to be "the most powerful drama of German literature"; Reinhardt's assessment was dutifully registered, without the slightest disapproval, in the Marxist playwright's *Arbeitsjournal*, the diary he kept during his exile.[40] With respect to his own drama, *Die Mutter* (*The Mother*), an "epic" play based on Maxim Gorki's revolutionary novel of the same title, Brecht stated that it was built according to "the classical German structure" distinguishing Goethe's *Götz von Berlichingen* as well as *Woyzeck*—he claimed, in a word, that it was itself classical.[41] Both these utterances (they date from May 20, 1942, and October 4, 1952, respectively) can be amply supported and supplemented by additional ones, which will be discussed in detail in the chapters to follow, as will the question of Brechtian and Büchnerian "epicity."[42] For the moment, suffice it to say that, time and again, Brecht returned to Büchner's dramatic writings, including *Leonce and Lena* and, notably, *Danton's Death*;[43] that he very often adopted for his dramas and productions the "ballad-like" treatment typical of *Woyzeck* in particular;[44] and that he may even have thought of dramatizing Büchner's life, in spite of the difficulties such an attempt would encounter.[45]

In sum, between 1913–14 and 1918–19, during the First World War, Georg Büchner at last came into his own. Ever since the breakthrough effected by those vividly remembered performances of *Woyzeck*, his fame has been on the increase, both within the German-speaking community and, especially after the Second World War, beyond. More and more essays and books, in a variety of languages, have been written and published on Büchner; more and more translations of his works have appeared; indeed, some of the most noteworthy productions of his dramas—spectacular as well as controversial—have occurred outside Germany. (*Danton's Death* as put on by Jean Vilar in Paris in 1952, or as staged for the opening of the Vivian Beaumont Theater in New York, are striking examples.) All three of Büchner's dramatic texts have successively been set to music, and made into operatic works: *Wozzeck*,[46] the first and indisputably most important of these compositions, by Alban Berg in 1925; *Danton's Death*, by Gottfried von Einem in 1947; and *Leonce and Lena*, by Kurt Schwaen in 1961.[47] However, instead of further disseminating such statistics, as illuminating as they are, I feel we had better call our chief witness in evidence: that is, summon the most recent Nobel laureate writing in the German language—the Bulgarian-born Elias Canetti, a novelist and dramatist, essayist and diarist of Spanish-Jewish descent, for whom German was a foreign tongue he had acquired as a schoolboy. The occasion on which he made the remarks in question is in itself an indication of the Hessian's established fame, for Canetti's words come from his acceptance speech delivered in Darmstadt in 1972, when he was awarded that year's Büchner Prize.[48] As usual, the talk was printed, and in it Canetti relates that Büchner brought about a change in his life "like no other poet" (*wie kein anderer Dichter).*[49] But he goes even further. Who, he asks rhetorically, would be so "foolhardy" (*tollkühn*) as to feel justified in placing words of his own alongside those of Büchner: "wen gibt es, in irgendeinem Lande der Erde, der ein Recht darauf hätte, neben diese Worte eigene zu setzen!"[50]

It is not surprising that *Woyzeck*—"the most consummate reversal and revolution" (*der vollkommenste Umsturz*) according to Canetti[51]—should again be singled out for special mention and exuberant praise by one whose German language and literature are a matter of choice rather than birthright. In 1931, when he read the play for the first time, so Canetti recalls, he could hardly believe anything like this existed;[52] yet he realized that it was to make an indelible impression on him. The then twenty-six-year-old was right: *Woyzeck* left an impression comparable to that of Sophocles' *Ajax* and Dostoevsky's *The Possessed*, as the mature author, an expert in literary history and criticism, confirms in retrospect.[53] "So will ich nur etwas sehr Einfaches sagen," he declares, "nämlich daß ich von keiner Ehrung weiß, die ich so sehr als Auszeichnung empfinde wie diese, und daß ich glücklich bin, sie noch zu erleben."[54] All he wants to say, and will eventually have said, is indeed very simple and touching, however insightful; but it is momentous, too. This future recipient of the Nobel Prize confesses straightforwardly that he doesn't know of any distinction whatsoever that would equal a prize bestowed on him under the auspices of Büchner! In fact, Canetti—who like his idol is also a scientist, in addition to being a man of letters—venerates the young Hessian as nothing less than "the pure exemplar" of humankind in its perfect potentiality: a model, that is, of "inexhaustibility," on the one hand, and of "never-to-be-accomplished wholeness," on the other. Büchner stands before us, we are told, "als das reine Beispiel des unvollendbaren Menschen. Die Vielfalt seiner Anlagen . . . bezeug[t] eine Natur, die in ihrer Unerschöpflichkeit ein endloses Leben fordert."[55] With that, Canetti's speech abruptly ends. For just as the genius would need an infinite span of time to fulfill himself and his purpose, so would, in all modesty, his critic.

4

How, then, are we to approach Georg Büchner? What is the proper way of dealing with him, his writings, his overall legacy? And what are their importance and meaning, indeed their relevance? In *The Southern Quarterly* of 1963, Gilbert Frederick Hartwig published an essay entitled "Georg Büchner: Nineteenth Century Avant-Garde." It will help us, not only further to illustrate Büchner's historical role and literary function, and to situate them in proper perspective, but also to point out the solution to our methodological problems, as well as the answer (if an answer is still necessary) to our evaluative questions. It will do so *ex negativo*, though, because this essay is also indicative of the halfheartedness and widespread indecision that have for a long time, with very few exceptions, ruled over even the more "advanced" wings of Büchner scholarship and research. Granted that Hartwig's title sounds quite promising—all the more disappointing is the conclusion he arrives at. Couched in poetic imagery, it runs as follows: "In the last analysis, it may be well to consider Büchner only as an isolated phenomenon with gossamer threads of connection extending in many directions, into the future as well as into the past. However, detailed analysis of the relationships seems to dull the iridescent shimmer of the connective threads and, finally, to cause them to break."[56] I maintain that the very opposite is true. The more closely one examines those connective threads, and the more carefully and attentively one pursues their manifold ramifications, the more they also reveal themselves as "unbreakable," if that is the word. They do hold, and hold together—not so much, to be sure, in token of "iridescent" relationships, but rather in terms of actual and essential affinities and, as often as not, demonstrable influences and effects. In short, Büchner is anything but an "isolated phenomenon," untimely though he was; he and his oeuvre are as firmly rooted in their past as they are tied to their future, and grounded in their present to boot.

Hence I propose to resort to a different, if somewhat related, imagery, to superimpose it upon the underlying, rectified and amended, concept of the preceding one, and, as far as seems feasible, adroitly to elaborate on both. For, rather than flying any "gossamer" webs and contemplating their fleeting "shimmer," it may be well to invoke three twentieth-century avant-gardists from Germany, the United States, and France, and to listen to what they have to say about the respective approaches—not to the Büchnerian oeuvre, admittedly, but to their own experimental works. Commenting, in an autobiographical account, on his anti-novel of 1944, *Roman des Phänotyp* (*Novel of the Phenotype*), the eminent German lyricist and essayist, Gottfried Benn, observes the following: "This novel has . . . the form of an orange. An orange consists of numerous sections, the separate parts of the fruit, the slices, all of them equal, side by side, equivalent; perhaps one slice contains a few more pips, another a few less; yet they all tend . . . toward the center, to the tough white root which we remove when taking the fruit apart. This root is the phenotype, the existential one, nothing but he, solely he . . ."[57] In a similar though more aggressive vein, William Burroughs reflects on the form of his novel-like prose work of 1959, stating peremptorily: "You can cut into *Naked Lunch* at any intersection point." According to him, this book "spill[s] off the page in all directions, kaleidoscope of vistas." It is composed of "units," Burroughs adds, "which be all in one piece and should be so taken, but the pieces can be had in any order."[58] And the boldly poeticizing Frenchman, Marc Saporta, describes his *nouveau roman* of 1962, *Composition no I*, by implicitly equating it with the abstract painting which figures in its narrative, but is already alluded to in its ambiguous title. "Each stroke," he says of the joint form of picture and book, "has its own life among the others, and this composes a world spinning on its own axis, caught in a cluster of meteors, in the bonds of shooting stars."[59] Obviously, that which all three images have in common—regardless of a vast heterogeneity I need not, nor wish to, belabor—is the idea of a circular, spherical, concentric structure the tensions, indeed dynamics, of which manifest themselves in either centripetal or centrifugal fashion, or as a combination thereof. To wit: Benn's antinovel "has . . . the form of an orange" (*ist . . . orangenförmig gebaut*), and each and every part of it tends "toward the center" (*in die Mitte*); conversely, the novel-like text of Burroughs virtually explodes, spilling off every single page, as it were, and not just "in many directions" but "in all directions"; and Saporta's aleatoric as well as fixed[60] *nouveau roman*, inasmuch as it composes "a world spinning on its own axis" (*un monde qui tourne autour de son axe*), actually subsumes and sublates both these contradictory yet complementary processes.[61]

   That, I contend, is an adequate depiction of Büchner's historico-literary situation and, as a consequence, a broad hint at the methodical procedure most apposite to dealing with him and his writings. There can be no doubt that Büchner occupies a position marking a veritable center, or hub, around which all kinds of connections radiate. And the converging ones are no less numerous and multifarious than those diverging.

To top it off, Büchner's own poetic creations can be shown to exhibit elements of a radial, circular, or concentric nature; his own creative processes and their results are, as a matter of fact, not dissimilar to the dynamic "compositions" I cited. The structure and structural workings of his dramas in particular, above all *Woyzeck* and *Danton's Death*, compare fittingly with the way his place in literary history has just been defined, as well as with the method a consequent historian might be driven to infer from it, and which would thus reveal itself as doubly appropriate and called for. To substantiate this second contention of mine, let me adduce but two salient features: namely, the heroes as they appear in Büchner's dramatic text, and the themes and events as they emerge in it. Both are, in most instances, "central" in our emphatic sense. *Woyzeck*, without fail, offers a perfect example of the former; *Danton's Death*, with equal stringency, one of the latter. As Volker Klotz, coining a neologism, put it in his pioneer study, *Geschlossene und offene Form im Drama* (*Closed and Open Form in Drama*): the erstwhile protagonist is reduced (or elevated, as the case may be) to a mere (or mighty) "monagonist." In pieces like *Woyzeck*, Klotz explains, the hero's antagonist is not an identifiable individual any more, nor even a single agent; instead, the whole world, "in the plenitude of its discrete phenomena," has assumed an antagonistic function and presses on the protagonist: "Rushing upon him from all sides, it turns the hero into a 'monagonist' while subjecting the action . . . to an indeterminate circular movement. Accordingly," Klotz concludes, "the dominant principle of composition is that of a rotating variation . . ."[62] In pieces like *Danton's Death*, on the other hand, everything is centered on a theme or event that constitutes the pivot of the play. Or as Wilhelm Emrich has it: "There is, in effect, no longer any action. . . . Rather, the catastrophe is already present before the drama begins. . . ."[63] All of which translates, in Emrich's opinion and slightly exaggerated diction, not only into *dramatis personae* rendered "puppets" devoid of will or power, but also into a "cosmic wheel" (*Weltrad*) spinning in endless circles of unchanging sameness.[64] "Antilinear, autonomous scenes," to quote a more restrained critic,[65] and "fragmented, paratactic dialogue": such are the textual components of the "new form," or "idea of a form" (*Formidee*), which is seen by Emrich, in a number of essays and articles, to permeate both the works of Büchner, the lone precursor of dramatic modernism in the 1830s, and those of Samuel Beckett, its towering representative in our time.[66] As directly as with the middle of the twentieth century, however, the Hessian has been connected with the late sixteenth and early seventeenth centuries. "What he accomplished," writes Richard Gilman, "was the greatest expansion of the procedural possibilities of drama, the widest accession of flexibility and diversity since the theater of Shakespeare."[67] I gladly subscribe to this comparison of Georg Büchner with the playwright of all playwrights. Yet was there, I cannot but ask, nothing between Shakespeare and Büchner or, for that matter, between Büchner and Beckett? Doubtless, one of the deepest experiences we owe the Hessian is what Canetti has so aptly termed the most consummate *Umsturz* in all literature, by which he means the "discovery of lowliness" (*Entdeckung des Geringen*)[68] achieved in *Woyzeck*. But, I must again ask, was this smashing discovery really so total a "revolution," so extraordinary a "reversal" as Canetti, who felt it most piercingly even in retrospect, would have us believe? Eric Bentley is more cautious in his *The Life of the Drama*, speaking technically, rather than existentially or sociologically: "Eloquent and expressive pages of dialogue can be made out of the stammering of semiarticulate people: Büchner's *Woyzeck* was perhaps the first proof of this."[69] Of course, what Bentley here submits, phrasing it ever so carefully, is entirely in keeping with Canetti's factual insight—whereas Gilman, in another statement involving the accomplishments of Shakespeare, seems to pronounce something quite disparate, indeed entirely contrary. For this American Büchnerian proclaims without hesitation that "Not since Shakespeare had drama been the source of such splendid rhetoric, such fiercely seized verbal truths."[70] Still, if we think of *Danton's Death* as well, not just of the omnipresent *Woyzeck*, both critics are, in a sense, right . . . and so is, on closer scrutiny, Canetti. Even Gilman's previous utterance, apparently out of any immediate context, is basically tenable.

To return to my initial contention: All the above observations, however different, trace or sketch as many convergent and/or divergent lines which meet and cross at our historical center; all grasp and identify many strands and forces and tendencies which intersect at that singular literary hub marked by Büchner and his texts. Moreover, the radial connections they point to or lay bare are mutually correlated also, in excess of being concentrated in *Danton's Death* and *Woyzeck*. The "open form" so keenly discerned by Klotz; Emrich's yoking of Büchner to Beckett and to others;[71] the yardstick, as applied by Gilman, of Shakespearean drama and speech; and, especially, the words of Canetti and Bentley concerning Woyzeck's lowly station and expressive stammering—the whole bundle of these truly "connective threads" (never mind the mixed metaphor) does belong together, their motley notwithstanding. They are interwoven and intertwined; in fact, they are as little "isolated" as are Büchner's own writings. Nor can they be said to be restricted to his two major plays. *Leonce and Lena* has been proffered no less eagerly, and assumed even more readily, as a forerunner of theatrical absurdism; for example, both Gilman and the leading German absurdist, Wolfgang Hildesheimer, consider it, if somewhat one-sidedly, a melancholy masterpiece and "tragicomedy of idleness, waste, and frustration" (*Tragikomödie des Leerlaufs und der Frustration*)[72] or a piece "that prefigures our theater of absurdity and verbal games."[73] And what about Büchner's epic work, *Lenz*? Wasn't it, as intimated earlier, recognized, hailed, and received long before the turn of the century? Indeed, ever since the 1880s, when Gerhart Hauptmann composed his Büchnerian tales,[74] has its influence manifested itself, from the Kaiserreich of yesteryear and its burgeoning letters right down to the divided Germany—though not always divided German literature—of today. Perhaps the best-known modern narratives echoing *Lenz* are Peter Schneider's West German novella of the same title, published in 1973, and Volker Braun's East German counterpart of 1975, *Unvollendete Geschichte* ("An Unfinished Story"). Each has been widely acclaimed, and proved to be highly successful.

The more we search and inquire, the more we sense Büchner's impact and presence. Everything he left testifies to his topicality or, as Robert Brustein phrased it, "the exceptional modern quality of his temperament."[75] Even when reading the Hessian's correspondence, his political insights and outcries in particular, we are hard put not to forget that he isn't our contemporary. Undismayed, it has been argued, he went beyond the boundaries of any revolution, bourgeois as well as socialist: "Büchners Briefe lesend, muß man sich mitunter mit Gewalt erinnern, daß es nicht die eines Zeitgenossen sind. Er griff nicht nur über den Horizont der bürgerlichen Revolution hinaus: auch an schönen Punkten über den Horizont der sozialistischen."[76] In contrast to such impassioned attestations to a universal revolutionary thrust, the homage paid to Büchner by the foremost novelist of German socialism, the late Anna Seghers, sounds rather scanty or, at least, strangely subdued. To her generation of the 1920s, so she confessed, Büchner's writings were but "a kind of prelude to modern literature" (eine Art Vorspiel der modernen Literatur). As she admitted further, however, one really didn't notice much difference then between Lenz and Franz Kafka's The Castle.[77] Which is, given the fame the latter enjoyed among the best of that generation, scarcely a mean assessment, no matter how distanced. Hence Seghers, too, bore ample witness to Büchner's overwhelming importance, as did so many before and after her, not only by offering a balanced account or, at times, overshooting themselves, but also by slanting their testimonies a bit or simply contributing their shares well-nigh unwittingly. In any case, writers and critics, practitioners of the theater and literary historians alike: all are, in effect, united in admiring, lauding, emulating, and continuing the heritage of the author from Hesse.[78]

Something else is equally noteworthy, though. In recent years Büchner's central position in history has been perceived and acknowledged both inside and outside Germany.[79] In a monograph titled Georg Büchner and the Birth of Modern Drama, David G. Richards, in near accordance with the view and approach I espouse, and certainly not at variance with the preceding dicta and documents, stated programmatically in 1977: "Büchner is one of those few seminal figures whose works constitute a turning point in the development of art: his three plays anticipate and have influenced almost every form of theater our century has created."[80] There is no need to elaborate on this; I merely wish to propose, in conclusion, to regard the Hessian's main achievement not as "a" turning point only, but as "the" decisive one, indeed the very nodal point in the entire history and development of modern drama. Indisputably, Büchner is, above all with *Woyzeck* and *Danton's Death*, "the first modern playwright"[81] and the ancestor, as it were, of a whole host of others; yet his own "forebears" are, of course, legion, as are his "descendants" and "contemporary kin" (either of which has succinctly been demonstrated already by Herbert Lindenberger,[82] whose terminology I am adopting). Nothing can better illustrate their clear and tight consolidation than our bunch of "gossamer threads" which have been alleged "to dull" and "to break" when subjected to "detailed analysis."

5

In the following investigations consisting of five independent chapters—accordingly, they will proceed both centrifugally and centripetally and, if necessary, synchronically and diachronically as well—an array of such connections will be taken up and pursued, albeit in varying manner and degree. Some of them, it is true, will barely be touched upon, notably those which have received satisfactory critical consideration, while others that have likewise not escaped the attention of Büchner scholarship will be reexamined and, as far as appears to be feasible, modified and broadened. A few, however, have hitherto gone unheeded, or been grossly neglected, although to my mind they are of singular weightiness; hence they will be uncovered here for the first time, and discussed in depth.

Those I shall treat in a more or less marginal way include, for instance: the development from sublime "stately hero" to lowly "proletarian hero" (and beyond)[83]—a trend that finds its most stunning expression in *Woyzeck*; the gradual change, though in itself not uninterrupted, from classical "Aristotelian drama" to modern "epic theater," even to the "documentary"—a process informing, and being informed by, *Woyzeck* as well as *Danton's Death*;[84] and the combination and dialectical interplay of comic and tragic elements, together with the tendency that then leads, as both gain momentum, to the rise of the modern genre, or mode, of the grotesque—all of which can be shown to reach an early flowering in the Hessian's dramatic output, permeating *Leonce and Lena* no less than *Woyzeck* and *Danton's Death*.[85] That we are speaking here of phenomena of world-literary dimensions, each likely to lend itself to a treatment of its own, is, I think, self-evident.

"More central" still, if I may say so, are the aspects of Büchner's work on which I have chosen to concentrate. They include primarily the two vast realms of "love and sexuality," on the one hand, and of "revolt, rebellion, and revolution," on the other; yet they are by no means limited to them. Their study will yield three major results: First and foremost, the enormous importance of the entirety of the erotic for Büchner's work as well as his life.[86] Second, the fact that Büchner's overpowering and all-pervasive eroticism (i.e., his "sexual revolt") is inextricably intertwined, indeed entangled, with the overall rebellion and revolution he lived and so intensely re-created in his plays and tale (i.e., his "aesthetic, social, and metaphysical revolt"). Third, the proper historical place and context in which Büchner's unique contribution is situated. Not only was it the first great repercussion, in drama and in literature at large, of the French Revolution[87] and the concomitant advent of European nihilism (witness comparisons with previous works, such as Goethe's *Egmont*), but it can also be seen as the first great anticipation of modern revolutionary drama[88] and theater and their respective theories. Both began to emerge around 1870, with the contemporaneous appearance of Naturalism in Europe and of Nietzsche's *The Birth of Tragedy from the Spirit of Music* in Germany,[89] and spread and developed until they ultimately attained to such extremes as Antonin Artaud's Dionysiac (but more-than-Nietzschean) "theater of cruelty" and Brecht's Socratic (but far-more-than-naturalistic) "theater of alienation."[90]

These as well as any other contentions I shall advance are based on a close reading of the pertinent texts—both by Büchner and a variety of authors—combined with a wide and diverse historical exploration that is, admittedly, centered on German literature, and German drama in particular, but not at all confined to either of them. In fact, the very comparativeness inherent in my approaches, along with their attempted ideological critique and methodological self-examination, may well account for the novelty I claim in my subtitle, the new perspectives I hope to have opened up. And a similar conjunction of textual and comparative historicity may also be reflected, however faintly, in the tripartite structure of the book as a whole. Each part, in any event, takes off from a general state of Büchner reception and research, in Germany or abroad, and subsequently goes on to unfold and evince the significance of the Hessian through a detailed analysis of his two main themes. This is most obvious in the chapters of Part 1, "Büchner's Paradox: The Modern Concept of Revolt" and " 'Cœur' and 'Carreau': Love in the Life and Works of Büchner"; yet the same principle applies to the chapters of Part 3, "*Danton's Death*: A 'Counterconception' to Goethe's *Egmont?*" and "A Dirge That Is a Paean: Paradox Once More." In addition, it should be emphasized that the first chapter seeks to explain the Hessian's relevance by probing into the works of his followers or heirs, and thus is oriented toward the future, while the fourth chapter concerns itself chiefly, though not exclusively, with his most revealing predecessor, and thus is directed toward the past, though again not totally. The third chapter (Part 2) fittingly joins and connects these two aspects: therefore, "Culmination, Conclusions, and a New Beginning: The Present State of Büchner Reception and Research" is located in the middle of the book. And as to the fifth and last chapter, it not only restates Büchner's paradox, both of revolt and of love, but also tries to sublate it on a higher level, and by that token to establish, if precariously, the paradoxical unity of his entire life, thought, and art.

All five chapters are to some extent independent of each other, for they originated as separate essays, speeches, and articles. While their chronological sequence has been preserved, no attempts have been made at concealing this independence, despite considerable reworking. Inevitably, as a consequence, there will be occasional repetitions, variations, even contradictions. But these occur in dealing with Büchner anyway, since perseverance plus variability or, in sum, contradictoriness is precisely that which characterizes his paradoxical unity. A closed piece of work—neatly rounded out, and ending, as it were, in harmony— on a man like Georg Büchner, the writer and revolutionary who could never be contained, would indeed be inappropriate, false, and altogether wrong. It would be a failure to begin with: an *œuvre manquée*.[91]

Part 1

1   Büchner's Paradox

The Modern Concept of Revolt

Pessimismo dell'intelligenza,
ottimismo della volontà.
—Antonio Gramsci

Though the English-speaking community has paid relatively little
attention to Georg Büchner and his writings, Anglo-American
scholars have managed to produce one of the worst as well as
one of the best treatments of this fascinating subject. I am referring, on the one hand, to Arthur Knight's un-Brechtian alienation of Büchner, published a quarter of a century ago—and, of
course, to Herbert Lindenberger's fine and perceptive study of
1964. The late Maurice B. Benn's contribution, the third major
monograph on Büchner to appear in English, seems to mark the
final turning of the tide.[1] This "critical study" clearly yet quite
independently continues the high standards established by
Lindenberger and might well succeed in securing a permanent
place for the German playwright not only in the classroom but
also among the Anglo-American reading public and even on the
stage. Enthusiasm, after all, is as contagious as the Artaudian
plague—all the more so if based on such solid ground and abun-
dant evidence as is the case with Benn's book. (And we do
have, at long last, reliable translations of Büchner: by Michael
Hamburger [1966], Victor Price [1971], and, most notably, Henry
J. Schmidt [1969–72].)[2]
    Why, then, emphasize the "critical" aspect of Büchner stud-
ies? The choice of this term is somewhat misleading, for it applies here merely in the limited (albeit most praiseworthy) sense
of meticulous scholarship and careful judgment. Benn scarcely
finds any fault with his hero. Drawing, as is indicated by his

35

title, on that modern philosophy Albert Camus expounded in
L'Homme révolté (*The Rebel*), the author sets out to demonstrate
that Büchner's work—not to mention his life—is permeated by
the threefold spirit of aesthetic, social, and metaphysical revolt
and thus constitutes both a ruthless rejection of older values and
the constant search, however difficult, for new ones. Despite dis-
illusionment and despair that nearly crushed him, Büchner's
works—*Danton's Death* and *Woyzeck*, as well as the masterly
novella *Lenz* and, to a lesser degree, the comedy *Leonce and
Lena*—all testify to the same revolutionary attitude, the same feverish and yet uncannily cold and scientific, almost objective,
approach. The young writer, filled with an unflinching sense of
truth and justice, as Benn so aptly observes, never ceased to
rebel against the principle and practice of "classical," idealizing
art and literature in favor of a powerful, indeed visionary, real-
ism; against oppression, exploitation, and misery in favor of a
truly "social democracy," a genuine "republic" which would do
away with class distinctions and privileges; against a human existence devoid of meaning and guidance, be it divine Providence
or some secularized Hegelian *Weltgeist*, in a chaotic, merciless
universe where nothing is left to suffering mankind but mutual
pity and understanding, humble friendship and solidarity. Re-
futing any and all attempts to deny this unity in Büchner, to belittle either his existential anguish or his political commitment,
Benn insists upon the whole man and the whole work being
at one.

I think he is basically right. Both the fervor and stringency
with which his image of Büchner is proffered will surely prove to
be one of the lasting merits of his contribution. But the very
force of Benn's argument betrays its inherent weakness. Those
three forms of Camusian revolt, while providing a convenient
framework in technical no less than in ideological terms, inevitably tend to exert a certain *Systemzwang* (i.e., a kind of slight but
pervasive schematism and compulsion) which becomes all the
more manifest, both in structure and content, if coupled with a
rigid dichotomy between negation and affirmation, as is the case
here. One cannot help feeling that this must have blinded the author to his deepest insight, an insight most strikingly evident (or
rather, blurred) toward the end of his book, when he does proceed—beyond such sporadic criticism as advanced, very cau-

tiously, against Büchner's aesthetics[3]—to an overall critical assessment. Partly aware of his problems, however, Benn is honest enough to include his own method in his critique.

That Benn's schema fails to do justice to everything he frankly admits; it is neither "comprehensive" nor "exhaustive."[4] In particular, Büchner's passionate "love of nature" and the tender "love of women" in his plays (although by no means ignored by Benn) are telling examples. The values they represent, so the author assures us, are "evidently not . . . values of revolt." But are they really not? Perhaps, one is tempted to suggest, Benn ought to have "supplemented" his reading of Camus with a few chapters from Ernst Bloch, the philosopher of hope.[5] And doesn't the former's treatise itself, this most thorough investigation of man in rebellion and revolution, culminate in expressly integrating nature and love, extolling "the brief love of this earth" (le bref amour de cette terre) without which that "strange joy which helps one live and die" (joie étrange qui aide à vivre et à mourir)[6] could never have arisen? For man's "happiness and joy" are intrinsically linked with the totality of his social and metaphysical, even aesthetic revolt. Büchner knew this; yet his critic, after years of patient research, maintains that "in Büchner's writings no adequate recognition is accorded it."[7] Benn seems to have been unable to conceive of the values of love and nature, frail happiness and defiant hope as being sublated in that same "rare synthesis" whose dialectics of "a pessimistic world view and a progressive social and political activism" he so admirably descried. It was only with "charity" or "hatred" that he could reconcile the "extraordinary paradox" of Büchner,[8] hardly with the "strange joy" which was experienced by Camus.

And not solely by Camus. Just as Büchner's "paradox"—I couldn't agree more with Benn—already foreshadows Antonio Gramsci's famous dictum, "pessimism of the intellect, optimism of the will," so the Frenchman's "absurd" experience that made him "imagine Sisyphus happy" (heureux)[9] clearly echoes such typically Nietzschean concepts as Eternal Recurrence, "Yea-saying to the world," and amor fati. Again, two ideas are inextricably intertwined, philosophically as well as historically: for what is Camille's hymn to nature, "which renews itself every moment in and around [us], glowing, rushing, luminous,"[10] other than a variation, albeit decades avant la lettre, on Friedrich

Nietzsche's Dionysian "pessimism"? And what else are the words of the poet Lenz about "an endless beauty moving from one form to another, eternally unfolding, changing"?[11] Proclaimed on the steps of the guillotine and on the verge of madness, as it were, these confessions from *Danton's Death* and Büchner's dramatic novella[12] reveal a synthesis no less paradoxical or extraordinary than that pointed out by Benn.

Yet for all that, neither Nietzsche nor Gramsci apparently ever took notice of Büchner; nor, as the critic himself has to concede, did Benn's mentor Camus.[13] On the other hand, this French existentialist's dependence upon Karl Marx is as obvious as is the even more surprising indebtedness of the Italian Marxist to the foster father of existentialism. There can be no doubt that Nietzsche, too, looms large in the realm of modern revolt, alongside Marx. But how incompatible are those two towering Germans of the nineteenth century, the prophet of the "superman" and the herald of "total man"? And isn't their contradictory relationship to each other—I hear the outcries of the orthodox—somehow prefigured by Büchner? If indeed we are to accept as our task not merely to investigate his life and work but, as Benn has suggested, "to pursue the investigation freely wherever it may lead,"[14] then we needs must arrive at such crucial questions. To answer them is certainly not easy; nevertheless, it can safely be said that references to Marx alone, useful though they are,[15] will not suffice for a discussion of the drama of revolt, especially under the aegis of Camus.

This is confirmed indirectly by the widespread efforts to revive and reevaluate Nietzsche—efforts particularly apparent among the heirs to Gramsci, the New Left in Italy. They come to the fore in philosophical works: for instance, in a book by Gianni Vattimo which deals with "Nietzsche and the problem of liberation."[16] Similar tendencies, sometimes unbeknown to the authors themselves, inform various literary and theatrical endeavors. An excellent case in point is the plea "for a political theater," dating from 1973, by Massimo Castri.[17] This highly stimulating and provocative treatise (note its allusion to Jerzy Grotowski's *Towards a Poor Theatre*, which advocates a decidedly nonpolitical view)[18] is all the more remarkable and controversial since Castri, director of the Teatro "La Loggetta" at Brescia and a learned critic to boot, successfully amalgamates the achievements of Bertolt

Brecht and Antonin Artaud, yet in doing so appears to be completely unaware of Nietzsche's impact on, or at least anticipation of, the teachings of either of them. It may be, of course, that the Italian, in his already sizable book, simply did not care to rehash the contribution of the alleged "forerunner of fascism" (Georg Lukács). After all, Castri pleads for socialism. Still, given his keen awareness of a Marxian "theater and its double," this blind spot is surprising.[19] Moreover, in spite of many differences, it bears a striking resemblance to what I find lacking in Benn's study of Büchner.

A sizable treatise would be required in order to analyze fully this second cluster of contradictory, seemingly incompatible relations and prefigurations. We would have to examine, on the one hand, the complex kinship of the Epic Theater to the Theater of Cruelty, including the interplay between their respective followers.[20] On the other hand, we would have to gauge the extent to which these seminal ideas, whether consciously or not, were derived from the theoretical writings of Nietzsche.[21] His most influential text in this respect is undoubtedly *Die Geburt der Tragödie aus dem Geiste der Musik* (*The Birth of Tragedy from the Spirit of Music*) or, as its re-edition was called, *Die Geburt der Tragödie oder Griechentum und Pessimismus* (*The Birth of Tragedy, or Greekness and Pessimism*)—a title that is bound to remind one of Büchner, although, unlike Nietzsche, the author of *Danton's Death* discovered the "horrifying fatalism of history" (*gräßlicher Fatalismus der Geschichte*)[22] while studying the French Revolution. To be sure, there is no real need to differentiate between the two versions of the *Birth of Tragedy*, since Nietzsche's key concepts remained identical. Yet when he added, in 1886, his brilliant "Versuch einer Selbstkritik" ("Attempt at a Self-Criticism"), he made it clear, once and for all, that the core of his argument was not, as is generally held, the juxtaposition of the Apollonian and the Dionysian, but rather the opposition of the Dionysian and the Socratic. To the attentive reader this opposition must have been evident from the beginning. Already in the *editio princeps* Nietzsche had stated his message in the strongest terms possible, as witness his words from §12: "This is the new opposition: the Dionysian and the Socratic" (*Dies ist der neue Gegensatz: das Dionysische und das Sokratische*).[23]

This new opposition, first announced in 1872, was meant primarily to explain the downfall of tragedy in ancient Greece. But now that over a century has elapsed, it takes on another, truly prophetic quality. For not only was it directed, quite intentionally and unmistakably, at Nietzsche's own time as well, but it was in fact to determine, far beyond the intentions of the lone philosopher, the course of Western theater ever since. In his *Birth of Tragedy*, as in other writings, he had pointed to a rotten bourgeois sybaritism and to filthy naturalistic art, according to him the worst outgrowths of Socratic thinking. Conversely, he had invoked a total work of art for the future: namely, the mythical *Gesamtkunstwerk* in the vein of Richard Wagner which, so Nietzsche hoped, would finally conquer the stage and reinstate Dionysus. (Alas, he returned only *in 69*.)[24] Looking back, one can hardly deny that the same basic opposition, though oftener in sequence than simultaneously, has kept recurring, both in theory and practice, in those ever more "modern" modes of drama and theater that have swept across the stages from Paris to Moscow and from Berlin to New York. In varying manner and degree, it characterizes all major movements, be they— to cite but a few—Expressionism vs. Naturalism, Surrealism vs. New Objectivity or, more recently, the ecstatic happening as opposed to a terse documentary style. Regardless of the values espoused and condemned, yet always sparked by a fierce disdain of what is summarily labeled "traditional" and "conventional," or bluntly denounced as "bourgeois," the opposition of 1872 and 1886—which coincides with the gradual revival of Büchner since 1879—has persisted till this day.

Its most important representatives, each emerging in the early 1920s but exerting his main impact only after the Second World War, are Brecht and Artaud. Their "Nietzschean connection," missed by Castri and almost everybody as yet, is anchored precisely in that dual principle of the Dionysian and the Socratic: the first pertaining to Artaud, who prophesied, but himself failed to accomplish, the rebirth of the old ritual theater; the second, to Brecht, who heralded, and succeeded in creating, a new theater of dialectical enlightenment, centered upon alienation. What Nietzsche cherished and glorified (compare his self-proclamations as disciple of Dionysus) was received and continued, or at least closely paralleled, by the Frenchman, whereas what he loathed and rejected was, after harsh scrutiny, either discarded or adopted, in order to be further developed, by the German. Artaud took up the Nietzschean element proper; Brecht, the proto-Marxian element—that is, Socratism with its trust in reason and the perfectibility of man and the world, and with its concomitant "epic" forms in the otherwise psychological and even naturalistic drama of Euripides. In short, Nietzsche laid the groundwork for an Artaudian theater of unbridled frenzy—plague and orgy at one and the same time—and for a Brechtian theater, sober but in no way pedestrian, "of a scientific age" (*des wissenschaftlichen Zeitalters*—as its founder repeatedly termed it, in his *Little Organum* and elsewhere in his formidable output of theory and dramatic criticism).[25] The *Birth of Tragedy*, in a word, prefigures both: Brecht's famous *Kleines Organon für das Theater* (*Little Organum for the Theater*) of 1948 and Artaud's *Le Théâtre et son double* (*The Theater and Its Double*), its equally famous counterpart of 1938.

Was it, then, mere coincidence that each of these men admired and loved Büchner, the frenzied playwright-scientist of the early nineteenth century who had anticipated not only a lot of Marx but also a bit of Nietzsche—indeed quite a bit, if one takes into account Büchner's much discussed nihilism and his pronouncements concerning God? Yet, ironically, Nietzsche had not the slightest knowledge of this radical precursor. Artaud and Brecht knew better. The former, for example, planned to produce Büchner's *Woyzeck* at his experimental Théâtre Alfred Jarry, while to the latter, although he never came to stage the play, *Woyzeck* was not merely the "first proletarian tragedy"[26] but the first modern drama to be written. Benn quotes from a report by Arthur Adamov in which Brecht, in turn, is reported to have declared, only a few months before he died, that Büchner's fragment "for him, too, marked the beginnings of modern theater."[27] This sounds impressive enough, but we need not resort to second-hand evidence, nor are such declarations confined to the mid-1950s. As early as the 1920s, Brecht's most iconoclastic period, he praised *Woyzeck* as "technically speaking, nearly perfect" (*technisch beinahe vollkommen*);[28] and later on, once more in the 1950s, he went so far as to establish a specific subgenre to accommodate this work. Together with the Goethean *Urfaust* (the embryo of the great drama) and the fragmentary *Robert Guiskard* by Heinrich von Kleist, it belongs, so we hear, "to a peculiar genre of fragments which are not imperfect, but masterworks penned down as wonderful sketches."[29] Though "incomplete," *Woyzeck* is by no means "imperfect" to Brecht's mind, but is "wonderful," a "masterpiece," a veritable stroke of genius. And we have every reason to believe that Artaud would have shared this opinion, if not its formulation.

Brecht was markedly less enthusiastic about the other works, not only Büchner's comedy but also *Danton's Death*. Or so it may seem at first sight. There is an entry in Brecht's diary, for instance, dated October 4, 1921. It contains the stunning remark: "Such [i.e., a play like *Danton's Death*] is no longer a model." However, the young writer added immediately: ". . . but powerful help."[30] This is, to say the least, a somewhat enigmatic statement, censure as well as praise and thus neither fish nor fowl. But it is based on a performance at the rather poor Stadttheater, the local stage in Brecht's native town of Augsburg; and we should not forget that we are back in the heyday of his youthful iconoclasm. Seen in this light, Brecht's remark is hardly so puzzling. In fact, to admit that a work from olden times was still helpful to the new avant-garde, though it could not longer serve as a model, amounts almost to a Brechtian eulogy in those years, especially when compared to the real Brechtian "vandalism" (as its perpetrator himself once called it).[31] The same entry describes *Danton's Death* as "magnificent" (*ein großartiges Melodrama*) and even relates it, not quite unfavorably, to Shakespeare. Shakespeare, to be sure, shows a roundness of characterization (*Plastik*) which Büchner lacks; but *Danton's Death*, among other things, is "more nervous, more spiritualized, more fragmentary" (*nervöser, vergeistigter, fragmentarischer*).[32]

Brecht defined this play as "ecstatic" as well as "philosophical" (*ein ekstatisches Szenarium, philosophisch ein Panorama*).[33] Doubtless, he must have sensed certain contrasting qualities—an inner dualism, as it were—which we might now be inclined to subsume under a more familiar heading. Or would it be too arbitrary to associate Brecht's impression, grasped so succinctly and soon, with the duality of the Dionysian and the Socratic, including their various ramifications? Was that which he felt merely a faint reflection of the then still rampant Expressionism? Yet if there is any epoch in German literary and theatrical life under the spell of both Büchner and Nietzsche, it surely is the decade of the Expressionist *Aufbruch*. Not only *Danton's Death* but also

Woyzeck had a tremendous impact on that generation; and as to Nietzsche, virtually no playwright or poet, critic or novelist, was to escape his influence. Benn gives some cursory hints of the influence of Büchner,[34] and we already have valuable contributions treating the repercussions of Nietzsche's works.[35] The same applies to Brecht. Having developed a strong dislike of Expressionism, he tried to criticize Büchner as well, if only on the spur of the moment; but his words, unwittingly or not, reveal rather the opposite. Like *Woyzeck*, *Danton's Death* ultimately became the object of Brecht's admiration, for in his later years, his verdict that this play was an impossible "model" for modern writers was to be reversed. In Brecht's notes on dramatic structure, "Verschiedene Bauarten von Stücken" ("Various Ways of Constructing a Play"), jotted down in 1955,[36] *Danton's Death* is listed with Kleist's fragmentary *Guiskard* (and also with Friedrich Schiller's *Demetrius*, another fragment) and expressly recommended as a model to be studied and emulated by young dramatists. Although Brecht singles out the *Massenszene*, the handling of large crowds in the script and on the stage, this is by no means the only merit he has come to acknowledge. Nor is *Danton's Death* the only play of Büchner's to be reconsidered. "What differences," Brecht goes on to exclaim, "between *Woyzeck* and *Leonce and Lena!*" (*Welche Unterschiede zwischen 'Woyzeck' und 'Leonce und Lena'!*) It is an exclamation of awe, denoting not a divergence of excellence but the overwhelming variety of ingenious suggestions offered in both of these works. And there are really not many plays that Brecht recommends. Apart from Shakespeare, who is inexhaustible, no more than eight from the classical German repertoire are mentioned: three by Goethe, three by Schiller, one by Kleist, and one by Gotthold Ephraim Lessing. Büchner, however, is represented not only by his drama on the French Revolution but also by his ambivalent comedy and his proletarian tragedy. In other words, his whole dramatic oeuvre is exalted here and finally raised to the status of an example to be followed.

But had it not been so ever since Brecht embarked on his career? Talking about himself in the third person, as befits not only Caesar but also, it seems, a Marxist writer, he reminisced in exile, sometime around 1940: "When World War I drew to an end, he was a young man studying medicine in Southern Ger-

many. There were two dramatists . . . who influenced him most.
[One of them,] Büchner, . . . was performed for the very first
time in these years and the playwright [*der Stückeschreiber*, as
Brecht used to refer to himself] saw a production of the fragment, *Woyzeck*."³⁷ This laconic report is Brecht's official testimony, so to speak, of his indebtedness to Büchner. Contained in
that gigantic torso of a Galilean dialogue on the theater called *Der
Messingkauf* ("Buying Brass"), the most ambitious theoretical
venture Brecht ever undertook, not only does it sum up his lifelong fascination with *Woyzeck*, with *Danton's Death* and *Leonce and
Lena*, and, in all likelihood, with *Lenz*. It also shows that Brecht
pictured himself as belonging to the same breed of playwright-
scientists as their author: materialistic writers, that is, whose
work does not spring from sheer emotion, an effusion of the
heart or outpouring of the soul, but is firmly rooted in thought
and knowledge, observation and experiment. Significantly, the
paragraph preceding Brecht's report begins: "Before the playwright became involved in the theater he had studied natural sciences and medicine."³⁸ (*Bevor der Stückeschreiber sich mit dem Theater befaßte, studierte er Naturwissenschaften und die Medizin*.) This
is a trifle exaggerated yet basically correct. Brecht, proud of his
early studies in medicine and the sciences, could claim to be
akin to Büchner in more than one way. The "playwright" tended
to adjust and stylize things a bit, it is true; but then Büchner—
who had founded the conspiratorial Society of Human Rights,
who had secretly written and published the rousing pamphlet,
The Hessian Messenger—was not merely a playwright-scientist,
either. He was, like Brecht, a playwright-revolutionary as well.

No, it is certainly not by chance that we find so many references to Büchner in Brecht's life and work. I shall agree, however, that they cannot possibly be matched by what we have
found in Artaud, whose brief reference, although again no accident, is an almost totally isolated one. Nevertheless, we ought
not to underestimate it. The Théâtre Alfred Jarry was a product
of the 1920s, after all, and the simple fact that a young writer in
France not only knew of Büchner at that time but boldly har-
kened back to him is most unusual. It is all the more astonishing
since Büchner's work, though hailed by the avant-garde, still had
to struggle for recognition even in Germany, at least in her academic circles. Under such circumstances, Artaud's intention to

stage *Woyzeck* is indeed highly illuminating and imbues his testimony with an authenticity almost as commanding as that of Brecht's. If the German felt attuned to his model, so did the Frenchman, albeit in a different key. And this double accord, together with its Nietzschean overtones, is borne out by any comparison with Büchner, be it in theory or in practice, on the printed page or on the boards.

But let us return once more to the notes and statements of Brecht. For is it not remarkable how consistently he connects Büchner's plays with the idea of fragmentariness? Not only does he stress such traits in the fragment *Woyzeck* (although, to be sure, he considers it a "complete fragment," as Thomas Carlyle would have said) but he also likes to group this play, as well as *Danton's Death*, with the unfinished works of Kleist, Goethe, and Schiller. *Woyzeck* is linked with *Robert Guiskard* and *Urfaust*; and *Danton's Death*, with *Robert Guiskard* and *Demetrius*. Nor has Brecht hesitated to proclaim, paradoxical though it may sound, the fragmentariness of *Danton's Death* itself. He maintains, on the one hand, that this drama is "more spiritualized" than a Shakespearean play while, on the other hand, he calls it "more fragmentary." But what exactly does Brecht mean by terming it *fragmentarisch[er]*? Of course, Büchner had to complete this work in an incredible hurry, ejecting it, as it were, within a few weeks, under the constant threat of being arrested, thrown into jail, and perhaps tortured and slowly put to death. Yet a look at the text will readily demonstrate that *Danton's Death* is definitely not a fragment but an aesthetic and philosophical whole. Obviously, then, what Brecht had in mind when emphasizing the fragmentariness in Büchner was not necessarily the idea of incompleteness, but rather something else. And what is this other than "the 'open' dramatic form" which Büchner's plays, as Benn rightly observes, have in common "with most of Brecht's"?[39] Didn't Brecht attribute this form to *Urfaust* as well? And also, some restrictions notwithstanding, to Shakespeare and the Elizabethan drama in general? According to the *Stückeschreiber*, they all share the same loose, ballad-like, detached structure—or, to be more precise, a seemingly loose structure combining, as a ballad combines its stanzas, a series of separate parts. Each of them forms an independent fragment, so to speak, within the whole fragment, which in a way is fixed, yet never tightly or closely.

In view of Brecht's penchant for punning, the very name he
adopted, *Stückeschreiber*,[40] might be interpreted as designating "a
writer of plays consisting of pieces or fragments" (the German
word *Stück*, similar to the English *piece*, can denote both). There
is ample proof in his *Little Organum* to substantiate this. "The
parts of the plot," so we read in §67, "have to be carefully set off
one against the other by giving each its own structure as a small
piece within the piece [or play within the play]" (*Die Teile der
Fabel sind also sorgfältig gegeneinander zu setzen, indem ihnen ihre
eigene Struktur, eines Stückchens im Stück, gegeben wird*).[41] Brecht's
examples—supplemented by his *Der kaukasische Kreidekreis* (*The
Caucasian Chalk Circle*)—are again borrowed from Büchner (*Woyzeck*), Goethe (*Faust*), and Shakespeare (*Richard III*). Schiller
and Kleist, however, are conspicuously absent (cf. §66),[42] and
for equally good reason. Their fragments, although unfinished
works in a literal sense, belong to the opposite type of drama:
namely, its "closed" form, represented not by Shakespeare, the
"dissolute genius" (*wüstes Genie*) chided in Nietzsche's *Ecce
homo*,[43] but by Racine and Corneille, the polished masters of the
tragédie classique, for whom Nietzsche, here as elsewhere, expresses such rare esteem and affection. The French, according to
him, at least tried to assume the heritage of the Greeks, the im-
peccably perfect Attic tragedy—perfect, that is, until Socratism
cast its evil eye upon it and destroyed it, leaving nothing behind
but the "deplorable rubble" of Euripidean drama. This hybrid of
art and dialectics is decadent, says Nietzsche, both in its "open"
structure and its "open" ideology. He would approve only of a
"closed," a genuinely tragic form. Yet that which Euripides, unwilling to reproduce this form any longer, happened to create
instead (or rather, to project into the future) was anything but
decadence: it was a new work of art, no less important and im-
perative than the old one. In Nietzsche's *Birth of Tragedy*, its seeds
are reluctantly registered as "a dramatized epic" (*ein dramati-
siertes Epos*);[44] in Brechtian terminology, it is known as "epic
drama" or "epic theater." Thinking of Brecht's early plays such
as *Baal* and, in particular, of Büchner, one might as well call it a
ballad for the stage.

More could be said about these correspondences between
Büchner and Brecht, but let us now turn to Artaud, for he, too,
subscribed to the idea of fragmentariness. That this Dionysian

maniac should side with rationalistic Socratism, if only briefly, may at first seem bewildering. However, what Artaud favored was not merely fragmentariness but outright chaos, and what he abhorred was dramatic form as such, be it "closed" or "open." His notorious slogans "Down with all masterpieces!" and "No more masterpieces!" ("En finir avec les chefs-d'œuvre," as a whole essay of his is entitled) were perhaps prompted by French classicism but are launched, expressly, against Sophocles and Shakespeare alike. Western drama in its entirety, the Greeks as well as "Shakespeare and his imitators," is rejected by Artaud because, as he curtly puts it, "they [the plays] are literary, that is to say, fixed." Although he specifies works that are "fixed in forms that no longer respond to the needs of the time," [45] his is a total rejection of any form, any finished text or artistic structure—in fact, of art and literature themselves. In plain but firm language, the prophet from Marseilles decreed: "We must get rid of our superstitious valuation of texts and *written* poetry." [46] The emphasis is Artaud's; for what he scorned and detested, despite his own hectic writing, was the written—that is, fixed or literary—word. Literature, Artaud insisted, must be banned both from poetry and from the theater. In any case, it must be reduced at all costs and as much as possible.

But he did allow for a few exceptions nonetheless. There were certain "great romantic melodramas" [47] that found favor (we remember the young Brecht's formula for *Danton's Death*), and there was, of course, Büchner's fragmentary *Woyzeck*. It appears to have offered Artaud a unique opportunity to experience what is proclaimed in his paradoxical confession: "Beneath the poetry of the texts, there is the actual poetry." [48] This implicit "valuation of a text" was due, on the one hand, to the condition of *Woyzeck* as a real fragment, barely "fixed" indeed, and, on the other, to the inherent structural "looseness" of the play, its ballad-like sequence of short, detached scenes, full of visionary atmosphere and wild, frantic gestures, embodied in a concise yet immensely rich dialogue. Büchner's play contained not a single trace of what Artaud rejected as "literature"; since it belonged to no recognizable tradition, the play was not besmirched by "bourgeois conformism," that abominable "idolatry of fixed masterpieces," as Artaud described it in his essay against the *chefs-d'œuvre* (from which all these quotations are taken). [49] On the contrary, *Woy-*

zeck, by its very form as well as its content, enabled Artaud to break through language in order to touch life (*briser la langage pour toucher la vie*)—which means, according to his preface to *The Theater and Its Double*, nothing less than to "create or re-create the theater" (*faire ou refaire le théâtre*).[50] Life, theater, and poetry (*poésie*, a concept far transcending the normal usage of this term) are united here as almost identical manifestations of one and the same "whirlwind of higher forces" (*tourbillon de forces supérieures*).[51] In other words, they are metamorphoses of his universal principle of cruelty.

Artaud's formulation has been much decried, and mostly misunderstood. "This cruelty," Artaud had to specify as early as 1932, "is a matter of neither sadism nor bloodshed, at least not in any exclusive way." And he goes on to explain, in this first of his three "Lettres sur la cruauté" ("Letters on Cruelty"): "I do not systematically cultivate horror. The word cruelty must be taken in a broad sense." It is, Artaud repeats, not synonymous with bloodshed, martyred flesh, crucified enemies. "This identification of cruelty with tortured victims is a very minor aspect of the question. In the practice of cruelty there is a kind of higher determinism." Such determinism, however, has to be a conscious one, Artaud stipulates; and he therefore hastens to add: "Cruelty is above all lucid, a kind of rigid control and submission to necessity. There is no cruelty without consciousness and without the application of consciousness."[52] In the threefold apology that was to be included in Artaud's book of 1938, these philosophical aspects of a fundamental cruelty (*cruauté pure*) are further developed and intensified.

Still, he does not lose sight of the theater. In his second letter, written some eight weeks later but also dating from 1932, Artaud declared:

> I employ the word "cruelty" in the sense of an appetite for life, a cosmic rigor and implacable necessity, in the gnostic sense of a living whirlwind that devours the darkness, in the sense of that pain apart from whose ineluctable necessity life could not continue. . . . When the hidden god creates, he obeys the cruel necessity of creation which has been imposed on himself by himself. . . . And theater in the sense of continuous creation . . . obeys this necessity.

A play in which there would not be this will, this blind appetite capable of overriding everything, visible in each gesture and each act and in the transcendent aspect of the story, would be a useless and unfulfilled play.[53]

Théâtre, for Artaud, constitutes a concept as far-reaching as *poésie*. And neither of them was "tacked on to [his] thinking." Like *cruauté*, they had "always been at home there" and he had only "to become conscious" of their implications.[54]

Thus in the last of his three letters Artaud gave full rein to his *idées métaphysiques*.[55] Having referred in passing to Gnosticism and its demiurge, he now proceeds to Hindu religion and philosophy, to suffering Brahma, to the juggernaut ("a terrible crushing and grinding") of all creation and existence. The whole universe is cruelty, he proclaims: "Eros is . . . cruelty . . . , death is cruelty, resurrection is cruelty, transfiguration is cruelty. . . . It is cruelty that cements matter together, cruelty that molds the features of the created world."[56] And though this be Artaudian madness, yet there is method in't. But shouldn't we also have expected a bit of another, more recent philosophy than Hinduism or Gnosticism? The correspondences, I trust, are evident. What Artaud designs is not only "a circular and closed world" but also a "closed space . . . fed with lives, and each stronger life tramples down the others, consuming them in a massacre which is a transfiguration and a bliss."[57] However more somber and ferocious, this universe of cruelty shows an unmistakable similarity to the Dionysian universe of Nietzsche.[58] Both are moving eternally in a closed sphere; both inflict, upon every being, endless pain, which coincides with boundless bliss; both are controlled by unbending fate or necessity and permeated by a blind life force which manifests itself as will to power. The same *amor fati* (note Artaud's obsession with the term *necessité*) and the same conscious yea-saying to the world in its totality pervade their ideas. Even a doubtful follower of Nietzsche's like Camus, even an unrecognized precursor such as Büchner seems to partake of this world view. For isn't Camus's "strange joy," the absurd happiness of his Sisyphus, comparable to Artaud's experience? Doesn't Büchner, too, share some of it, although he seldom, and much less exuberantly, expressed it?

At any rate, there are enough instances of cruelty in his works, in *Woyzeck* as well as in *Danton's Death*, the "concrete symbol" of which, "integrating and unifying" the entire play, is, after all, the guillotine. As Benn stresses, it is "oppressively" evoked from the very beginning and "we feel it looming ever nearer, until . . . it actually dominates the stage in all its hideous reality."[59] Other examples of such cruelty—both physical and mental, even metaphysical—could be gathered from the torment of the poor soldier Woyzeck, downtrodden and abused by everyone; from the lust for life of his woman, Marie, who betrays him and whom he kills; from the tortured mind of Lenz, the doomed poet, slowly mangled by the advance of madness; or again, from *Danton's Death* with its orgies, nightmares, and frenzies. But there is no more need to enumerate these antecedents of the ideas of Artaud than to detail, either structurally or ideologically, those pointing to Brecht. The correspondences are self-evident. Nor is there any reason to speak of the massive amount of documentary material incorporated, as is well known, in *Woyzeck*, in *Lenz*, and, above all, in *Danton's Death*. Büchner's many sources have been investigated long since. From those concerning the French Revolution, for instance, one-sixth of the text of the whole work was lifted, in part verbatim, when Büchner wrote his historical drama. Truly, the theater of revolt he created is both "cruel" and "epic-documentary."

And so, to a certain degree, are the theaters created by Brecht and Artaud. The correspondences just observed can also be discerned—with Nietzsche and Büchner acting as catalysts—between the avowed Marxist from Germany and the unpredictable Frenchman, who sometimes had very different inclinations. (As a matter of fact, Artaud dedicated a poem to Adolf Hitler.)[60] Left is Left and Right is Right, to be sure; but occasionally the twain do meet. Just as Artaud reveled in "fragmentariness," an element of Brechtian epic theater, so Brecht, at least for a while, indulged in "gruesomeness," an element of Artaudian cruelty. Scenes of cruelty are embedded not only in Brecht's *Aufstieg und Fall der Stadt Mahagonny* (*Rise and Fall of the City of Mahagonny*) and *Badener Lehrstück vom Einverständnis* (*Baden Didactic Play of Acquiescence*), but also in works such as *Baal* or *Im Dickicht der Städte* (*In the Jungle of Cities*) and, especially, *Leben Eduards des Zweiten von England* (*Life of Edward the Second of England*). This adaptation of Marlowe's famous play, retranslated by Eric Bent-

ley under its original title, reaches its climax in the cesspool of
the tower, where King Edward is imprisoned and tormented in
order to "ripen" (*mürb [zu werden]*): that is to say, finally to con-
sent to abdicate. Standing in a hole, "up to the knees in sewage
water," and kept awake day and night by incessant drumming,
he is "unnaturally exhausted"—and yet, "he sings"! "If you
open that trap," his hangmen tell each other, "you hear him
singing." For, paradoxically, all this misery, all the sufferings
Edward has to endure in his "cage," only serve to "harden his
limbs" and fill him with "boundless greatness," as he ecstatically
exclaims: *Abwasser härtet / Meine Gliedmaßen . . . Geruch des Abfalls
macht mich noch / Maßlos vor Größe.* Not only does Edward resist;
he openly triumphs. And only minutes before he is choked to
death, this most miserable of all kings breaks into the most extraordinary hymn to cruel life:

> Rain was good. Not eating filled the belly.
> But the best was the darkness.
> All were irresolute, many reluctant, but the best
> Betrayed me. Therefore
> Who is dark, let him stay dark,
> Who is unclean, let him stay unclean.
> Praise deficiency, praise cruelty, praise
> The darkness.[61]

In a scene so Artaudian, Bentley's free rendering of *Mißhandlung*
("physical ill treatment," also "injury" and "abuse") is thoroughly justified.[62] What is meant here is indeed utter cruelty.

Moreover, as might be inferred, these are not merely the words
of an unusual character in an unusual play. King Edward speaks
as the young writer's mouthpiece. In one of Brecht's most personal confessions, his book of verse called *Hauspostille* (*Manual
of Piety*), the same ideas and images not only recur but are uni-
versalized. In fact, his atheistic prayer book contains a poem
which, forming a choral variation on Edward's hymn of praise, is
expressly entitled "Grand Hymn of Thanksgiving." This "Großer
Dankchoral" culminates in a line echoing almost literally the paradoxical ecstasy of Brecht's martyr-king: "Praise ye the coldness,
the darkness, the decomposition!" Yet in order to feel the whole
impact of such pious blasphemies, one has to be familiar with

their frame of reference. What Brecht alludes to is a well-known Lutheran hymn, "Praise ye the Lord," written three hundred years ago by Joachim Neander but still sung today in thousands of churches in Germany and beyond. Only by juxtaposing Neander's *Lobet den Herren, den mächtigen König der Ehren,* that passionate outburst of Christian belief, can Brecht's jubilant nihilism fully be grasped in its dark power and glory: *Lobet die Kälte, die Finsternis und das Verderben!*[63] It should also be noted, of course, that the word *Verderben* suggests far more than just "decomposition" or "decay." Rather, at least in Brecht's usage during the early 1920s, this and similar concepts tend to be nearly as all-embracing as their Artaudian counterparts. *Verderben* and *Finsternis,* it is true, may not qualify as "metaphysical ideas"—and Brecht would surely have refuted, and been disgusted with, any such classification. Nevertheless, he must have conceived of, and undoubtedly has created in certain works, a universe of cruelty of his own. His "Great Hymn of Thanksgiving" and his adaptation of Marlowe's tragedy—reminiscent, in several ways, of Artaud's adaptation of Shelley's melodrama, *The Cenci*—are but two random examples which could be augmented at will. In this the young poet and playwright came astonishingly close to a world view espoused by Artaud as well as by Nietzsche and Camus. Brecht, too, worshiped the Dionysian, despite all Socratic appearances. Even after his conversion to Marxism, his existential delight in the "terror of . . . unceasing transformation" (*Schrecken [einer] unaufhörlichen Verwandlung*), as extolled at the end of his *Little Organum*[64] or as contemplated in his favorite image of an eternally changing "stream of happening" (*Fluß des Geschehens*),[65] did not subside but was simply sublated.

Incidentally, this river or flow[66] is not only Heraclitean but also Nietzschean. One cannot ignore the fact that Brecht's dialectical sublation, though never quite explicitly, resulted in a notion of history as linear and cyclical at the same time. Repeatedly in his later work, Progress and Eternal Recurrence are about to coincide.[67] The mature Marxist author—fairly cognizant of the situation, if we think of his lifelong struggle to subjugate the Dionysiac Baal—preserved a good deal of those early views and attitudes paralleled so closely by Nietzsche and Artaud. And Camus, in his philosophy of the absurd, presents an even more striking correspondence, especially to the ensuing paradox of history. This is perhaps best illustrated by the telling symbolism used, say, in Brecht's "Lied von der Moldau" ("Song of the Vltava") and in *Le Mythe de Sisyphe* (*The Myth of Sisyphus*). Camus resorted to antiquity in order to convey his modern message: "The Gods had condemned Sisyphus to ceaselessly rolling a rock to the top of a mountain, whence the stone would fall back of its own weight. They had thought with some reason that there is no more dreadful punishment than futile and hopeless labor."[68] Brecht, on the other hand, drew upon the Middle Ages but wrote a proletarian folk song. It is included in his stage version of Jaroslav Hašek's novel *Osudy dobrého vojáka Švejka za světové války* (*The Adventures of the Good Soldier Schwejk in the [First] World War*) and its decisive stanza reads:

> The stones on the Vltava's bottom go shifting
> In Prague three emperors molder away.
> The top won't stay top, for the bottom is lifting
> The night has twelve hours and is followed by day.[69]

Brecht's "Song of the Vltava"—composed in 1943, only a year after the essay on Sisyphus was published—occurs twice in his *Schweyk im Zweiten Weltkrieg* (*Schweyk in the Second World War*) and proves to be no less important than Camus's myth.

What the song and the myth have in common is obvious. Both contain a central image: for Camus, it is Sisyphus rolling his rock a long way uphill only to see it tumble down again and be forced to begin anew; Brecht focuses on the stones on the bottom of the river, quietly turning and wandering, with the regular change from night to day and day to night as the decades, the centuries go by. Each author pictures a process that combines a linear with a cyclical movement. Progress and Eternal Recurrence coincide. For Camus, this is a real paradox which he consciously accepts. The dynamics of past and future have been replaced by a static present, and Sisyphus, whom we have to imagine "happy," holds that this, as everything, is "well" (*tout est bien*).[70] "The absurd man says yes," Camus concludes, "and his effort will henceforth be unceasing."[71] The cycle prevails. It is different, however, with Brecht: what prevails for him is the linear movement. His words express hope instead of happiness; the will to change and a sense of the future instead of acceptance and absurd "yea-saying." In the second stanza of his song, he stresses repeatedly: "Times change" (*Es wechseln die Zeiten*).[72] Unlike Camus, who admonishes us that "it is essential to know the night" (*il faut connaître la nuit*),[73] Brecht emphasizes the dawn and the day. Things will be changing, he assures us, for the times change, too. Brecht paradoxically claimed that, in spite of "wandering in circles," man does "advance" (*Im Kreise laufend kommen wir weiter*, as his pseudo-Chinese sage, Me-ti, would have it, if only in regard to a frustrating debate).[74] Contrary to the convinced existentialist, the convinced Marxist was intent on rejecting any wholesale absurdism.

Yet the mature Brecht's paradox of history is a real one. It can by no means be exhausted, much less resolved, with mere intentions. Implicitly, by converting historical processes into cycles of nature, as well as by postulating change that never ends, Brecht accepted—as had Friedrich Engels in his *Dialectics of Nature*—the great chain of cruel being, the coincidence of an infinite linear progress and a never-ending cyclical recurrence. (And are they not ultimately identical, much as two parallels meet at infinity? Brecht was well read in mathematics and the current astrophysical theories, as witness notes such as "Der gekrümmte Raum" ["Curved Space"], also to be found in his prose collection, *Me-ti*.)[75] In his youth, at any rate, Brecht not only accepted but consciously affirmed the cyclical nature of history, deriving, like Camus, happiness and a strange joy from the absurdity of all existence. Once more, Brecht's *Edward II* offers the prime example. This entire play, both in its structure and its ideology, is a rotating wheel of Fortune, a dramatic emblem of enormous dimensions, symbolizing the rapid alternations of human fate.[76] An absurd and merciless unity emerges through the workings of the wheel as it performs, ever faster, its senseless circles. History and time themselves, so essential to a "Chronicle Play," are crushed and ground, as it were, to an amorphous mass of unceasing change and unchanging present. What remains is a static futility. Paradoxically, the more Brecht's wheel turns, the less it moves.

Small wonder, then, that all the main characters in his play experience the lot of Sisyphus. I must refrain here from a further comparison of the works of Brecht and Camus, though it would certainly be warranted.[77] Just consider Mortimer, King Edward's antagonist. Again using a most significant image, he exclaims toward the end of his "rise and fall":

> Hoisting a small load out of the primeval
> Slime—my own strength ebbing with the years—I can't
> help seeing, stuck to it,
> The human algae. More and more.
> As I pull myself upwards I
> See ever more dead weight.
> Around the knees of the last one, another
> Last one. Ropes of people. And at
> the pulley-wheel of these ropes, breathless,
> Dragging them all up: me.[78]

Mortimer's is a travail as useless and hopeless as that imposed on Sisyphus. And later in this scene Queen Anne, once Marlowe's "fair Isabel,"[79] bursts into absurd, hysterical, almost uncontrollable laughter: she laughs, as she intimates, "at the world's emptiness" (*über die Leere der Welt*)[80] yet at the same time, full of insatiable lust, professes her delight in it and her desire to continue to enjoy it. Anne, to be sure, doesn't quite "praise" darkness and cruelty; but can she be too remote either from Sisyphus or his elder brother? For what else is her husband, Brecht's jubilant martyr-king of 1924? More than anyone in this powerful drama, King Edward psalming in the cesspool as he awaits his death is a grotesque prefiguration—admittedly "dark" and "unclean"—of what Camus was to personify, so nobly and heroically, by reinterpreting the Greek myth. In Brecht's early play, both a cyclical view of history and a universe of cruelty affirmed in the spirit of Dionysian *amor fati*, are epitomized in an exemplary manner. Nihilism and absurdism converge.

Which brings us back to Büchner. The theater he created, so we found, is "cruel" in the sense of Artaud as well as "epic-documentary" in the sense of Brecht. (We need not add the name of Erwin Piscator.) But while such theater may also be "absurd" in the sense made famous by Camus, it is hardly, as some critics would have us believe, "absurdist" in the sense of Eugène Ionesco. In this respect, an anticipation or possible connection has been grossly exaggerated, particularly with regard to *Leonce and Lena*. What informs Büchner's comedy is not so much absurdism à la Ionesco but alienation à la Brecht. Benn makes a strong case for this proto-Brechtian "comic alienation,"[81] and given the many grotesque and satirical elements not only in *Leonce and Lena* but in Büchner's work as a whole, he is absolutely right. Most of them, at least in our context, have been unduly neglected.[82] To spot a German precursor of Ionesco and his kind, one ought to look not at Büchner, but rather at his most gifted and extravagant colleague in those years, Christian Dietrich Grabbe. In addition to ambitious tragedies, Grabbe left a single comedy, elaborately entitled *Scherz, Satire, Ironie und tiefere Bedeutung* ("Jest, Satire, Irony, and Deeper Significance"). This play, if any, foreshadows—via Alfred Jarry and the French Surrealists, including the German-born Dadaist Iwan Goll—the absurdist theater of the 1950s.[83] And this is an ancestry not merely to be surmised or construed. Jarry himself—perhaps the first to plead overtly for the absurd in modern theater—translated the ribald "Lustspiel" of Büchner's contemporary and staged it, under the new title *Les Silènes* ("The Sileni") in 1898. If we remember Artaud's Théâtre Alfred Jarry and its program, or ponder the role played by Silenus and the satyrs (or sileni) in Nietzsche's *Birth of Tragedy*, we must concede a splendid serendipity to the author of *Ubu Roi*. What he discovered and aptly put into practice was, beyond any doubt, "an extraordinary German play" (*une pièce allemande extraordinaire*).[84]

Jarry's phrase is inserted in a speech on puppets ("Conférence sur les Pantins") treating a favorite image of his, which was equally dear to Büchner and Artaud. Evidently, these various types of absurdism are tightly intermingled. But instead of going on to differentiate them, we had better return to Büchner's "extraordinary paradox" of a "pessimistic world-view and a progressive . . . activism" and ask ourselves whether it should not be extended. Does it not comprise, in Benn's excellent wording so reminiscent of Gramsci, a paradoxical view of history as well? That is to say: Does it not also reflect, albeit on strictly conceptual and biographical levels, the coincidence of a cyclical recurrence and a linear progress? Büchner's famous letter to his fiancée—his "fatalism letter"—is highly instructive:

I studied the history of the [French] Revolution. I felt myself crushed by the terrible fatalism of history. I find in human nature a horrifying sameness, in the human condition
an inescapable force, granted to all and to no one. The individual merely foam on the waves, greatness sheer chance,
the mastery of genius a puppet play, a ludicrous struggle
against an iron law: to recognize it is our utmost achievement, to control it is impossible.[85]

Not only these lines, but most of the writings of Büchner abound
with such moods and ideas, poignant images and compelling
formulations. Here it will suffice to comment on but two aspects of this text.
First, Büchner's letter is permeated with the gloomy atmosphere
engendered by an "inescapable force" turning both nature and
history into a "horrifying sameness" and leaving man "crushed"
under the "terrible fatalism" it entails. We all know this "iron
law." What it represents is the same "cruelty" which manifests
itself in the senseless rotation of Brecht's wheel of Fortune, and
what it produces is the same static futility, the same "savage misery of man's condition" which pervades Brecht's play. Missing
from Büchner's letter, though surely not from his oeuvre as a
whole,[86] is the equivalent to a Brechtian hymn of praise. Unlike
the modern King Edward and his creator, he appears to have
been unable (or merely unwilling) at this point to revoke their
desperate outcry: *O wilder Jammer menschlichen Zustands!*[87]

Second, the concept of a circular process is not only implied in
Büchner's letter but is actually present. There is indeed an analogy to those emblems and images—be they from Brecht or
Camus, Artaud or Nietzsche—depicting a similar experience.
The last called man a "speck of dust" (*Stäubchen vom Staube*) and
spoke of the "eternal hourglass of existence" (*ewige Sanduhr des
Daseins*) which runs incessantly, being turned upside down
again and again.[88] Büchner, for his part, pictured man as mere
"foam on the waves" (*Schaum auf der Welle*), choosing a totally
different image yet achieving an almost identical effect. Both express, as do the others we have investigated, essentially the
same thought. For is it really so farfetched to read Büchner's image of the "wave[s]," by definition rising and falling in all eter-

nity, as a circular and cyclical one, a symbol or emblem imparting an absurd notion of change without change?

Such, at any rate, must have been the way Brecht, one of the keenest of readers, reacted when he studied Büchner's letter, probably sometime during the early 1920s. And, it seems, Brecht's impression was to last. As late as 1938, looking back at his formative years dominated not only by Büchner but influenced also by Nietzsche,[89] he, too, visualized the individual as nothing but foam on the wave(s) of an ever-changing, never-changing ocean. He put it as follows: "White spray flew from a muddy wave."[90] It is true, this image has a more active sound and a critical edge to boot; yet who would deny its resemblance to that of Büchner? In addition, Brecht is quite specific. His isolated verse—rather obscure unless placed into perspective—belongs to a fragmentary sonnet, "Über Nietzsches *Zarathustra*" ("On Nietzsche's *Zarathustra*"). Neither man in general nor just any individual is envisaged here, but rather the teacher of Eternal Recurrence. The dazzling work and dismal fate of Nietzsche: they are fleeting foam, the "white spray" flying from a "muddy wave," that is, a world of dirty exploitation and decadence. I do not have to belabor the Marxist allegory hidden in Brecht's verse. Nor do I have to dwell upon the wheel, the ball, the globe or sphere, and the many similar signs and movements, circular as well as cyclical, in *Also sprach Zarathustra* (*Thus Spake Zarathustra*). Their meaning and importance are truisms. But the fact remains, and is all the more remarkable, that the tragic philosopher and his euphoria were accorded by Brecht (who was used to weighing his words carefully) the very same image that Büchner had employed to utter his anguish and despair.

Büchner's "iron law" (*ehernes Gesetz*), that vicious circle of sameness and sempiternal present, forms merely one half of his paradox of history. The other half is formed by the law of the straight line aimed toward the future. As in previous instances, although much more forcibly, the ring of repetition and the arrow of progress meet, at least collide. And, finally, they also coincide, for Büchner literally incorporates them. If his letter is the climactic testimony of his pessimistic world view, then his life, contradicting such a view every day, is the continuous proof of his social and political activism. His knowledge and bitter insights, resulting in a paralyzing nihilism, are countered over and over by an untiring determination to revolt against all injustice, oppression, and misery. To reiterate Gramsci's dictum: "Pessimism of the intellect, optimism of the will." Only if the two are hammered together, both in historical and philosophical terms, does Büchner's full paradox emerge. That the same man who felt himself crushed (*wie zernichtet*) by the immutability of the human condition should found, at about the same time, a secret Society of Human Rights intent on radical change, planning to overthrow the government and trying to revolutionize the people, is almost inconceivable—and yet this is precisely what Büchner did! If anything, this beginning anew, after having been crushed so dreadfully, recalls the attitude of Camus's Sisyphus who, knowing that his lot will never improve, bends forward, reaches down for his rock, and leans firmly against it to move it uphill once more. Sisyphus will continue forever, as Büchner continued after the devastating failure of his short-lived Society of Human Rights, the members of which were jailed, tortured, and murdered, or had to flee into exile. Like Camus, Büchner was an unflagging rebel. "Let our hope lie in the passage of time" (*Hoffen wir auf die Zeit*), he defiantly wrote in 1835.[91] The "nihilist" accepted defeat just "for the time being" (*für jetzt*) and the "absurdist" sternly prepared for the future.[92]

This "extraordinary paradox," says Benn, is Büchner's "rare synthesis." Nevertheless, Benn himself ascribes it not only to Camus—though restricting it, oddly enough, to *La Peste* (*The Plague*)—but attributes it also to Ernst Toller. Indeed, he goes so far as to name it, vaguely generalizing, "a peculiarly modern attitude" which might well be the last one "that can still seem valid."[93] But neither such speculations nor Benn's arbitrary restrictions are tenable. The truth lies in between. Those who indulge in plain pessimism, as those who indulge in plain optimism, will always outnumber the few embodying both—of whom Toller, to be sure, is a most informative example. To include him seems, therefore, quite appropriate. From the prison cell where he served a five-year sentence for his leadership in the abortive German revolution, Toller voiced his paradox of agonizing awareness and indefatigable will. And like Gramsci, he did not shrink from combining it with a Nietzschean concept, calling upon the "strong," the "men with a will—although they know," as he worded it in a letter to Stefan Zweig, dated June 13, 1923.[94]

Benn quotes from this letter extensively, and rightly so; but it is by no means the only evidence of Toller echoing Nietzsche, anticipating Gramsci and Camus, and "joining hands" with his "brother" of a century before, Büchner.[95] Unmistakably, the young prisoner cried out against the cyclical return in history and invoked the proverbial myth which was to be transformed, two decades later, into the core of Camus's philosophy. Toller lamented, and simultaneously braved, the depressing "recurrence" (*Wiederkehr*) and "identical circuit" (*gleicher Kreislauf*) of things and events, as well as the "Sisyphean labor" (*Sisyphusarbeit*) faced by all revolutionaries, particularly in Germany.[96] Already these early documents indicate the direction of his whole life (just think of how frantically Toller worked during the Spanish Civil War) and they could easily be supplemented by others testifying to his despair and his desperate efforts to overcome it—not to mention Toller's creative work, which offers ample proof of a similar kind.[97]

Regardless of the historical situation, the same predicament elicits the same response, if only among those few. There is no question, however, that their philosophies, or the ideologies involved, may differ drastically. Even more telling examples are provided not merely by Brecht but once again by Nietzsche who, while praising the return of everything, yet announced the advent of a novel era. Both men, each in his own way, carried Büchner's paradox to extremes. Even Brecht (not the young writer, naturally, but the Marxist) confessed how he had to dissuade himself from trusting his very senses; how he had to force his mind wilfully to perceive darkness as though, "perhaps," it were light. In an almost imploring quatrain, he exhorted himself and his reader:

> Do not trust your eyes,
> Do not trust your ears.
> You perceive darkness,
> Perhaps it is light.[98]

Conversely, not even he who preached the recurrence of the identical, the joyous yea-sayer to the world in all its manifestations, was willing to abandon the idea of progress. Despite his acceptance of the iron ring of necessity, Nietzsche celebrated—for instance, in *Thus Spake Zarathustra* and in his *Götzen-Dämmerung oder Wie man mit dem Hammer philosophiert* (*Twilight of the Idols, or How to Philosophize with a Hammer*)—the "arrow," the "straight line," and their ultimate "aim" in "distant futures," to which he "blissfully" aspired. He had Zarathustra, his main spokesman for his prophecy of the "superman," project himself repeatedly as a shivering *Pfeil* soaring *durch sonnentrunkenes Entzücken*, tending *hinaus in ferne Zukünfte* that nobody ever dreamt of. In such enravished flight through the "blaze of the sun," as in the ecstasy of the circle, Nietzsche thought he had found a perfect image for his Dionysian experience. "Formula of my happiness" (*Formel meines Glücks*), he emphatically exclaimed in one of his "arrowy" sayings. And truly philosophizing with a hammer, he defined his formula thus: "a Yes, a No, a straight line, a goal" (*ein Ja, ein Nein, eine gerade Linie, ein Ziel*).[99]

How it all ended with Nietzsche is well known. Incapable of enduring so glaring a light any longer, he collapsed in 1889 and spent the rest of his days in the darkness of insanity. The terrible tension between pessimism and optimism virtually tore him asunder. But let us not forget that Toller, too, proved unable to endure this everlasting tension, to sustain the paradox of intellect and will. In 1939, shortly before the outbreak of the Second World War, his steadfastness gave out and he committed suicide after years of unwavering struggle. To his friends, it is true, this was not totally unexpected. Toller had long since, not unlike Büchner's Danton, yearned for a place of refuge in nothingness. He had a profound "home sickness," as he confessed from his cell, going on to explain: "And the home's name is nothingness" (*Und das Heim heißt: Nichts*).[100] Yet neither Danton nor his author, in spite of so many declarations, laid hands upon himself. Only Toller took his own life. Büchner persisted, as did Camus, Brecht, and Gramsci. To impute that Büchner gave up would be utterly wrong; but it has been a common prejudice—so deeply ingrained, in fact, that very few seem to be able to get rid of it. The early exception worthy of note (if we ignore the victims of a "progressive fallacy," rare but no less one-sided than the former) is Hans Mayer. He, at any rate, has realized Büchner's paradox from the beginning and stated it in all its contradictoriness. His

Georg Büchner und seine Zeit ("Georg Büchner and His Time"), written in exile during the 1930s and first published in 1946, portrays the author of *Danton's Death*, *Woyzeck*, and *The Hessian Messenger* under the double heading of an "'optimistic' or 'pessimistic' world view, of progress and freedom . . . or circuit [*Kreislauf*] and constraint." Also, Mayer convincingly argues that it was indeed love—though surely not love of nature alone, as he claims—which, in the long run, enabled Büchner to persist and "to live face to face with the Medusa" (*im Angesicht der Medusa zu leben*).[101]

The definitive edition of Mayer's book dates from 1972. But as late as 1974, homage paid to Büchner was still marred by the old misunderstanding. The following epigram, modest as it may sound, offers a weighty case in point. Although consisting of just three laconic lines, it attains special weight because it comes from a writer who simply ought to know better. He is Heiner Müller, the East German dramatist born in 1929. Müller uses the same device as Brecht but, apparently, feels content to be addressing solely himself. At most, he is talking to readers from his own generation:

> OR BÜCHNER, who died in Zurich
> 100 years before your birth
> age 23, from a lack of hope[102]

It is plain that the figure "100" marks a slight poetic license, since Büchner died on February 19, 1837. Otherwise the data are correct, but the drift of the poem is wrong. Whereas Toller is quite likely to have died "from a lack of hope," Büchner decidedly did not. As we have seen, he "always" despaired and yet, in utmost defiance, "never" ceased to hope and to plan for the future. Büchner upheld his gorgonizing paradox until the end of his life.

Müller's miniature epigram is not his only text which is relevant here. It belongs to an entire series, or cycle, of poems. Müller aptly calls them "Lektionen." In most of these lessons he reflects upon the lives and works of earlier authors, especially revolutionary ones, investigating their hopes and despairs, their achievements and failures and, above all, the final "solutions" at which they arrived. Suicide, madness, or the holding out against any and all afflictions: such are the possibilities he has to ponder. Two of his poems are of particular interest. The first is dedicated to Brecht; the second, immediately preceding his verse on Büchner, to Vladimir Mayakovsky. Why did a writer like Mayakovsky, the poet of the Russian Revolution, choose the fatal bullet? Or as Müller, in a magnificent couplet derived from his model, phrases it:

Mayakovsky, why
The leaden full stop?

After all, weren't the poet's life and work surrounded by a successful revolution? What on earth, then, was his reason? Was it really—as has been suggested of Toller—disappointment in love (*Herzweh, Wladimir?*) that caused Mayakovsky to kill himself? And if so, are we not again to remember Büchner? Do not his plight and his perseverence call for a comparison with Mayakovsky? Yet Müller continues in an almost flippant tone:

"Has
A lady
Closed herself up to him
Or
Opened herself
For another?"

Müller's poem seems to allow for nothing but a petty affair and its carnal complications, which he takes up, toys with, and quickly brushes aside. Or rather, he abruptly breaks off, since his answer is given subsequently, if implicitly. Having dismissed the assumption of *Herzweh* altogether, so we are led to believe, he now juxtaposes a dynamic emblem of irresistible revolution and ultimate victory (namely, Mayakovsky's bayonet in the fists of his comrades) with an equally stark and compelling sign of stagnation and bitter defeat. It is the fate of the German predecessor of Büchner, Friedrich Hölderlin, who had succumbed—like Alexander Blok, another Russian to be mentioned here—to the onslaught of insanity. Without any comment, Müller quotes the ending of one of the most touching of Hölderlin's fragments, "Hälfte des Lebens" ("Half of Life"). Its four italicized lines (at least in Müller's version) form the conclusion of "Majakowski":[103]

> *The walls stand*
> *Speechless and cold,*
> *The wind-swung*
> *Weather-vanes clatter.*[104]

Such verse has been praised and interpreted as "purely poetic" and/or "cryptically existential" for decades. However, combined with the fate of Mayakovsky and the symbolism thereby laid bare, it gains the quality of the paradox of revolution. This paradox is as permanent as the revolution itself, according to Müller, and thus yields an overwhelming reason indeed. None other, it seems, is necessary. Hence this poem must be understood, despite its dash of benevolent irony, as no less earnest and momentous than the epigram (or epitaph) devoted to Büchner. Müller's opening, "OR BÜCHNER," makes their connection unambiguously clear. There is no intent on his part to belittle or ridicule the agonizing contradictions faced by his fellow writers and revolutionaries; quite to the contrary.[105]

Still, he does rule out, albeit not explicitly, what proved to be of such vital importance to Büchner. Müller completely bypasses it when dealing not only with him but also with Hölderlin; and though undeniable, Mayakovsky's "woe" is shrugged off as immaterial. Love and happiness are at best assigned a subordinate role. Moreover, Müller views them differently. What he advocates is neither the hectic bliss of Nietzsche nor the brief joy of Camus; neither the charity of Hölderlin nor the more worldly feelings of Mayakovsky. Instead, Müller wants to promote a "new concept of happiness." This *neuer Glücksbegriff* is pithily summarized in a discussion published in 1966. "There is [under socialism] no private, noncommittal happiness any more, no happiness of pensioners and consumers," Müller decreed.[106] Admittedly, this sounds promising enough; but it results in an old and fairly shopworn dichotomy which, in turn, endows the "new" in Müller's concept with a rather pale, idealistic hue. Happiness that isn't a profoundly personal and individual experience must needs be vague and somewhat anemic. Or to put it bluntly: Ideology as such, however passionately embraced, is a frigid bedfellow. Besides, most of the characters in Müller's work belie his own postulate happily; they show no lack of private fulfillment but plenty of love and lust and an oftentimes "Baalish" quest of sheer consumption. Discussing his drama *Der Bau* ("Construction") of 1963–66, the author himself had to concede this basic "defect in the play." His statement speaks for itself: "The new concept of happiness is presupposed, not formulated."[107] The reverse, of course, is equally true. The new concept may reign in theory, while the old practice continues unabashed.

Almost all revolutionary writers are haunted by this same dichotomy. If they respond to it, their answers seem to be twofold—depending, though not entirely, on the historical situation. What prevails in a socialist society is the difficult task of attempting a synthesis, as exemplified by East German playwrights such as Peter Hacks or Volker Braun (with *Moritz Tassow* and *Kipper Paul Bauch*, respectively); Hartmut Lange (with *Marski*, completed before its author moved to West Berlin) could be adduced as well. These writers' principal aim is the redemption, as it were, through socialism of that wild Dionysiac Baal with whom even Brecht, in spite of his constant endeavors, was unable to come to grips. Yet during the ongoing revolutionary struggle—especially if it is seen as a permanent one—socialist writers tend to suppress their dilemma without trying to resolve it and to concentrate, all the more seriously and searchingly, on the fundamental paradox of revolution. Very seldom do they encompass both: tackling the dilemma on the one hand and pursuing the paradox on the other. However, that is what distinguishes Müller. He solemnly pledged to remedy the defect in his work ("That has to be corrected")[108] and yet, simultaneously, learned and taught quite a different lesson.

In this regard, as in so many others, Müller is "Bertolt Brecht's most consequential and important successor,"[109] for Brecht had already encompassed both dilemma and paradox. Despite being torn by contradictions, which he stated in no uncertain terms, he did not hesitate to proclaim his view of happiness. More categorically than his most fervent disciple, he declared in a conversation with the composer Paul Dessau: "Happiness—that is Communism" (*Das Glück ist der Kommunismus*).[110] Brecht tried time and again, in his plays and elsewhere, to reconcile this "new" concept with the "old" practice, as is apparent in his programmatic lines from *Der gute Mensch von Sezuan* (*The Good Woman of Szechwan*):

> To let no one perish, not even oneself
> To fill everyone with happiness, even oneself
> That is good.[111]

Like a tender sister of Baal, the "good woman" celebrates love and nature, if only from the jungle of her city (see, for instance, scene 4).[112] Indeed, a host of Brecht's characters indulge in such sentiments, whereas Brecht himself, in an elegy no less touching than Hölderlin's, felt obliged to disavow a great deal not only of his writings but also of his doings:

> Love I practised carelessly
> And nature I looked on without patience.[113]

Yet the mere fact that entire anthologies of Brechtian poems about "earthly love and related enigmas"[114] can be amassed amply demonstrates how essential, how vital all this was to "grim" Brecht. His life and work actually abound with such experiences (and, by the way, with friendliness). Brecht hardly handled his love of women carelessly[115] nor did he treat nature with impatience or indifference. Rather, each may be seen as constituting a central "unifying theme" of his life and work although, by and large, his attitude toward nature was more complex.[116]

In any case, it ought to be evident why Müller, in the following "Lesson," took his cue not only from the aforesaid elegy but also from Brecht's verse on darkness and light quoted earlier. "An die Nachgeborenen" ("To Those Born Later") starts with the elegiac exclamation, "Truly, I live in dark times!"[117] Based on the same somber metaphor, Brecht's quatrain reads:

> Do not trust your eyes,
> Do not trust your ears.
> You perceive darkness,
> Perhaps it is light.

The two texts are combined by Müller, who more than agrees with Brecht, drawing on him nearly verbatim:

Truly, he lived in dark times.
The times have brightened.
The times have darkened.
When brightness says, I am darkness,
It has told the truth.
When darkness says, I am
Brightness, it does not lie.[118]

Yes, Brecht lived in dark times. Have they come to an end? In what way do they differ from ours? There is more light now, says Müller, but there is also more darkness. So if the light claims to be darkness, it must be telling the truth; and if the darkness claims to be light, it can't be accused of lying. Has anything changed at all? Nothing has changed, according to Müller, and yet everything has changed. His "Brecht" is the most thorough, most poignant lyrical expression of the extraordinary paradox of revolution and history in general. Stripped of all personal feelings and moods, Müller's lines present the bare historical, or revolutionary, process in its permanent interchangeability of movement and stagnation, advance and reverse, progress and recurrence. It is couched, quite fittingly, in an imagery evincing the dialectics of enlightenment—those insoluble dialectics which, regardless of how they are stated, leave the mind caught between hope and despair, and more often than not, wavering from optimism to a pessimism that only an almost absurd act of the will can overcome. Even the author of the *Little Organum* of 1948, who extolled the terrors of unceasing transformation and advised us to enjoy them "as entertainment,"[119] was not fully proof against such trials. In his quatrain dating from the late 1940s he sounds rather uncertain, allowing but for a faint possibility of darkness turning into light, light shining in darkness (or *Lux in tenebris*,[120] to parody one of his own parodies); whereas Müller, more Brechtian than Brecht himself, conceives of them as inextricably enmeshed and entangled, and establishes his insight as a universal law. To be sure, it lacks the serenity and poise of the *Little Organum*; and the seeds of this "dark enlightenment," so to speak, are to be found not only in Brecht but also in Nietzsche. Müller's poem as a whole is, in fact, reminiscent of both: with its startling antitheses and chiasms as well as its (seemingly) monotonous parallelisms and repetitions. He owes an immeasurable amount to Brecht but also, to some degree, poetizes—or rather, philosophizes—with a Nietzschean hammer. At least in this text, there appears to be not the slightest difference between the struggle for socialism and its accomplishment, between a pre- and a postrevolutionary situation.

However, is there really none? If we study "Brecht" attentively, I think we'll have to modify our judgment. Müller's "Lesson" does convey change, though on a strictly formal and structural level. Its design betokens a subtle, almost imperceptible movement from darkness to light, precisely because the former (cf. "dark times," line 1) governs the outset, while the latter (cf. "brightness," line 7) dominates the end. Progress wins out in Müller's lines, their overpowering "darkness" (mentioned four times in German) notwithstanding. And once again, Brecht provides a persuasive model. It is the ending of his play on Galileo as he produced it at the Berliner Ensemble in 1956. (When Brecht died, Erich Engel took over the production.) The final darkness that enveloped the theater, both concretely and figuratively, and the last piece of dialogue uttered in this scene flatly contradicted each other; yet the form of their clash, its mere structure and texture, signaled hope. Charles Laughton's version, written in collaboration with Brecht, comes perhaps closest to the original. Galileo is sitting upstage; his daughter, Virginia, has moved to the window:

> GALILEO: How is the sky tonight?
> VIRGINIA: Bright.[121]

Müller may well have been inspired by this ending since his verse stems from 1956—as does, incidentally, the main part of his cycle. He may have composed it under the dual impact of Brecht's sudden death, on August 14, and of events such as the hapless Hungarian uprising in November.

That second thoughts are in order is further borne out by Müller's twofold poem, "Zwei Briefe" ("Two Letters").[122] These epistles, much more discursive than most other "Lessons," gradually introduce the author of *Galileo* and group him, significantly enough, side by side with the author of *Danton's Death*. While Büchner's anguish is stressed without comment, Brecht's work— despite Müller's sincere admiration—is classified as preliminary and his death, naturally, as premature; but "great tenacity" is attributed to him as an individual, as well as to his lifelong search for a "possibility not to kill his neighbor," that is, for mankind to live in peace. Only shortly before he died did he catch a glimpse of this possibility. At long last, Müller says, it began to emerge, albeit still "afar" and "half hidden by a bloody fog." These concepts and metaphors had already been employed by Brecht himself and they appear, for good reason, either in his play on the birth of science or in his elegy on the dawn of socialism. "Our goal," he confessed in "To Those Born Later,"

> Lay far in the distance;
> It was clearly visible, though I myself
> Was unlikely to reach it.[123]

Similarly, his Galileo comes to profess (again in the Laughton translation of 1947, which is actually a second version): "This age of ours turned out to be a whore, spattered with blood. Maybe, new ages look like blood-spattered whores."[124] Or as Brecht/Galileo put it in 1938, when the first version of the play was completed: "Ich bleibe . . . dabei, daß dies eine neue Zeit ist. Sollte sie aussehen wie eine blutbeschmierte alte Vettel, so sähe eben eine neue Zeit so aus."[125] Both Brecht and Müller use the imagery of blood in order to characterize the new age or its emergence; and each time the ultimate "goal" is far away and unattainable—although for Brecht, contrary to Müller's contention, it was at least "clearly visible." As of necessity, however, Brecht made Galileo announce, immediately after the sentences just quoted: "The breakthrough of light occurs in the deepest darkness."[126] Obviously, the dialectics of enlightenment cannot be absent, either.

But they are prone to shifts of emphasis. Doesn't Müller here sound far more pessimistic than the Brechtian texts to which he alludes? Nevertheless, he maintains that there had been "some hope," not sheer "lack of hope" as ascribed to the young revolutionary from Hesse. Müller opens his centerpiece on Brecht, in his "Two Letters," with lines which can hardly fail to remind us of his verse on Büchner, including his own misunderstanding:

> Or the misunderstood Bertolt Brecht
> With great tenacity and some hope
> *Not even he could do more than bend the bow*

How many blockheads survived him.
All his life he searched for a possibility
Not to kill his neighbor. Toward the end
He had perceived it from afar
Half hidden by a bloody fog.

Brecht's utopia—in whatever "distant futures," as Nietzsche
would add—has a place in history, if only for those "born later."
To those living today, on the other hand, no more is allotted,
even in a socialist society, than the tiny "span between nothing
and a little." Such, in concluding, is Müller's humble message,
the "Lesson" he has learned and decided to teach: *Für uns die
Spanne zwischen Nichts und Wenig.*[127] Yet quite contradictorily, in
his "Construction," the hero is proud and eager to declare: "I am
the pontoon between the Ice Age and the Commune."[128] And
this message, contained in the selfsame volume as the previous
one, is surely no less peremptory. Once more, it is pronounced
by, and addressed to, the revolutionary builder(s) of socialism.
Though changing but "a little," or perhaps "nothing," during
their brief span of life, they know they are living bridges span-
ning the immense distance between the "Ice Age" and the
"Commune," the horde and the collective, and thus changing
everything. Time immemorial and distant futures—prehistory
and posthistory, as it were—must be welded together, according
to Müller, in order to create a concrete utopia. Which is to say
that one paradox, paradoxically, is being countered by another.
But man's vicissitudes continue.

It may seem arbitrary, at least at first sight, to associate Müller
directly with Nietzsche. To associate him with Camus, however,
is anything but arbitrary.[129] Just as the French existentialist of the
early forties chose the myth of Sisyphus to express his innermost belief, so did the East German Marxist when, in 1955/61/
74, he wrote and rewrote his play, *Traktor* ("Tractor"). Of course,
the context is totally different in each case, for Müller's elaborate
image, inserted in a drama on agricultural productivity achieved
under the most adverse circumstances, is indeed, despite the
"absurdity" inherited from Camus, "poetic material for and
within the building of socialism."[130] Moreover, Müller carefully
avoids citing Sisyphus' name. But both the ancient myth and the
modern meaning it has acquired make themselves felt all the
more intensely:

Forever to roll the same rock up the forever same mountain. The weight of the rock increasing, the worker's strength decreasing, proportionate to the growing steepness. Stalemate just before the peak. The race with the rock, which rolls downhill many times faster than the worker had been rolling it upward. The weight of the rock increasing, the worker's strength decreasing, relative to the steepness. The weight of the rock decreasing absolutely with every uphill movement, faster with every downhill movement. The worker's strength increasing absolutely with every shift (to roll the rock uphill, to run downhill, before beside behind the rock). Hope and disappointment. Roundness of the rock. Mutual wear and tear of man, rock, mountain. Up to the dreamt-of climax: release of the rock from the attained peak into the abyss beyond. Or to the dreaded point of exhaustion just before the no longer attainable peak. Or to the conceivable point zero: no one moving nothing on a plain. STONE SCISSORS PAPER. STONE WHETS SCISSORS SCISSORS CUT PAPER PAPER BEATS STONE.[131]

Of the paradox of revolution and history, this text is the most compelling and complex presentation that has ever been published, at least by a Marxist writer. However obscure it may seem, it is a highly revealing document. Not only does it offer a whole series of variations on Sisyphus rolling his rock uphill and helplessly watching it tumble down again, but it also equates his predicament, by picturing him as "the worker" (*der Arbeitende*), with the frightening travail of those who are working for socialism. Over and over, Müller ponders the paradoxical coincidence of advance and return, rise and fall, progress and recurrence inherent in this symbol, and the cycle of "hope and disappointment" it implies. One might even be tempted to conclude, in view of his choice of vocabulary, that he takes the word "revolution" in its most literal sense (i.e., connecting the very concept of it with the notion of a circular movement). At any rate, his predilection for the verb *wälzen*, "to roll," is quite obvious. (And *Umwälzung*, instead of *Revolution*, it should be noted, was a favorite term of Brecht's, too.)

It ought to be evident that Müller combines myth and history. This tendency of his is by no means restricted to *Traktor* but equally rampant in other works. For example, in *Zement* (*Cement*), Müller's stage version of F. V. Gladkov's novel of the same title, there erupts a veritable geyser of myths and legends, sputtering forth Prometheus and Hercules as well as Ulysses, Medea, and Achilles. And *Cement* takes place right at the hub of history: namely, in Russia during the revolution! As Müller's adaptation was written only in 1972, this can hardly be attributed to a juvenile phase in his development. In fact, it permeates his entire oeuvre. I cannot see any dichotomy between Müller's "production of history" and an alleged "incest of myth" (as it has been claimed by an American critic).[132] On the contrary, his combination of myth and history corresponds exactly to his blend of a mythical theater of cruelty à la Artaud with a dialectical theater of history à la Brecht. We need only consult plays such as *Schlacht* ("Battle," with the implication of "Slaughter") or *Germania Tod in Berlin* ("Germania Death in Berlin")[133] in order to realize that Müller, like Peter Weiss, is one of the most consequential successors of either of them.[134]

This peculiar amalgam is clearly reflected in a style characterized, as witness the sentences quoted from *Traktor*, by a singular mixture of scientific and poetic language. Talking almost like a physicist, Müller meticulously discusses the increase or decrease of the weight of the rock and how that affects the strength and capacity of the "worker"—yet he elaborates with additional imagery that raises myth and metaphor, and their concomitant meaning, to an even higher power. He draws upon chess and athletics, for instance, speaking of a "stalemate" (*Patt*) between Sisyphus and the rock before they approach the summit, and of a subsequent downhill "race" (*Wettlauf*) between the two; yet he also deliberates, in plain terms, what might conceivably put an end to Sisyphus' struggle. There are three possibilities, so we are told: the "climax" or culmination (*Höhepunkt*), which would actually mean man's ultimate victory over his fate; the "point of exhaustion" or termination (*Endpunkt*), which would indicate his final defeat; or else, a "point zero" (*Nullpunkt*), which would amount to a kind of entropy. Such thinking, of course, is not only discursive but also "linear" since it tries to break away from the vicious circle; however, it is immediately overwhelmed by yet another "eruptive cascade of metaphors"[135] which repeats and reaffirms "cyclical" thinking. For "STONE SCISSORS PAPER" refers to the German game *Knobeln*, based on gestures, and used in lieu of throwing dice: a game which is by definition both aleatory and circular. All we have to do is read on where Müller stops, and complete his enumeration—"SCISSORS PAPER STONE PAPER STONE SCISSORS"—until we have come full circle. Significantly, his text expressly emphasizes the growing "roundness of the rock" (*Rundung des Steins*) beforehand. But once more the circle is met by the straight line; the ring, by the arrow. For doesn't the very roundness of the rock also contribute to its maneuverability? In other words: Isn't the stone ever easier to handle the smoother it gets? We must be careful lest we fall short of Müller's mark. His ambiguous myth calls for a close reading in every respect. In particular, such caution applies to *Knobeln*. Anyone familiar with that game will notice, upon rereading Müller's sentence, that here again the choice of vocabulary is significant. Instead of employing the ordinary terms which suggest the mutual destruction of stone, scissors, and paper, and would invest the whole passage with a negative quality, Müller seems to have searched for productive alternatives that subtly endow his image with a more positive meaning. This is unmistakable in STEIN SCHLEIFT [i.e., "whets," or "sharpens"] SCHERE, where almost any trace of the usual wrecking, destroying, demolishing is missing; but even in SCHERE SCHNEIDET PAPIER, what we have is not so much a destructive "cutting up" as a rather productive "cutting out." The reckless *zerschneiden*, in short, is replaced by a regular [*zu*]*schneiden*. By thus startling the expectations of his audience, Müller has already obtained a slight ambiguity which then, at the end, becomes altogether outspoken. The normal expression, in the last triad of words, would have been *einwickeln* (i.e., "to wrap up," or "to envelop"); yet Müller has selected a synonym, [*ein*]*schlagen*, and by dropping its prefix evokes, naturally, the original meaning as well: namely, "to beat"—a verb which in German, as in English, signifies also "to defeat, to overcome, to surpass." As a result, PAPIER SCHLÄGT STEIN, though caught in an endless cycle, simultaneously breaks away from it, turns off into a linear, a forward motion. Progress and productivity, however ambiguously, win out over the barren recurrence of the identical.

And this paradoxical breakthrough is in turn echoed by the ending of the play itself. Here, a *Traktorist* who had served as a soldier under Hitler reminisces—without any pangs of conscience, by the way—about how he and his comrades had killed an old Russian peasant, member of a collective farm, in front of a gigantic corn field. Because they were drunk and in a generous mood, they deigned to grant him a favor, letting him dig his own grave in his own ground:

> We had schnapps, the lieutenant was in the mood
> He said: Tell the bolshevik, because
> I like his beard I will permit him
> To dig his last hole in his own field.[136]

So they ask the peasant to show them his field amongst those thousands of acres of corn. But the old man simply replies "Thisallmyfield." He doesn't even remember where his own lot used to be before the kolkhoz went into effect. His sole answer is an all-embracing gesture:

> We asked him where his field was. Says the old man:
> Thisallmyfield. We: Where his field had been
> Before it all became collective. That one merely gestures,
> Like the owner of a large estate, round the land
> Where breast-high stood the corn for miles.
> He had plainly forgotten where his field had been.[137]

These are the concluding lines of Müller's play. Their message, it would appear, is unequivocal. However, it has to be read, or received, against the dual background of the somber myth of Sisyphus and of a history of violence and war, devastation and genocide. Such is the "bloody fog" present not just through him who relates the murder (a builder of socialism!) but still threatening all over the globe. In verse preceding this scene, and preformulating the message it is to convey, Müller states in no uncertain terms that, though Hitler's war was over, the battles continued—and will continue to rage, so we must infer, for a long time to come:

AND WHEN THE BATTLE WAS LOST
THEY RETURNED HOME THE BATTLEFIELD IN THEIR HEARTS
AND MANY A ONE WAS BROUGHT TO RUIN YET
A WEAPON AND AN ENEMY TO HIMSELF.
AND MANY A ONE WHO WAS NO MORE STILL TRIUMPHED
AS GRASS GROWS FROM THE DEAD EARLY EACH YEAR [138]

While sounding a final note of hope, in history as in his version of the myth, Müller does maintain his precarious balance. He, too, upholds his extraordinary paradox till the very end. And therefore, not unlike Jean Genet, the author of the most ambiguous play on revolt and revolution in French literature, Müller might proclaim: "It is a matter of holding out the ambiguity to the very end" (*Il faut tenir l'équivoque jusqu'à la fin*).[139] *Le Balcon* (*The Balcony*) and *Traktor* both date from about the same time and both writers have by no means altered, but rather deepened, their primary conceptions.

To be sure, Genet, another follower of Artaud, is a bitter foe of Brecht and, what is worse, has revealed himself as a rabid reactionary.[140] Our fleeting comparison, then, was merely formal—although, if pursued in a different direction, it would gain immediate significance.[141] More than formally, however, the position, attitude, and ideas of Müller emerge if gauged, for instance, by those of his East German colleagues, Reiner Kunze and Volker Braun, for these two mark the concrete pitfalls Müller has managed to avoid. Neither has he (though indebted not only to Artaud, but also to Camus) ever denied the possibility of effecting change, not even for himself; nor has he (though trying to sublate Brecht, as do so many dramatists in the GDR) indulged in shallow optimism. But Kunze, in an interview with the West German newspaper *Die Zeit*, flatly confessed that he feels much closer to Camus than to Karl Marx. According to the reporter, Kunze "doesn't believe in changeability at all."[142] To Kunze's mind, it is the human condition as such which constitutes an insoluble, a hopelessly "antagonistic" contradiction. And he is quoted here verbatim: "To live face to face with nothingness and, in full awareness of the absurdity of this existence, to will one's human(e)ness, to prove oneself human(e)."[143]

Volker Braun, on the other hand, declares that he has arrived at a stage "beyond Brecht" and has already entered the Promised Land Marx predicted; for him, the "most stirring contradiction" (*aufwühlendster Widerspruch*) still left to the revolutionary builder of socialism is but "the novel one" between "the political leaders" and those who are "being led" by them (*zwischen den politisch* Führenden . . . *und den* Geführten). Although he admits that ours is a period of transition that doesn't exclude the GDR, he is convinced that, "obviously," such new contradictions are assuming more and more weight and importance. But, of course, they are "nonantagonistic." Deceptively similar to Brecht in style and method, he posits a "new dramaturgy" which, both in terms of its content and by its rules and guidelines, claims to supersede the Brechtian model once and for all.[144]

Braun, it is true, shares a number of ideas with Müller and he is certainly one of the more talented East German writers—as is Kunze, the author of a book with the highly ironical title *Die wunderbaren Jahre* ("The Marvelous Years"). Yet neither of them seems to be able or willing to endure and to sustain the agonizing paradox of revolution and history. Only Müller does. This is what distinguishes him from any of his colleagues, be they from the GDR or from other socialist countries. His dramas have been labeled "Optimistic Tragedies,"[145] but in reality, and despite all attempts at disassociation, they are far more akin to Brecht and Büchner than to Vsevolod Vishnevsky who, in 1932, published the original *Optimisticheskaya Tragediya*. Müller's "optimism" bespeaks the same "progressive absurdism," the same *coincidentia oppositorum* so blatantly manifest in Brecht's dictum from his *Galileo*, "The breakthrough of light occurs in the deepest darkness." For, after all, what does Müller's contention amount to in his "Tractor" rendition of the Camusian myth? To state that Sisyphus grows all the more powerful and sovereign the more he has to toil and to labor (*Die Arbeitskraft absolut zunehmend mit jedem Arbeitsgang*) is surely no less paradoxical. Clearly, Brecht and Müller are united in the same absurd and admirable belief in progress whose earliest roots are apparent in the life and works of Büchner. One might well call it a modern *credo quia absurdum*, a dialectical materialist mysticism.

In summing up, I could also have invoked the paradox of Gramsci once again (who, by the way, died exactly a hundred years after Büchner, in a fascist dungeon in 1937). His creed, as well as that of Brecht and Müller, or even Camus, is miles apart from the complacent absurdism of an Ionesco which some people would like to detect in Büchner. Compared to this giant, Ionesco and his kind, with their stale and stagnant products, strike me as dwarfish and ridiculous, almost silly.[146] Nevertheless, in all fairness one cannot but concede that, ever since the young playwright was rediscovered toward the end of the nineteenth century, writers and readers alike have always appropriated their own Büchner: which is, in fact, the touchstone of every great historical figure in literature or the arts, whose works invariably attain mythical dimensions. Each admirer, whether creative or not, singles out what he needs most. Such was already the case with the German Naturalists; but even nowadays, both in Germany and abroad, the same can be observed. Yet neither were the Naturalists the first nor will our contemporary authors—let alone countless readers and theatergoers—be the last to succumb to the spell of Büchner. And in between there was the expressionist generation, to recall but the most conspicuous movement. Nietzsche alone sticks out, oddly enough. The rediscovery of the tragic world of Büchner, soon after the *Birth of Tragedy* had appeared and caused its scandal, seems to have gone completely unnoticed by this ardent lover of any reevaluation of the past. That Nietzsche ignored so influential a precursor of his is one of the whims and ironies of *Geistesgeschichte*, but not only of *Geistesgeschichte*. For wasn't he, on the other hand, quite notorious for his hatred of practically everything connected with the French Revolution?

However, *les extrêmes se touchent*, and the "dialectics of enlightenment" have become ever more penetrating. Nowhere can this be seen more clearly, in all its paradoxical, already paralyzing contradictoriness, than in a recent statement by Heiner Müller, issued as a facsimile in an anthology of "Plays from the Twenties," the very selection of which is highly telling. The Nietzschean heritage of Artaud and Brecht has been welded together, at long last, by the East German playwright; but the shadow of Büchner also looms large, although his name is not mentioned. In fact, I feel Müller's "Note on Antonin Artaud" might justly be read as a fitting if all too somber—and, to be sure, quite one-sided—summary of what I have tried to explicate in my foregoing considerations. Thus, then, spake Heiner Müller:

> Artaud, the language of pain. To write out of the experience that the masterworks are accomplices of power. To think at the end of Enlightenment, which began with the death of God—Enlightenment being the coffin wherein He is buried, and rotting away with His corpse. To live, locked in this coffin.
> THINKING IS ONE OF THE GREATEST PLEASURES OF THE

HUMAN RACE thus Brecht has Galileo speak before they
show him the instruments. The stroke of lightning which
split Artaud's consciousness was Nietzsche's experience it
might also be the last. Artaud is the decisive case. He has
wrenched literature away from the police; the theater, away
from medicine. Under the sun of torture, which shines simultaneously upon all the continents of the planet, his
texts are flowering. Read on the ruins of Europe, they will
be classical.[147]

The reference to Brecht's *Galileo* is most revealing indeed. And it
also indicates to what extent Müller's sum total does in fact differ
from mine. Namely, while Galileo the scientist continued to believe in and struggle for progress in spite of his recantation,
Müller the Marxist seems to have recanted for good. What is imparted by his words is no longer a concept of genuine revolt, of a
mundane *credo quia absurdum* as it was embodied, for the first
time in history, in the life and work of Georg Büchner; rather,
those words betray sheer absurdism and despair, even delight in
despair. Could it be that Heiner Müller, the author of the most
compelling and complex formulation of the modern concept of
revolt, as well as of its most poignant expression in lyric poetry,
has also become the first to signal its final demise?[148]

Yet can one ever forsake such a paradoxical belief? The very
question is enigmatic: "The text breaks off and calmly the answers keep rotting on."[149]

2 "Cœur" and "Carreau"

Love in the Life and Works of Büchner

Έρος δαὖτέ μ' ὁ λυσιμέλης δόνει
γλυκύπικρον ἀμάχανον ὄρπετον.

—Sappho*

What the texts contain is clear—and clearly the critics, virtually without exception, have chosen to avert their eyes. Let us begin by simply listing what the reader encounters.

Two women commit suicide out of love for their men: one while in the grip of madness, the other through a conscious decision (decades before Wagner's *Tristan and Isolde*, she dies a veritable "love-death"). And there are men no less extreme in their passions: one drowns himself after having nearly strangled his lover; another attempts to take his own life in a similar manner— in a state of erotic intoxication, already anticipating ultimate fulfillment. A third, seized by blind despair, compulsively and methodically murders his woman, stabbing her to death in an almost ritualistic process of judgment and execution. All this in only three dramas, one of which is a sketchy fragment; dramas, moreover, teeming with true love and trollops, lovers and libertines, the most delicate tenderness and the most drastic lasciviousness, dramas in which flies mate on people's hands, curs couple in the streets, and we are confronted by the question: "Don't you feel like . . . tearing off your pants and copulating over someone's ass like dogs . . . ?"[1]

*For an English version of the epigraph, see Sappho, *The Poems and Fragments*, Greek text with an English translation by C. R. Haines (London and New York, n.d.), p. 116: "Love's sweet palsy yet again my limbs doth wring, / That bitter-sweet resistless creeping thing." A German rendition which is closer both to the spirit and to the letter of Büchner would read: "Schon wieder schüttelt mich der gliederlösende Eros: / Bittersüß, unbezähmbar, ein dunkles Tier."

I am speaking of *Danton's Death*, of *Leonce and Lena*, of *Woyzeck*. I am speaking of Georg Büchner. Of all the many dozens of studies, monographs, and dissertations that have been devoted to this writer, not a single one actually deals with love; and among the hundreds of essays and articles on Büchner, there is, according to the existing bibliographies as well as the most recent handbooks and commentaries,[2] only one short article entirely devoted to this subject. It comes to us from Brazil, was authored by Erwin Theodor [Rosenthal], carries the title "Büchners Grundgedanke: Sehnsucht nach Liebe" ("Büchner's Fundamental Idea: The Longing for Love"), and was published in 1962 in the journal *Revista de Letras*.[3] Today, almost 150 years after the young writer's death, this is all that "the literature" has to offer regarding a theme which an insightful critic (one of the few) has described—albeit only in passing and in a manner which both exaggerates and is overly cautious—as functioning for Büchner as the "core [*Angelpunkt*] and meaning of life."[4]

The core and meaning of life for this writer? The scientist and revolutionary? The author of a seditious pamphlet? The fugitive conspirator who, at the age of twenty-three, died in exile in Switzerland, then the most proper and prudish of lands? His "fundamental idea," his overpowering "longing" was for love? But I must ask: What do we really know about Georg Büchner's view of love? What have we *dared* to know? In point of fact, we have only Rosenthal and a few scattered attempts.[5]

And yet, the very first scene of Büchner's first play begins with lines which unambiguously define the way this theme will be presented. A card game is in progress; and the figure who initiates the dialogue as well as the "love interest" is none other than Georg[es] Danton. He turns to his wife Julie and remarks: "Look at Madame over there—how sweetly she fingers her cards. She knows how, all right—they say her husband always gets the *cœur*, the others the *carreau*. You women could even make us fall in love with a lie."[6] The symbolic implications of the card suits mentioned by Danton are unmistakable. This is true of the "cœur," the heart, which traditionally has expressed a concept of love containing both Amor and Caritas. It is equally true of the "carreau" or diamond: here Büchner sets up a frivolous, obscene counterpart to the heart, using a sign the shape of which is decidedly suggestive. Contrary to one critic's ponderously naive thesis, it is surely not intended to serve as a metaphor for the "world theater."[7] Rather, what Büchner is referring to is something much more intimate, though no less universal. His friend Hérault develops and concretizes the reference when he takes the card names literally and declares that young ladies should not "play games like that. The kings and queens fall on top of each other so indecently and the jacks pop up right after."[8] (The reader will, I trust, forgive this Büchnerian smuttiness; the playwright could not have his "bandits"—to use his own hyperbolic term—talk like parsons' daughters, even though he himself was engaged to the daughter of a parson.)

What the duality of "cœur" and "carreau" conjures up from the very beginning is the entire range of the erotic: from the purest, indeed most chaste, affection as expressed by that ancient emblem the heart, all the way to the crassest carnality, which is denoted by the red diamond. And the two areas are not kept separate from one another but are closely bound together, in however daring, unbourgeois, and unstable a manner. Their common denominator is love—but not love as a mere concept or some anemic "fundamental *idea*," but rather as an all-embracing fundamental *experience*, an experience which is at once joyous and overwhelming. For let us not forget that Julie and Danton, whose gentleness and kindness toward each other ("dear heart," she calls him)[9] culminate in Julie taking her own life for the sake of her beloved, exist alongside of Hérault and his promiscuous "queen of diamonds," a woman who can make a man fall in love with a lie. What is more, these two radically dissimilar couples are joined by Camille Desmoulins, who exhibits what is perhaps the most faithful and selfless love to be found in Büchner's works—yet it is precisely this figure who calls for the elemental "limb-loosening, wicked love" of Sappho, with "naked gods and bacchantes" and, again completely uneuphemistically, "Venus with the beautiful backside"![10] Unvarnished sexuality, the most tender affection, and a classical Greek sensuality which the declaration that Venus, along with Epicurus, is to become the "doorkeeper of the Republic"[11] clearly endows with emancipatory and even utopian traits: all this is present in Büchner's images and allusions, as well as in his invocations of Renaissance licentiousness. Attentive readers cannot fail to note that in the opening scene of his first drama the playwright sketches out a full panorama of the world of Eros; he develops, or at least alludes to, all its various manifestations, which not only recur in, and color the rest of, this drama of revolution, but also suffuse Büchner's comedy *Leonce and Lena* and, to an even greater extent, his proletarian tragedy, *Woyzeck*.

Yet there is more. This fundamental experience is not limited to Büchner's plays nor even to those of his writings which have been preserved. It can also be found in that "complete fragment," the novella (or story) *Lenz*, and must have been present in his play, apparently lost forever, *Pietro Aretino*—present, once again, unless all indications are wrong, in the most multifarious manner. What, after all, do we learn about that unhappy writer, Lenz? Does his breakdown not result in part, indeed primarily, from the collapse of his love for Friederike? Does he not fall apart because her "happiness," which always made him so "calm," no longer washes over him, and instead her "fate," as well as his own, lies on his heart "like a hundredweight"?[12] These are all direct quotes which, it must be added, occur directly before the central passage in which Lenz is seized by the "obsession" of resurrecting a dead girl, something he attempts to carry out with "all the misery of despair" and all the force of will he still possesses. It is surely no coincidence that the child at whom he vainly hurls his demented "Arise and walk!" also bears—or bore—the name Friederike.[13] And we find this blasphemous phrase repeated word-for-word in Leonce's frenzied ecstasy of love;[14] moreover, the underlying concept also crops up in Büchner's letters to his fiancée, Minna Jaeglé. In February of 1834, while at the university of Gießen, he wrote: "I am alone as if in a grave; when will your hand awaken me?" To this he added the highly allusive line: "They say I am mad because I have said that in six weeks I will rise again, but first I will ascend into heaven, in the diligence [to Strasbourg] that is."[15] Clearly, Büchner was not reluctant to mingle erotic allusions with references to Christianity and the Bible. This connection between his letters to Minna, his comedy, and his narrative dealing with Lenz can also be developed out of another passage in the story, the section which describes the religious ecstasy that the tormented writer experiences with such intensity after he preaches: "Now, another existence, divine, twitching lips bent down over him and sucked on his lips; he went up to his lonely room. He was alone, alone! Then the spring rushed forth, torrents broke from his eyes, his body convulsed, his limbs twitched, he felt as if he must dissolve, he could find no end to this ecstasy." [16]

Let us here carefully note Büchner's choice of words! Not only does he mention "ecstasy," he also causes the Ἔρως λυσιμελής of Sappho, referred to by Camille as "limb-loosening love" (*gliederlösende Liebe*), to spring from overheated piousness. It is important to see the connection here to the love scene in *Leonce and Lena* [17] and, above all, to Büchner's "fatalism letter" of 1834, in which he tells Minna: "I glowed, the fever covered me with kisses and enfolded me like the arm of a lover. Above me there were waves of darkness, my heart swelled in infinite longing, stars forced their way through the gloom, and hands and lips bent down." [18]

The almost mystic undertones of this erotic fever-fantasy are as evident as is the startlingly erotic quality of Lenz's pietistic experience of transcendence. But even there, is not all "heavenly" love—if in fact such a thing is present in Büchner's writings— overshadowed by a love which is thoroughly worldly? When we seek to categorize the causes and effects of Lenz's madness, it is clear that those of a philosophical and social nature play an important role. [19] Yet should we not also look elsewhere, not so much in the area of religion—which lately has been stressed to the point of excess [20]—as in that of sexuality? Both in regard to Büchner in general, and in this context in particular, the emphasis on religious elements reveals itself as a highly dubious approach. Granted, certain remnants of Christianity are present in Lenz; after all, the man had studied theology. But are these remnants not thoroughly secularized by Büchner, just as he secularized so many other references to Christianity and the Bible? Indeed, to pose a rather heretical question, should not Lenz's mad attempt at resurrecting the dead Friederike be viewed as an attempt at reviving the bliss he experienced with the living Friederike? The shattered man, in the utter demise of his joy and happiness, prays "that God should grant him a sign and revive the child"! [21] And Büchner chose these words, too, advisedly.

Or consider *Pietro Aretino*, Büchner's supposed "obscenity" dealing with the renowned eroticist of the Renaissance, a man who, like the Marquis de Sade, won for himself the cynical and yet admiring epithet, "the divine one." God knows, it is high time that the information which has been preserved or can be deduced[22] regarding this work is taken seriously, rather than being brushed aside with an embarrassed blush. Let us dare to admit that Büchner wanted to write about this man precisely on account of, and not despite, Aretino's having written the *"Sonetti lussuriosi"* ("Voluptuous Sonnets")—on "sixteen positions of a pair of lovers *in coitu*" after drawings by Giulio Romano—as well as the so-called *Ragionamenti*, his notorious "Conversations" among courtesans. Because, not in spite of, Aretino's "vigorous sensuality" in both life and art, the young German writer found him a fascinating figure. It is actually of little import whether the "legendary 'Aretino' drama" (thus Walter Hinderer)[23] was almost complete or only a conception, whether it was intentionally destroyed or lost in some other way. What is important is the subject matter and the fact that Büchner concerned himself with it. Quite recently, this work—or conception—has been the object of further speculation by a scholar, on the one hand, and a writer, on the other. According to the literary historian Hermann Bräuning-Oktavio, the drama would have been a historical "painting on a colossal scale," a gigantic fresco portraying the "power and greatness of human passions";[24] according to Gaston Salvatore, in whose play *Büchners Tod* ("Büchner's Death") the fevered deliria of the dying poet are haunted by Aretino,[25] Büchner would have linked the Italian not only to questions of revolution and class conflict but also to modern concepts regarding the problem of the intellectual's servile role in society—a favorite topic of Bertolt Brecht, by the way.[26]

It may well be that Bräuning-Oktavio's hypothesis possesses a certain validity; in any event, it is more convincing than Salvatore's notion of how Büchner would have portrayed this man who was known and feared by all Europe; who—for this reason—was showered with gifts, honors, and bribes; whom the great Ariosto apostrophized as the "scourge of the princes";[27] indeed, who liked to refer to himself proudly as "a free man by the grace of God" (*per divina grazia uomo libero*).[28] There is something colossal, almost monstrous, about this *condottiere* of the pen, something of a "Great Dane with dove's wings," to use the phrase which Büchner applies to Danton.[29] And yet, if one takes a closer look, it appears that in the case of Aretino, too, it was love that was of primary importance. Even a cursory glance at the Italian's life leads one to believe that the play dealing with him—as far as we know, Büchner's last or next-to-last work[30]—would have repeated and intensified, nay, virtually doubled, the theme of love which the young writer had developed in his previous literary efforts. In 1829 his contemporary, Christian Dietrich Grabbe, published *Don Juan und Faust*, and I for one am convinced that in 1837 Büchner would have followed suit by providing us with a work which would have amounted to a *Danton and Woyzeck*.

Aretino lends himself to an undertaking of this sort not only through his insatiable "affirmation of pleasure in every form," nor his endless "series of loves, love affairs, and love encounters" which, as was the case with Danton, caused him to be involved with women of all social strata, "the highborn and the low, those with intelligence and those with a price."[31] At the same time, he was also hopelessly in love with *one* woman who, having brought him great happiness, betrayed him—just as Marie betrays Woyzeck. For the rest of his life, Aretino was caught in the toils of an obsessive love from which he was unable to free himself even after this woman's death. His declarations of passion for the young Perina Riccia remind us, in their sensual intensity, of Danton's stammerings to Marion,[32] just as his searing lamentations at her deathbed recall Woyzeck's desperate grief as well as that felt by Lenz. We even hear echoes of some of Büchner's own statements.[33] (Salvatore, despite the many problematical aspects of his play, at least gives us some sense of all this when he has Minna appear before the feverish, sexually aroused Büchner as a courtesan.) In recent times, it has been regretfully noted that "we have not a single really good play about the Cinquecento."[34] It is my firm conviction that Büchner's *Pietro Aretino*, marked by both "cœur" and "carreau," was, or would have become, the work that could have filled this gap.[35]

But let us concentrate on the texts we possess, let us return to Büchner's first and most important work, *Danton's Death*. For I wish to commit yet another heresy by declaring that in this play the theme of love is no less central than that of revolution. Indeed, the two are inseparably intertwined. Even if we limit ourselves to the main characters, we see that this is true not only of Julie and Camille's wife, Lucile, but also of the "grisette" or "hetaera," Marion.[36] All three of the leading female figures in

Danton's Death contribute—each in her own way—to the exemplary unleashing of both the dialectic of revolution, with all its contradictions, and of love "in every form." As has been indicated, Julie and Lucile belong together, even more so at the end of the play than in the early scenes. Critics have noted that *Woyzeck* and *Leonce and Lena* exhibit elements of a circular structure in that their endings, to a certain extent, flow back into their beginnings.[37] However, something that has hardly been noticed, let alone investigated, is the circular construction of *Danton's Death*[38] and the concomitant function which is assigned to the two female figures as well as to love. This oversight is the more surprising since all these elements are particularly noticeable in Büchner's drama of revolution. One need only compare the first scene ("Danton on a footstool at Julie's feet") with the last scene where Lucile sits "on the steps of the guillotine":

DANTON. No, Julie, I love you like the grave. . . . They say in the grave there is peace, and grave and peace are one. If that's so, then in your lap I'm already lying under the earth. You sweet grave—your lips are funeral bells, your voice my death knell, your breasts my burial mound, and your heart my coffin.

LUCILE. (*enters* . . .) I'm sitting in your lap, you silent angel of death. . . . You dear cradle, you lulled my Camille to sleep, you strangled him under your roses. You death knell, you sang him to the grave with your sweet tongue.[39]

The connection between these images, the cyclical way in which they anticipate and echo one another, can hardly be overlooked, especially since they are so boldly unusual. There can be no doubt that Büchner created this connection intentionally; the references to sweetness and love, peacefulness and silence, the correspondence established in both instances between a lap (*Schoß*, which can also mean "womb") and a grave—all this is simply too exact to be regarded as accidental. Even the cradle, which at first is missing from the opening scene, soon puts in an appearance. Before the next scene begins, we encounter the line, "having coffins for cradles,"[40] a phrase which clearly anticipates

Lucile's speech at the end of the play; and, of course, the evocative rhyme of "womb" and "tomb," of "cave" and "grave," is something of which psychoanalysis has long been aware. In the programmatic writings of Norman O. Brown, to which I shall eventually return, one finds the laconic yet unambiguous words: "Birth, copulation, and death, equated." [41] This is precisely what Büchner accomplishes: "cradle," "womb" (*Schoß*), and "grave" are—as Danton himself declares—"one and the same." When Lucile utters the phrase "dear cradle," she is addressing the dreaded guillotine, the killing machine she also refers to as an "angel of death" and a "death knell"; and when Julie reaches for the vial of poison from which she imbibes her love-death, she does so with the words: "Come, dearest priest, your amen makes us go to sleep." [42] Both of these death scenes are love scenes, just as both figures are, above all else, women in love. True, it seems at first that Julie regards Danton's words as frivolous and shocking, for she turns away from him with an almost Kleistian "Oh." However, she quickly regains her composure, and with it her love for Danton, a love in which she henceforth abides with steadily increasing confidence and unreservedness until finally, with the words "sleep, sleep" on her lips, she follows Danton and the darkling world into the "slumber" of death. [43]

The same development can be discerned in Danton's much-cited loneliness: from his fatalistic and seemingly resigned declaration, "we are very lonely," [44] to the fervent intimacy he shares with Julie in the aftermath of his agonizing nightmare. In the latter scene, which occurs in the second act, Danton is able to say, "Now I'm calm"—and are we not forced to envision him in his wife's arms, not just in her presence? "Completely calm, dear heart?" she asks, full of concern, and he replies: "Yes, Julie, come to bed." [45] That all this is connected to various aspects of the play's concluding scenes—for example, to the revolutionary's fear of the loneliness of death, a fear which is so difficult to reconcile with the philosophy he manifests in other situations, [46] and, above all, to Julie's actions and attitude, to the extraordinary love-sacrifice she offers—cannot be ignored. The correspondences extend even to specific words and phrases, something which is particularly evident in Danton's cry: "Oh Julie! If I had to go *alone*! If she would abandon me! And if I decomposed entirely, dissolved completely—I'd be a handful of tormented dust. Each of my atoms could find peace only with her. I can't die, no, I cannot die."[47] As a comforting answer, Julie has a messenger carry a lock of her hair to the imprisoned Danton: "There, bring him that and tell him he won't go alone. He'll understand. Then come back quickly. I want to read his looks in your eyes."[48] And, once again, Danton is freed from his agony. "I won't go alone," he says to himself as if he has been saved, "thank you, Julie."[49] Now he is able to face the guillotine, composed and calm.

Julie's love-sacrifice is indeed extraordinary. What renders it even more extraordinary and even more indicative of the importance Büchner attached to love is the fact that it has absolutely no basis in historical reality. It did not at all occur to the real Julie (who was actually named Louise) to accompany her Georges in death. Not only did she survive him by decades, but she had also no compunctions about remarrying—although, admittedly, this did not happen until she had mourned Danton for a few chaste (or, at least, relatively chaste) years.[50] The banality of these facts is sobering; yet it also serves to establish irrefutably that the heroic transfiguration effected by Büchner evinces his own concerns and conceptions. And then there is Lucile, who is presented as deriving a limpid, self-effacing happiness from the love she shares with Camille. Even with this character, Büchner departs from what he read in his history books. Instead of having her arrested, condemned, and executed on the basis of Laflotte's denunciation, which is what actually happened,[51] he causes her to provide a second example of transfiguration achieved by means of a luminous love-sacrifice. Like Julie, Lucile is cloaked in radiance. Or, as Maurice B. Benn puts it: "Against the dark background [of the play, these] two pure figures . . . appear in an almost radiant light."[52] Of course, Julie chooses death without hesitation and in the full freedom of her spirit, while Lucile, like Ophelia, falls victim to madness and is able to return to herself only at the very end of the play. Yet this ending, one of the most moving and magnificent in all of world drama, not only presents, in the words of Benn, "a sudden return of lucidity"[53] for Lucile; it also crowns and confirms the triumph, the limitless glorification of love in Büchner's drama of revolution. The passage in question is deceptively brief; it begins with the entrance of a militia patrol and then breaks off with Lucile being led away to her death:

> A CITIZEN. Hey—who's there?
> LUCILE. Long live the King!
> CITIZEN. In the name of the Republic! (*She is surrounded by the watch and led off.*)[54]

These lines must be read with the utmost attentiveness and exactitude. On the one hand, they serve to close the circle of the play's "love interest" which begins at the gaming table with the bantering about "cœur" and "carreau"; on the other hand, in testifying to the power of love, they also provide a final manifestation, indeed a proclamation, of the republic, and with it, the revolution. The part of the play's action which is connected to the revolution is encompassed by the theme of love. Even the scene in which Danton and his followers are executed, a scene in which their severed heads kiss "at the bottom of the basket,"[55] is framed by—and one might say, sublated into—this theme as it is developed in the two scenes devoted to Julie's and Lucile's acts of self-sacrifice and transfiguration. Yet, at the same time, the part of the play which deals with love is also subjected to a sublation. In that final scene, in which love shines forth one last time and reaches what could be termed its apotheosis, Lucile is, in a very literal manner, "surrounded" by the power of the revolution in its most concrete form.

The vividness of this action, which is truly theatrical in the best sense of the word, is no less striking than the imagery Büchner utilizes at the beginning and end of *Danton's Death*, or, for that matter, the basic circular structure of the play as a whole. Here, both themes are fused together in a relationship as inseparable as that of form and content. Comfort and hope, refuge from the present and assurances regarding the future, all are intertwined in Büchner's play. Truly, for individual human beings, love is all that remains. For humanity, however, there is the revolution. Although conservative critics would have us believe that the notion of progress and the linear movement of history is flatly rejected, and in its place a Spenglerian "circular movement

of all history" is glorified,[56] this conclusion cannot be substanti-
ated, regardless of whether one concentrates exclusively on *Danton's Death* or examines the young writer's entire oeuvre and biography.[57] Büchner was a man who despaired and yet continued
to fight, a militant who founded the Society of Human Rights,
wrote *The Hessian Messenger*, and yet admitted that he "felt as if
[he] were crushed under the terrible fatalism of history."[58] If ever
anyone had a right to lay claim to that dictum of Gramsci, "pessimism of the intellect, optimism of the will,"[59] then it was surely
Büchner, a revolutionary in that most reactionary of times, the
German Vormärz period. However, what sets him apart from
Gramsci, and even raises him above the Italian's paradox, is the
fact that he was a great writer and, both as a writer and a revolutionary, a man who loved. Büchner wanted "life and love" among
human beings to be "one and the same"; he wanted love to be
life and "life [to be] love."[60]

I believe that one can legitimately take these words, which
come from a fragmentary scene not included in the final version
of *Leonce and Lena*, and apply them in a general sense to Büchner's entire concept of love.[61] For are they not equally true of
Marion, the third major female figure in *Danton's Death*? Does
not this "grisette," in an exemplary manner, live a life of love? In
her existence, are not life and love in fact identical? Admittedly,
this is yet another heresy, and one especially offensive to those
who, while not necessarily conservative in their political views,
are nonetheless rigorously moralistic.[62] But have the numerous
attempts to explain Marion with concepts such as "tragedy" and
"guilt" really helped us to understand this figure? Should we de-
prive her of what she terms "the only thing,"[63] and instead burden her with "a dark, animalistic sadness," in effect, a bad conscience?[64] Ought we not instead approach both Marion and
Danton as well as their relationship with one another—and, by
extension, Georg Büchner's treatment of love in its entirety—
with very different concepts and values? That it is not enough
simply to rattle off a few of the fashionable phrases of the playwright's era, such as the well-known "emancipation of the flesh,"
is, I would hope, obvious. It was no accident that Büchner repeatedly distanced himself from the Saint-Simonians and the
Young Germans.[65] As for the latter group, their supposedly daring heroines[66] resemble, when compared with Marion, nothing

more than "marionettes with sky-blue noses and affected pathos," the fleshless and bloodless constructs for which Büchner mocked the "so-called idealist poets."[67] But should we descend to the opposite extreme and—utilizing a word which carries with it the most repulsive of associations—see in Marion "something subhuman" (*Untermenschliches*)?[68] Neither this dubious concept nor the "uncontrollable animalistic lustfulness" which has been linked with it nor, by any stretch of the imagination, the insipid sensuality of the Young Germans can touch the essence of Marion's being; and the yammering and howling, the erotic spasms and convulsions which fill Peter Weiss's *Marat/Sade* also have very little to do with the serenity and delicacy, indeed the poetry of Marion and her scene.

Unfortunately, there is not enough space here to quote the love scene between her and Danton in its entirety. I can only point to the naturalness, the lyrical-idyllic simplicity and yet eloquence with which Marion—sitting "at the feet" of Danton, according to a telling stage direction—narrates the story of her life, which is to say the story of her love. "My mother was a smart woman. She always said chastity was a nice virtue." Thus Büchner, taking a sly jab at bourgeois morality, has Marion begin her account: "When people came to the house and started talking about certain things, she told me to leave the room. When I asked what they wanted, she said I ought to be ashamed of myself. When she gave me a book to read, I almost always had to skip over a couple of pages."[69] Marion goes on to recall how once, in springtime, while still a girl, she found herself "in a peculiar atmosphere," an atmosphere which "almost choked me." Luckily, a young man appeared who, though he often said "crazy things," was "good-looking." In time, Marion says, "we couldn't see why we might not just as well lie together between two sheets as sit next to each other in two chairs." Then, soon thereafter, she declares with calm frankness: "But I became like an ocean, swallowing everything and swirling deeper and deeper. For me there was only one opposite: all men melted into one body. That was my nature—who can escape it?"[70]

When the young man, who believed Marion was his alone, learned of her activities, he kissed her as if he wanted—again that word—to "choke" her: his arms wrapped tight around her neck; she was "terribly afraid." But he released her and then

went off and drowned himself (an event which is conveyed to
us only by Marion's indirect and highly evocative remarks; see
chapter 5 below). "I had to cry," she admits, "that was the only
break in my being."[71] Since then she has lived in complete unity
and harmony with herself:

> Other people have Sundays and working days, they work
> for six days and pray on the seventh; once a year, on their
> birthdays, they get sentimental, and every year on New
> Year's Day they reflect. I don't understand all that. For me
> there is no stopping, no changing. I'm always the same, an
> endless longing and seizing, a fire, a torrent. . . . It's all the
> same, whatever we enjoy: bodies, icons, flowers, or toys,
> it's all the same feeling. Whoever enjoys the most prays the
> most.[72]

Marion's autobiographical account closes with this avowal, which
clearly provides the philosophical, or ideological, highlight of
the entire scene. Büchner was not, however, content to stop
here. The ensuing dialogue between Marion and Danton provides yet another highlight—in this case, one which is lyrical-
idyllic, even lyrical-utopian, in nature:

> DANTON. Why can't I contain your beauty in me com-
>   pletely, surround it entirely?
> MARION. Danton, your lips have eyes.
> DANTON. I wish I were a part of the atmosphere so that
>   I could bathe you in my flood and break on every
>   wave of your beautiful body.[73]

It is at this point that Lacroix, loud-mouthed and vulgar, enters
the scene. Accompanied by a pair of common whores, he fills
the air with crude remarks; and thus the scene ends on a jarringly discordant note that tears apart the idyl briefly shared by
the two lovers.[74]

I would like to ask: Could a playwright possibly express more
in a single scene? Could a scene be any more unambiguous?
How can it be that Büchner has been so completely misunderstood here by so many experts, by virtually the entire corps of
critics? Or, phrased more maliciously: How is it possible to react

to such a text—particularly when it is part of Büchner's drama of revolution—in a way which is so blind to history and so indifferent to art, so joyless and so dismally sanctimonious? It is perhaps not entirely accidental that the only voice which has been raised in favor of Marion comes to us from Sweden![75] Everything else one encounters reeks of puritanism and philistine narrowmindedness. The eternal bourgeois (who, by the way, lurks not just in "bourgeois" critics) is not only repelled by a "soulless whore" or, at best, a "hetaera"; he finds her positively frightening. Indeed, Marion "is obviously a very dangerous person," we are informed in all seriousness.[76] Critics' sensibilities—not to mention their senses—have failed to grasp this woman and her message even though, beginning with the very first scene and Camille's proclamation of Venus and Epicurus as the patron saints of the republic, it pervades the entire drama and stands inscribed as a secret motto over the events of the revolution. Of course, we also notice a marked heightening of the current of eroticism: Camille merely *demands* primal love and Greek sensuality, while Marion actually *manifests* these ideals, actually lives and proclaims them with her own flesh.

After Marion's scene, there can be no doubt that the erotic-utopian qualities which the play first presents in a purely theoretical manner or in broad outline, have now become elements of concrete praxis and thus must be recognized as a crucial dimension of the entire theme of revolution. And how could it be otherwise? Are not love and sensuality of every sort, as well as the achievement of full happiness in this life, integral and inalienable aspects of the complete and liberated human being, the *total* human being, and hence essential components of any full concept of revolution? If one draws on Camus, as does Benn, and speaks of Büchner's "threefold concept of revolution," which combines sociopolitical rebellion with metaphysical revolt and an overturning of established aesthetic norms[77]—then why not also acknowledge Büchner's liberation of Eros, that is to say, his sexual revolt? Are we not forced to do so by what we encounter in his works? I can no longer ignore the testimony of these texts. "Cœur" and "carreau" speak with a clarity that leaves little to be desired; what they say to us is far clearer and more convincing than any painstakingly assembled collection of quotations from Arthur Schopenhauer, whom some critics want to drag into the

discussion of Büchner at all costs.[78] But so be it! If, in 1813, the
year of Büchner's birth, this notorious reactionary and misogynist among German thinkers examined the "fourfold root of the
principle of sufficient reason," then Büchner, the loving rebel
among German writers, in *Danton's Death* dealt with the fourfold
root of the principle of revolution. Indeed, it seems to me that
even if one were to ignore the play, it still would be possible to
establish the necessity of Büchner's support for a fourth revolt,
the revolt of Eros:

> For what would it be this revolution
> Without universal copulation?[79]

Here we clearly have an area of intersection between Büchner
and the author of *Marat/Sade*, regardless of how crude the latter's
intentionally primitive slogans may seem when compared with
Marion's scene. When Bo Ullmann, who is responsible for the
aforementioned contribution from Sweden, refers to her message as a "utopia of unmutilated, total humanness," a "utopia of
the erotic negation of both self and possession,"[80] he merely provides more restrained but, by the same token, considerably more
apt formulations of what Weiss, his German-born countryman,
has in mind.

But though it is an admirable virtue, the open-mindedness *in
eroticis* displayed by Ullmann and Weiss is not in itself sufficient for a full understanding of Marion. The same is true of
some "sisterly" insights; however knowing they may be, they remain incomplete or even lead to new varieties of misperception.
Margaret Jacobs, for example, starts out on the right track when
she writes of Marion: "In a special sense she is natural, but one
must beware of assessing her as naive."[81] Precisely in its contradictoriness, this statement is directly on target. Unfortunately,
Jacobs fails to perceive the full implications of her own *aperçu*, for
she immediately lapses into a moralizing approach and decides
that there is "something undeniably gruesome" about Marion.
Even the moment of illumination provided by our Swedish critic
flickers, dims, and finally disappears. In spite of all his accurate
perceptions, Ullmann not only pushes Marion in the direction
of "childishness" and "foolishness"[82] but feels compelled—even
while acknowledging her "innocence" and "purity"—to describe

her as "dirty"! Finally, he judges Marion to be "truly unfit for a utopia" because, as he goes on to inform us, she is "scarcely a person of this world"! (Wouldn't "although" make more sense?) Thus a utopian presence is registered, but only in order to be denounced as a failure. What seems to exert a certain fascination is not so much utopia itself as its supposed collapse. That this perspective involves a distortion, indeed almost an inversion of the concept of utopia is quite obvious. In actuality, Büchner is concerned neither with the "abandonment" nor with the "defense" of an erotic utopia, but rather with imagining and manifesting it. The fact that the present, even when it is revolutionary, fails to live up to the utopian goal does not refute the latter any more than the temporary collapse of the ongoing sociopolitical revolution refutes or even "compromises" its particular utopian vision.

However tempting it may be, one cannot connect Marion with Marie of the *Woyzeck* fragment;[83] nor can one view the proletarian tragedy as a necessary continuation of *Danton's Death*, much less its recantation.[84] This would presume, within Büchner's oeuvre, an evolution which has never been convincingly demonstrated. And if indeed one is willing to make the interpretive leap of associating the suicide of Marion's lover with the murder of Marie by the pond, why not link the young man's death with Leonce's loudly announced decision to plunge into the river and drown, a decision motivated not by despair, but rather by the ecstasy of love? In other words, one could just as easily concentrate on the laughable consequences of Marion's "terrible dangerousness" as on those which are somberly serious. Of course, it cannot be denied that she admits: "My mother died of grief, people point at me." But she adds: "That's silly"[85]—a comment that Büchner meant to be taken seriously. Marion's mother, who is so ironically characterized as wise and moral, can hardly be regarded as tragic; if anything, she is to be pitied. And Marion's first lover is not only pitiable, he is comical. To say this obviously involves a degree of exaggeration—but is not the death brought on by grief a standard element of cheap melodrama? And does not the young man's impetuous suicide smack of a certain callow foolishness? The playwright, in any case, speaking through that incorrigible materialist, Valerio, describes such deeds as "lieutenants' romanticism."[86] Even the phrase "a foolish thing" is

supplied by Büchner himself.[87] He refrains from condemning
Marion morally—or, for that matter, in any way. She exists outside of the traditional value system which bases itself on Christian ethics and hence she cannot be defined in terms of its conception of morality. Marion does not have a faulty or corrupted
conscience, she has no conscience at all. She is not an evildoer,
not a sinner, not laden with guilt. In the final analysis, she is not
even immoral. She can only be termed amoral. As both elemental nature and its utopian projection, she exists *before* as well
as *after* and *above* all traditional, which is to say bourgeois, moral
strictures and sexual mores. Marion is entirely natural and yet at
the same time she presages a perfect utopia. The first of these
aspects serves as an anticipatory manifestation, a poetic image,
of the second aspect. Or, to draw on yet another notorious
thinker, though he certainly was not always a misogynist: Marion, as a living revaluation of all the values of love, stands both
before and beyond good and evil (and, by the way, completely
removed from the world of work). She is the "restoration of
nature, free from false moralism [*moralinfrei*]," to use Nietzsche's
lapidary description of this condition.[88]

It is only through an appreciation of such paradoxes that we
are able to understand Marion, her relationship to Danton, and
the function of her scene. On the one hand, she is nature in its
purest form and yet, on the other, she is not at all natural. Actually, she is caught between two sets of constraints: she is acutely
susceptible to those of nature and she finds herself a prey of
those of society. Only gradually is she able to overcome the
double disharmony caused by these forces and mechanisms.
This is revealed to us twice—here Büchner is quite exact—in the
oppressive feeling of suffocation or choking which is so vividly
visited upon Marion before she finally is able to become herself.
In the midst of spring's luxuriance, it symbolizes the powerful
drives of nature; in the enraged embrace of her disappointed
lover, it represents society's insistence upon possession. For
Marion, both issues now belong to the past; life and love have
long since become one and the same. When this feeling of suffocation recurs at the end of the scene, it is no longer associated
with her but instead with Danton. Coming on the heels of his
strained debate with Lacroix and Paris, it is symptomatic, both
specifically and in a broad sense, of an external compulsion to

"exertion" and "work," to purposeful "action" in general;[89] symptomatic, moreover, of the individual's renunciation of pleasure and obsession with productive accomplishment, as well as of that sad state of affairs in which people mutually oppress one another. Referring to his friends, Danton might well have repeated his line from the opening scene: "Their politics [i.e., their plans, their appeals, their demands] are getting on my nerves."[90] Marion, however, uses a different image in conveying this thought to Danton: "Your lips are cold, your words have stifled your kisses."[91]

Even in her lament, Büchner's grisette manifests, as a utopian projection, precisely that which Büchner's revolutionary, who is trying to blaze a trail to utopia, would like to achieve in historical reality: the realm of untrammeled pleasure. Marion is actually able to live the existence Danton demands, impatient and audacious—and hence burdened with guilt. She is able to be what he can only long for. The playwright has allowed her to rise above all constraints and enter that much sought-after realm. As Ullmann points out, Marion has attained complete and unmutilated "humanness" (*Menschennatur*); she has managed to transcend all notions of private property, an achievement which allows her to possess the entire world. Moreover, she has dissolved her sense of self; thus her existence, while totally unfragmented, is marked by infinite multiplicity. However, such fulfillment can only exist as the projection of a possibility; this perfect unity of being can only reside on the periphery of history, where origin and goal flow into one another. For the revolutionary who lives in the midst of a bloody reality, all this is unattainable. Danton, entangled in history, thoroughly caught up in the developments of each new day, must remain in a state of inner disharmony from which he can escape only for a few moments at a time. His agonizingly acute consciousness, which constantly disturbs his peace of mind, and Marion's seamless, almost unconscious, happiness are discordantly juxtaposed, their compatibility and loving encounter notwithstanding. Büchner's grisette manifests a tangible utopia, a concrete praxis of erotic liberation; in Büchner's revolutionary, we see a concretization of utopia's dependence on history and its concomitant contradiction of reality.

Yet the difference between Danton and Marion is not presented simply as a painful disharmony, but instead primarily in terms of a reconciliation. For this is the central meaning of the brief, lyrical exchange that consummates the idyl shared by the two lovers. Does it not almost resemble a duet? While it seems to begin so abruptly, the dialogue actually is a logical continuation of what has already been said, a final, poetically terse evocation both of the undistorted nature that preceded man's descent into history and of the erotic utopia that lies somewhere in the future. These lines are not intended to provide contrast; instead, they represent a culmination.[92] What does it mean when Danton voices his ardent desire to enfold Marion "completely" inside himself and feels a need to become "part of the atmosphere" so that he might "bathe" his lover in his "flood" and "break on every wave" of her "beautiful body"? And what are we to make of that seemingly cryptic line in which Marion reproachfully tells Danton that his lips have eyes? Should we follow the lead of formalist criticism and conclude that this is nothing more than a bold image that anticipates Rimbaud and the Dadaist Hans Arp? Should we accept the judgment of the critic and poet Walter Höllerer and view it as "surreal estrangement"?[93] But does not Hinderer offer a more convincing explanation when he speaks of a "metaphor for Danton's inability to turn off his consciousness"?[94]

Yet even this interpretation, while establishing a persuasive connection between form and content, provides only half the answer. The other half can be found in a book which makes no reference to Büchner, a book which carries the trendy—and yet appropriate—title, *Love's Body*. Experiences of the sort described by Marion are, the author emphatically informs us, "polymorphous perversity, the translation of all our senses into one another, the interplay between the senses," which is to say "the metaphor, the free translation."[95] And in truth, however suspicious we may be of faddish prophets and lecture-circuit revolutionaries, could we find a better description of Büchner's "new, previously unarticulated sensibility"[96] than this passage by Norman O. Brown? Does not the concept of "polymorphous perversity," the interplay of all the senses, provide, if not *the*, at least *a* key to Danton's lips that have eyes? Or, to phrase the question differently, is not the "metaphor" also a sensual reality? This notion, among others, is elucidated as Brown, proceeding in his inimitably eclectic manner,[97] issues a prophecy regarding an erotic utopia: "The human body would become polymorphously perverse, delighting in that full life of all the body which it now fears. The consciousness strong enough to endure full life would be no longer Apollonian but Dionysian—consciousness which does not observe the limit, but overflows, *consciousness which does not negate any more.*"

Does this not constitute a summation, and a rather detailed one at that, of both the dialogue and the relationship between Danton and Marion? Are they not, like the fervent disciple of Freud, though in a much more direct way, involved in the "complete abolition of repression" and the "resurrection of the body"? As if he were not only allowing Marion to reflect, but also seeking to outdo Danton's "laziness," [98] Brown announces: "The riddle of history is not in Reason but in Desire; not in labor but in love."

To be sure, Brown is indulging in extreme understatement when, in his earlier and better known book, *Life Against Death*, he refers to all this as "a little more Eros." [99] There is no denying that his writings run the risk of making an absolute of erotic liberation. Yet it is by no means mere eclecticism that leads him to draw not only on Nietzsche and, especially, Freud, but also on Marx, whose concept of the "total person" he blends with ideas taken from the other two thinkers. [100] (The concept, it will be remembered, first appeared in the *Economic-Philosophical Manuscripts* of 1844, that is to say, seven years after Büchner's death.) The necessity of connecting Marx and Freud, perhaps Nietzsche as well, and, in any event, Marxism and psychoanalysis, social and sexual revolution, was perceived long before Brown came on the scene. One need only think of Wilhelm Reich and, above all, Herbert Marcuse and his book, *Eros and Civilization*. [101] Actually, it is of secondary importance which of these thinkers one relies on for supporting testimony. What is crucial—as well as astounding—is the fact that in Büchner's works we encounter a thoroughly modern view of revolution, one which is not just twofold but actually fourfold; indeed, I would go so far as to say that in his oeuvre every conceivable variety of revolt is not only present but is developed to its fullest extent. Both love and revolution are here in all their various forms; both possess central importance and, at the same time, are inseparable from each other. Nowhere is this more evident than in the female figures of *Danton's Death*, and most of all in Marion.

Thus it is no exaggeration to say that Marion, the embodiment

of sexual liberation, can be viewed as the pleasure principle incarnate: a notion which—let me make this point one last time—
involves absolutely no value judgment. Nothing could be further
off the mark than to dismiss Marion as an inferior variant of her
partner by declaring, "[Her] insatiability . . . is a distortion, a
vulgarization of Danton's." [102] For if one were carefully to compare the two figures, would it not emerge that the very opposite
is much closer to the truth? Certainly, the playwright did not
hesitate to underscore Danton's own naturalness and sensuality;
in fact, he even relates these qualities to Marion's versions of
them by having his protagonist anticipate, almost word-for-
word, one of her key statements. Prior to the grisette's declaration, "that was my nature," her visitor has candidly announced,
"That's my nature." [103]

Denigrations of the sort we have cited are grossly unpercep-
tive; they are rooted in a latent machismo, an outlook no less be-
nighted than the pseudofeminist laxness which has nurtured its
own brood of false conclusions, such as the judgment regarding
Marie in *Woyzeck*: "She knows [!] that [she] is justified in sleep-
ing with the drum major." [104] No, we cannot grasp love in Büchner with such simple-minded pronouncements. But everywhere
one turns, even among the most insightful critics, one encounters simplifications of this sort. I have no desire to list them all;
let a few egregious examples suffice. Rosetta in *Leonce and Lena* is
surely more than the "withered utopia of hetaerism"—the label
that Ullmann, trapped in his own schematism, feels compelled
to assign. [105] On the other hand, the Drum Major in *Woyzeck* is
indeed a virile "provincial Don Juan," but, contrary to what
a rather overheated Benno von Wiese would have us believe,
surely not a "sleek and fiery man-beast." Like Woyzeck, he is a
soldier bound by military discipline, and thus he is at most a
"stud-bull . . . with a ring through his nose." [106] Or again, having
recognized that love is the "core and meaning of life" for this
writer, how can one go on to speak repeatedly of the "failure"
and "foundering" of love in Büchner and his works, and even
advance the notion that not just in his writings but even "in his
life" love was "at most [!] a hope"? And how—this dismal list,
I see, is easier started than concluded—how can one declare
that the "real subject" of Büchner's comedy is the "miracle [!] of
love," and still reach the conclusion that the play ends with a "de-

feat"? All these contradictions can be found in interpretations produced by a single critic, the distinguished French scholar, Gonthier-Louis Fink.[107] In the final analysis, Fink's underestimation of love in the works of Büchner is as one-sided and inaccurate as is the rosy overestimation offered by Rosenthal, for he imagines the presence of an entirely unmenaced "belief in love," and therefore contents himself with ascertaining whether or not Büchner's plays possess happy endings, determining that *Leonce and Lena* does, while *Woyzeck* and *Danton's Death*, alas, do not. I am almost moved by the fervor of Rosenthal's pathos when he says of Büchner's revolutionary: "Now [i.e., near the end of the play] he knows that the attempt to establish contact with Julie, which he doubted in the first scene, would have been successful—but now it is too late!" The conclusion that follows this observation is also endearingly heartfelt, but must likewise be regarded as idealistic and romantic: "For Büchner, pure human love is the most important element of existence and the main characters in his dramas urgently desire its manifestation."[108] That there is a grain of truth in it goes without saying, just as the contradictions in which Fink finds himself entangled are not entirely absent from the works he is interpreting. Nevertheless, one cannot extract from Büchner's oeuvre a saccharine "pure human love," any more than one can say that the great gamble of love—even though it is confronted by dangers of which the young writer was fully aware—ends in complete "failure." And to maintain that the comedy ends in a defeat! What a grievous misjudging of both the play's world and the rules of the genre to which it belongs, a genre which always—and *Leonce and Lena* is no exception—culminates in the γάμος, the love-festival of the wedding.[109]

In Büchner's works no clear distinction is made between carnal desire and spiritual love; hence it is entirely mistaken to draw a value-laden dichotomy between "love" on the one hand and "lust" on the other (as does Fink).[110] We must avoid tearing apart in dualistic fashion the realm of love as presented by Büchner; we must reject the conclusion that Marie and Woyzeck repeat "the constellation Marion and Danton" and implicitly exemplify the "familiar opposition of spirituality and sensuality."[111] In reading Büchner, we encounter *differences*[112] between spiritual and sensual affection, but in no way do they constitute an *opposi-*

tion. Büchner's view of love is not typified by "cœur" *or* "car-reau," but rather by "cœur" *and* "carreau." Throughout his works, love is consistently affirmed in both its aspects, in a virtually indivisible unity of the heart and the senses. Even Lena, for all her ethereal shyness and incorporeality, finally "leans against" Leonce.[113] Are we to believe that he, the former lover of Rosetta, plans to have a celibate marriage with Lena? The man who refers to love's endless variations and his own need to experience them all? "My God," he cries, "how many women does one need to sing up and down the scale of love? One woman is scarcely enough for a single note." He even goes so far as to pose the question: "Why is the mist above the earth a prism that breaks the white-hot ray of love into a rainbow?"[114]

Strong stuff, admittedly; but at least it has protected Leonce from those pious canonizers into whose hands the hapless Woy-zeck has fallen, recently having been forced upon a pedestal and labeled a Christian saint![115] But he who, after all, has fathered a child with Marie, can hardly be termed a wan ascetic. Of course, as she points out, Woyzeck is "seeing things" and thus at times even fails to notice his own son;[116] but he is by no means monk-ish or sanctimonious. He certainly never fails to notice Marie. True, this proletarian "man of sorrows"—which is what he actu-ally is—laments to his comrade: "But Andres, she was one in a million."[117] But even while we are moved by the simplicity and restraint of this line, we must not forget that Woyzeck jumps up violently with a wild passion when he spies his woman dancing with the Drum Major: "The bastard! Look how he's grabbing her, grabbing her body! he—he's got her now, like I used to have her!"[118] Even at the pond, just before he murders Marie, Woyzeck, this supposed Christ figure, moans: "How hot your lips are! Hot—the hot breath of a whore—but I'd give heaven and earth to kiss them once more."[119] For Woyzeck, her sensual allure is so great that he is willing to give up his own eternal salvation in or-der to possess her. But then, are we not forced to admit that even Büchner's tortured theologian, who is surely no less disturbed than Woyzeck[120] and goes so far as to attempt an *imitatio Christi*—albeit one which is not altogether religious in its inspiration—exhibits a significant amount of sensuality, though it is entirely frustrated?[121]

Those who find all this too heretical ought to take another look at Büchner's drama of revolution. What sort of relationship does the play's main character have with women? Does Danton's Julie want to read Young's *Night Thoughts* with her husband when she calls him "dear heart" and the two of them—as Büchner explicitly notes—go "to bed"?[122] Can one separate this "big, white, wide bed" (as Brecht would put it)[123] from Julie's gentle kindness?[124] Can one separate sensual and spiritual love here? As for Marion, I would hope by now the inappropriateness of any such division is obvious. Are there still those who would obdurately insist that the relationship she shares with Danton is devoid of deep feeling, of any tenderness and affection? If this were the case, why would Büchner have introduced Rosalie and Adelaide, the two other grisettes, from whom Marion is as clearly different as is Danton from that "confirmed scoundrel"[125] Lacroix in whose company they appear? Why is it Marion who utters that uninhibitedly pagan (and only seemingly blasphemous) credo, according to which "whatever we enjoy" involves "the same feeling"—thus justifying the conclusion: "Whoever enjoys the most prays the most"?[126] The answer is obvious. Marion is not exclusively passion, let alone "concupiscence," just as Julie is not exclusively "love" in any limited sense; instead, both women—Büchner, after all, was a realist—partake of both varieties of feeling, though in varying degrees. The same is true of Lucile and Lena and, of course, Marie. But most of all, this unity and wholeness is exhibited by Danton himself who stands between his two female counterparts. In the first scene he sits "on a footstool at Julie's feet," while Marion, in her scene, sits "at [his] feet."[127] The function of this triptych is clear. Here, as is so often the case in his works, Büchner has concretized his statement into a sign which is visibly manifested on stage: Julie next to (or above) Danton; Danton next to (or above) Marion. From this, one might wish to construct a hierarchy of love; but such an undertaking would be beside the point. What is crucial here is not the differences that distinguish these characters, but rather their basic similarity: each of them partakes of the entire spectrum of Eros—*as does Büchner himself*. Is it possible to ignore this aspect of his oeuvre and the message it proclaims? Can one deny that "cœur" and "carreau" are not only reconciled with one another but are in fact inseparably bound together?

There is something else which must be mentioned. Even "neutral" concepts like spirituality and sensuality lead one dangerously close to the Young Germans and Saint-Simonians upon whom Büchner heaped such mordant scorn. Moreover, one becomes trapped in a thought pattern which is far older than these fleeting movements. For, in spite of their supposed progressiveness, concepts of this sort perpetuate the age-old Christian duality of spirit and flesh, soul and body, a duality which over the centuries has been modified and trivialized, but never entirely abandoned—and which so strongly affected the way women have been regarded and the position they have been accorded in our society. It is no secret that women, in the Christian tradition, have been portrayed either as naked, soulless whores or as incorporeal saints, as objects of unbridled lust or as objects of pious veneration. On the one hand, they have been viewed as snares of diabolical seduction, on the other, as mediators of divine mercy. Most notably, this dualism manifested itself in the typology of Eve and Mary. The medieval "Melker Marienlied" ("Melk Song of Mary"), to cite but one example, names both figures, denouncing one and praising the other.[128]

From the very beginning, it is Woman who, as the devil's tool, lures Man into sin and carnality, leading him away from the narrow path of virtue. Seduced by Satan, she is responsible for the Fall and the banishment from Paradise; as a result, she embodies the principle not just of iniquitous desire but rather of evil in general. And yet, she also embodies atonement and sanctification, indeed the principle of good in its entirety; for, as the Mother of God, she herself has, in a certain sense, accomplished the salvation of all humanity. These extremes have proven to be equally deleterious in their effect on the way women are viewed. Sensual pleasure and spiritual love have remained hopelessly cut off from one another, whether in the Middle Ages or, later, in that musty world of Pietism from which Büchner drew heavily, yet ambiguously. In the nineteenth century, there developed a crusade of sorts against both distortions, against the entire dualistic categorization of Woman as either "something to enthuse about and idealize" or a "sex object" (thus Egon Friedell as early as 1927).[129] However, this effort to break with the past was unable to avoid a more up-to-date, that is to say bourgeois, division of women into disreputable wenches and respectable spouses (or, at best, consorts). The contradiction was virtually inescapable; even a man like Heinrich Heine was unable to free himself from it—not to mention the lesser lights of his generation.

Here, too, it is Büchner alone who stands out as the true progressive, as a man manifestly ahead of his time. How else are we to explain his decision to endow both Marion, that embodiment of pagan sensuality, that pleasure principle incarnate, and Marie, a woman who perceives herself as being lustful and sinful in the Christian sense, with the name of the immaculate Virgin?[130] Can one really maintain that the playwright did this unintentionally, that in selecting these names he was guided only by chance or whim? Instead, are we not led to the conclusion that they reflect a conscious desire to break with the tradition of opposing sensuality to spirituality, an attempt to underscore both the falseness of this opposition and the necessity of a resolution? And, once we become attuned to such matters, there are other things that meet our eye. For example, is it only an accident that the most chaste and virginal of Büchner's female figures, Lena, bears the name of the Gospel's archetypal fallen woman, Magdalene (German: Magda*lena*)? Does not this, too, constitute a rejection of that age-old dichotomy of spirit and flesh, a rejection the playwright may well have had in mind when he christened this delicate character? Furthermore, does not Büchner actually go so far as to expunge—in a way that avoids all heavy-handedness—the stain of evil, of the demonic and the diabolical, which has marked sensual pleasure ever since the advent of Christianity? For though he had to rely on Pastor Herder's translation to conjure up the Eros of the Greeks,[131] it is clear that the verse of Sappho which he quotes is endowed with a tone that is unmistakably his own. In Büchner's play, the reference to "limb-loosening, *wicked* love" possesses an undercurrent of irony, a sovereign sense of playfulness and serenity. It is the same playful and gaily ironic tone that we encounter in a letter the young writer sent to his bride-to-be on January 27, 1837, a few weeks before his death: "Soon I must again draw nourishment from your inner blissfulness, from your divine lack of self-consciousness, your lovely frivolity, and all your wicked qualities, you wicked girl. Adio [*sic*] piccola mia!"[132] Lines like these are just as important for an understanding of Büchner's concept of life and love as are the oft-quoted statements found in his "fatalism letter."[133] Do not the twenty-three-year-old's phrases of endearment, which glide over into Italian, recall the world of the "divine" Aretino, and with it the *leggerezza* and *disinvoltura* of the Renaissance? And are they really so far removed from the image of the South, from the gaily sovereign approach to love and life invoked by Leonce and Valerio at the end of Büchner's comedy?[134]

Wherever one looks in this writer's life and works, one encounters Eros, and always in its full extent and in every conceivable form. Even in *The Hessian Messenger*, which Büchner wrote together with the impassioned parson, Ludwig Weidig, this topic is not excluded: "The princely cloak is the carpet on which lords and ladies of nobility and the court roll over each other in their lust. . . . The daughters of the people are their maids and whores."[135]

In spite of such righteous indignation (and in spite of the tract's motto, "Peace to the huts! War on the palaces!"), Büchner was anything but a bluenose progressive, a repressed and desiccated "virtuous one"[136] of the sort he portrayed in Robespierre—portrayed, it should be emphasized, without condemning. In his passionate sense of outrage carrying with it a current of bitterness, Büchner was in fact much closer to Danton, although it would be a grave mistake to posit a thoroughgoing identity between the writer and this figure. He managed to combine within himself both positions (which is not to say he was simply the sum of the two characters he used to manifest these positions). Büchner was an eroticist *and* a revolutionary; he was an erotic revolutionary and a revolutionary eroticist. For him, the slogan *amour, charité, fraternité* was no less important than *liberté, egalité, fraternité*. He was always concerned with the well-being of humanity as well as the happiness and fulfillment of the individual; his fraternal realm of love is always marked by Amor *and* Caritas, Eros *and* Agape. The totality of love stands as the only consolation, the only refuge and salvation in a world of cruelty, suffering, and pain, a world which is seemingly unchangeable and yet which *must* be changed.

It is only in this sense—but, in this sense, absolutely—that love is the highest value for Büchner, not merely a "longing" or a "highest hope," but indeed the "most important aspect of existence" and the "core . . . of life." And its antipode, the loss of love, loveless isolation, is the most terrible fate that can befall a person. Lenz, for instance, lives out his life in this "emptiness": repeatedly, the point is made that he is "terribly lonely," "alone, alone," "completely alone."[137] Both Lena, before she finds Leonce, and Woyzeck, after he loses Marie, experience this sense of existential abandonment; even Danton is touched by it. In Büchner's comedy, moreover, the feeling is alluded to in a manner which is at once free from embellishment and highly poignant: "We all walk alone and reach out for a hand to hold until the undertaker separates the hands and folds them over our breasts."[138] But there can be no doubt that it is expressed most movingly in *Woyzeck*—namely, in the grandmother's "fairy tale." Here, even the last traces of faith and hope, which survive in the image of hands being folded, have completely disappeared; and the utter starkness of the old woman's language only serves to underscore this fact:

> Once upon a time there was a poor little child with no father and no mother, everything was dead, and no one was left in the whole world. Everything was dead, and it went and cried day and night. And since nobody was left on the earth, it wanted to go up to the heavens, and the moon was looking at it so friendly, and when it finally got to the moon, the moon was a piece of rotten wood and then it went to the sun and when it got there, the sun was a wilted sunflower and when it got to the stars, they were little golden flies stuck up there like the shrike sticks 'em on the blackthorn and when it wanted to go back down to the earth, the earth was an upset pot and it was all alone and it sat down and cried and there it sits to this day, all alone.[139]

In this fairy tale devoid of all happiness, an "anti-fairy tale" if ever there was one, the mood of isolation and abandonment takes on truly cosmic dimensions. What Büchner has created here is the bleak image of a world *completely devoid of love*.[140] Yet precisely by means of this powerful, indeed starkly terrifying, evocation of the absolute disappearance of love, of the absence of all kindness, warmth, and refuge, he succeeds in incalculably heightening the value of these categories—which is exactly what he intended to do. For can love and human contact be celebrated more intensely, can they be praised more unconditionally or exalted more unreservedly than through a myth of total isolation and universal loss of love, such as Büchner's?

But Büchner would not be Büchner if he limited himself to glorifying or liberating love, and failed to present its dark and threatening aspects, its compulsive and mechanical side. He regarded it in much the same way he regarded the revolution, raising not only love's redeeming value but also its repellent wildness, not only the sweetness but also the bitterness of "bittersweet Eros," to a universal, indeed cosmic, level. Büchner's pansexual images extend from the flies on our hands [141] to the sun in the firmament. [142] If in Danton's eyes untrammeled desire retains a certain gaiety, Woyzeck perceives its descent into crude, animal-like lust, its transformation into open bestiality. [143]

"Life" itself, which unleashes a pandemonium of promiscuity, "is a whore, it fornicates with the whole world": thus the fatalistic conclusion drawn by Danton. [144] Or conversely, as Valerio puts it in his equally all-inclusive and fatalistic description of human beings, specifically those who are "highly educated": "Nothing but cardboard and watchsprings." [145] For Büchner, nature's drives and society's imperatives are equally ambiguous. It is certainly not just sexuality that he subjects to critical scrutiny; he also regards with skepticism, indeed with merciless irony, the "idealistic" love of those who possess such a "fine sense of propriety" that they have "no word for the concept 'pants.'" [146] When Leonce and Lena are ushered in "masked" as upright "members of human society," they are "very noble" and "very moral," [147] but in their mechanical rectitude they are as constrained as the compulsively lascivious men and women who inhabit Büchner's drama of revolution and his proletarian tragedy. Introducing these "two persons of opposite sexes" in a manner strongly reminiscent of how the sideshow operator in *Woyzeck* presents his trained horse and his apes, Valerio declaims:

> Take note, ladies and gentlemen: they are now in an interesting state. The mechanism of love is beginning to function—the gentleman has already carried the lady's shawl several times, the lady has turned her eyes up to heaven. Both have whispered more than once: "Faith, love, hope!" Both already appear to be completely in accord; all that is lacking is the tiny word "amen." [148]

With this condemnation of "love in the *juste milieu*," Büchner takes a position similar to that adopted by Heine, even if the latter phrased his gibes more in terms of national peculiarities, maliciously remarking, not of women in general, but specifically of "German women": "Gently they yearn / And sigh about love, hope and faith."[149] Not only did Büchner exalt what Fink labels "concupiscence" as well as what this critic deems worthy of the term "love"; he also regarded both of them skeptically and critically. The latter has pleased the literary-critical proponents of morality; the former (insofar as it has even been acknowledged) has found only grudging acceptance with them. Yet is it not time—or so certain people might ask nowadays—that their skepticism be expanded to include Büchner himself? Are we not forced to subject him to the rigor of his own critique and indict him for grievous offenses? For what are we to make of Leonce's "scale" and "rainbow" of love for which one requires an infinite number of women? Does this not bespeak male chauvinism of the worst sort? Indeed, are we not informed that no less a personage than Danton adheres to an approach of this type? "He's searching for the Venus of Medici piece by piece among all the grisettes of the Palais Royal," Lacroix tells us. "He's making a mosaic, as he says."[150]

But let us not forget that Leonce is a comic figure who, besides being the butt of our laughter, is at least partially cured of his notions regarding love. Moreover, Lacroix's lines occur immediately after the scene with Marion. If Danton is using the grisettes to fashion a mosaic, Marion declares that "all men" have melted together into "one body."[151] The difference, I submit, is really not all that great. For information that is truly illuminating, we must look elsewhere. Namely, is it not necessary to take Lacroix's words in the most literal fashion? Was it not Venus, together with Epicurus, who was to serve as the "doorkeeper of the Republic," thereby placing her seal on a state of utopian perfection? And now, is she not in actuality scattered (indeed painfully "cut up . . . into pieces")[152] among the impoverished whores in a brothel? It is not her liberated (and liberating) sensuality—except in the case of Marion[153]—that suffuses the Palais Royal; what is revealed there is simply naked need. "Hunger goes whoring and begging"[154] in these wretched women, just as it does in the daughter of Simon the prompter, whom we encounter near the beginning of the play. Hence, must not Danton be counted among those who "prostitute the daughters of the people"?[155] Is he not doing something that Büchner, in *The Hessian Messenger*, denounced as one of the crimes of the exploitative nobility? Why is the Palais Royal mentioned twice with such emphasis?[156] We know full well who "these marquises and barons of the Revolution" are, the men condemned by Robespierre for "marrying rich wives, giving sumptuous banquets, gambling, keeping servants, and wearing expensive clothes."[157] As might be expected, the "virtuous one" views all this from his own austere perspective and does not hesitate to define "vice" as "the mark of Cain on the aristocracy."[158] For the "impotent Mohammed,"[159] luxury and vice are synonymous; in assessing Danton, he cannot see the connoisseur of pleasure, but only the parasite.[160]

As always, though, the playwright saw both sides. Robespierre is correct in his view of Danton, just as Danton is correct in his view of Robespierre. Büchner remains the proponent of a social as well as a sexual utopia, advocating that humane luxury of the "extra" which, according to Brecht,[161] is what people are really fighting for when they man the barricades. If Danton is laden with guilt, it is only because he attempts a premature and one-sided realization of something that lies in the distant future and can only be attained through long and laborious effort. This is the historical-philosophical critique contained in Büchner's revolutionary play; yet as propounded by Robespierre it amounts to an equally one-sided condemnation of his opponent's outlook as vice-ridden and parasitical, as nothing more than a relapse into feudalism, and thus results in the stern judge himself being enmeshed in guilt. Büchner, however, is present in both characters and in both positions. Instead of softening or obscuring the contradictions, he presents them with the greatest possible clarity. It is no accident that he sends Lacroix crashing into the utopian idyl of Danton and Marion, an intrusion which not only diminishes, but also brutally demolishes, what the two lovers have shared:

> (*Lacroix, Adelaide, Rosalie enter.*)
> LACROIX. (*Remains at the door.*) Oh, that was funny!
> DANTON. (*Indignantly.*) Well?
> LACROIX. The street!

DANTON. And?

LACROIX. There were dogs on the street, a Great Dane and an Italian lapdog—they were trying to have a go at it.

DANTON. So what?

LACROIX. I just thought of it and I had to laugh.[162]

The contrast to the glimpse of utopia we have just been given could scarcely be more glaring or grotesque. But is the same glimpse not rendered all the more bold and radiant by the somber shadows that surround it? Those shadows, too, have already been discussed at length, and by many a critic. Rather than contenting myself with the orthodox view, I will instead close with one last bit of heresy. This time it is purely philological in nature and consists, *horribile dictu*, of my doing something which no serious scholar should ever dare to do. Without consulting the original manuscript, I want to suggest an emendation in the text of *Woyzeck*. Yet I am so confident in the matter that I must in all modesty request that this new reading be regarded as obligatory from now on. Each and every complete edition of Büchner, from Bergemann to Lehmann,[163] contains a passage which was struck by the playwright and which reads as follows (Woyzeck, here still referred to as Franz, apparently is speaking to Marie): "I want to tell you, I had a doggy [and] it kept sniffing at a big *hat* [*Hut*] and couldn't get on. So, out of kindness, I helped him out and set him up on top. And the people stood around and [*remainder illegible*]."[164] Do we not hear Lacroix's wanton laughter resounding in our ears? "There were dogs on the street, a Great Dane and an Italian lapdog—they were having a go at it." But surely, even without this parallel, the glaring incorrectness of the established reading is apparent. Even if Büchner did clearly write "hat" he meant to write "dog": "I had a doggy [and] it kept sniffing at a big dog [*Hund*] and couldn't get on. So, out of kindness, I helped him out and set him up on top."[165]

Animal lusts, the lowest type of sex, and human kindness, a generosity which is extended even to unthinking beasts—the two are joined together here in programmatic fashion. Indeed, it is not "cœur" *or* "carreau," but rather "cœur" *and* "carreau," in their full extent and in their every form, that typify love in the works and life of Georg Büchner.

Part 2

3   Culmination, Conclusions, and a New Beginning

The Present State of Büchner Reception and Research

> *Solche Werke, wie diejenigen Büchner's, kommen nie zu spät.*
>
> —Wilhelm Schulz

Let us not deceive ourselves: The founding of a Georg Büchner Gesellschaft ("Georg Büchner Society") and the publication of a *Büchner Jahrbuch* ("Büchner Yearbook") are separated by a century and a half from the life and works of the man to whom they are dedicated. Christian Dietrich Grabbe and Friedrich Hebbel, two writers often—though not always justifiably—associated with Büchner, possess their own Societies, as do Joseph von Eichendorff, E. T. A. Hoffmann, Jean Paul, and even Johann Joseph von Görres—not to mention Goethe and Schiller. And all of these associations, some of which have been in existence for many years, publish yearbooks or at least proceedings. There has been a Brecht Society for more than a decade, albeit—and this is no accident—founded outside of Germany (indeed, in the United States). Also, there is a Carl Zuckmayer Gesellschaft which came into being even prior to the death of this writer who hailed from the same part of Germany as Büchner, and who, like the latter and like Bertolt Brecht, was forced to flee his homeland. Georg Büchner, however—who surely must be regarded as being at least the equal of all but a few of the writers I have listed; who, although I am always reluctant to proffer such judgments, is more important than quite a number of them—was not accorded such an honor until 1979, exactly one hundred years after the publication of the first edition of his collected works. This fact alone, it seems to me, tells us something about his fate among the Germans.

115

Or only among the Germanists? I have no desire to repeat the dreary song of self-accusation that is, or at least was, so popular in our discipline. But the fact remains: among the discoverers of Büchner, one does not meet any of the august personages who were our predecessors in the lecture halls, libraries, and archives. This honor belongs exclusively to others, most particularly to a number of writers and critics. In addition to the friends and contemporaries of Büchner who sought to further the young writer and his work, men such as Wilhelm Schulz and Karl Gutzkow, there was the writer Karl Emil Franzos—himself currently being rediscovered—to whom we owe the first collected works of 1879. Between that important date and the publication of the first significant scholarly treatment of Büchner, a sensitive study by Paul Landau,[1] again almost a generation was to pass. In the meantime, the young Naturalists, playwrights such as Gerhart Hauptmann and Frank Wedekind, had become vociferous supporters of Büchner and had drawn inspiration from his writings; their enthusiasm was such that they even made pilgrimages to his grave in Zurich. Later, this same type of creative reception—which over the years has evoked a sizable body of works dealing with and/or dedicated to Büchner—could also be found among the Expressionists and the practitioners of the so-called New Objectivity (*Neue Sachlichkeit*). It managed to survive the dark years between 1933 and 1945 and has continued down to the present day, growing steadily in intensity and breadth. And in the process, it has by no means remained limited to those areas in which German is spoken. For example, in France, a land which played so decisive a role in Büchner's life and thought, a comparable pattern of reception emerged at an astoundingly early point.

And yet these developments beyond the Rhine, indeed almost all "foreign" creative responses to Büchner, have been largely ignored, while the appropriation of Büchner by German-speaking writers—as well as composers—has, for the most part, been recognized and subjected to scholarly scrutiny. Just recently, several anthologies and investigations of this type of literature have been published in Germany.[2] Nevertheless, a brief review seems in order before we proceed to Büchnerian aspects which have not yet been dealt with. A particularly illuminating example is provided by the Expressionist poet Georg Heym who, though he first noted he "knew little" of Büchner, soon thereafter was so overwhelmed by him that he wrote in his diary: "Received Georg Büchner and placed a new god . . . on my altar." The entry dates from January of 1909.[3] Three years later, Robert Walser demonstrated his ties to the author of *Danton's Death* and *Woyzeck*;[4] and four years after that, in a collection of novellas entitled *Das rasende Leben* ("Raging Life"), Kasimir Edschmid honored the "memory" of his "very great dead brother."[5] Rainer Maria Rilke, though of a temperament entirely different from Büchner's, was compelled to acknowledge in a letter of July 1915 that the *Woyzeck* fragment was an unparalleled drama, "something astounding";[6] and Robert Musil, a writer known for the acuity of his critical sensibilities, betrayed a similar degree of enthusiasm in regard to *Danton's Death* and its "poetic vision."[7] Even Hugo von Hofmannsthal strove to come to terms with this play, despite his own desire to produce a body of work that would negate the revolution. On the other hand, years later, his favorite director, Max Reinhardt, attempted to transform the Beggar in Hofmannthal's adaptation of Calderón's *El gran teatro del mundo*, the repentant rebel with an axe, into a pious Danton who, like some figure in a legend, undergoes a miraculous conversion.[8] However, neither this drama nor Alban Berg's twelve-tone opera entitled *Wozzeck*, the work which first secured a degree of international recognition for the Hessian writer, should blind us to the other developments that occurred during that period. The years preceding 1933 generated Franz Theodor Csokor's "play concerning Büchner," a work which bears the programmatic title *Gesellschaft der Menschenrechte* ("Society of Human Rights"), as well as Arnold Zweig's ambitious *Versuch über Büchner* ("Essay on Büchner").[9]

Admittedly, not even Zweig's lengthy study of 1925 has been recognized by the German academic establishment as a "genuine scholarly contribution." This refusal should come as no surprise in view of the fact that the same establishment, gravid with degrees and titles, has felt compelled to regard Franzos as a mere "dilettante," even while reluctantly acknowledging the services he has rendered.[10] Today it seems all too obvious that academicians would be well-advised to abandon their stubborn conviction that the only useful ideas and insights are those which have been spawned within an institution of higher learning; input from the "outside world" can be extremely helpful, regardless of whether it functions as a corrective to established notions or simply as a stimulating provocation. And this is particularly true of the texts which in recent years have been written about, to, for, even against Büchner.

It is neither possible nor even necessary here to offer a detailed discussion of these writings and the issues they raise. Let a few brief observations suffice. First of all, it must be evident that in the years following 1945 a large and multifarious body of literature has developed out of an ongoing process of creative confrontation with Büchner, a process involving a number of the German language's most talented writers. The texts that have been produced range from the three-line epigram to the drama, the novella, and the novel; in some cases, one encounters only isolated elements, figures, or motifs sprinkled through a larger text, but there are also entire works that—in one way or another—have been inspired by the nineteenth-century author and his oeuvre. His writings are alluded to, quoted, and echoed in variations; they are rethought and continued; they are used as the basis for what, since Brecht, has been referred to as "counter-conceptions" (*Gegenentwürfe*). And these efforts to come to grips with Büchner have involved all his works—literary, political, and scientific—as well as his personality and biography.

1956: Heiner Müller writes the poem "Or Büchner" as part of the cycle "Lessons." 1958: Max Frisch begins his parable-play *Andorra*, which he then completes in 1961; its central figures, Barblin and the Soldier, are clearly modeled after Marie and the Drum Major in *Woyzeck*. 1964: Peter Weiss finally finishes *Marat/Sade*, a work whose debt to *Danton's Death* is somewhat less direct, but nonetheless fully evident. 1965: Hans Magnus Enzensberger publishes a new edition of *The Hessian Messenger* and in his afterword strives to place it in the "political context" of struggles for national liberation in the Third World.[11] 1966: Kasimir Edschmid publishes his lengthy historical novel, *Georg Büchner*, a book which carries the provocative subtitle *A German Revolution*. 1972: The Hessian State Theater stages the world première of *Büchners Tod*, a play written in German by the Chilean Gaston Salvatore. (Born in 1941, Salvatore lived in West Berlin during the era of the student protests; in 1969, he was sentenced to nine months in prison for his involvement in a political disturbance.)

As anyone who is familiar with recent German literature will realize, this list is far from complete. Additional works that need to be included are Peter Schneider's story *Lenz* from West Berlin and Volker Braun's *Unvollendete Geschichte* ("An Unfinished Story") from East Germany, as well as Braun's essay "Büchners Briefe" ("Büchner's Letters").[12] For it should be noted that the creative appropriation of Büchner is no less lively and fruitful in the GDR than in the FRG—a fact that stands in marked contrast to the sadly hidebound approach that long has dominated East German scholarly treatments of this most revolutionary of writers. Significantly enough, the current pinnacle of the literary reception of Büchner is provided by Heiner Müller's *Der Auftrag* ("The Mission"), an East German piece which is part drama and part narrative. It would appear that in Müller's work, which appeared in 1979, both the historical material that Büchner dealt with in *Danton's Death* and the Hessian writer's life and thought are subjected to a thoroughgoing sublation, in the Hegelian sense of the word. This interpretation is virtually forced upon the reader from the very outset by the text's evocative subtitle, *Erinnerung an eine Revolution* ("Remembrance of a Revolution").[13]

However, the example of Müller is particularly illuminating insofar as it demonstrates that the exchange between creative literature and scholarship need not (and should not) flow in only one direction. We already know his three-line epigram of 1956 in which the poet addresses himself:

OR BÜCHNER, who died in Zurich
100 years before your birth
age 23, from a lack of hope[14]

Granted, Müller has chosen his words (as well as his punctuation) in such a way as to invest these lines with a high degree of "openness"; nevertheless, this is a case in which scholarship clearly needs to come to the aid of poetic intuition rather than the other way around. Büchner very definitely did not die from "a lack of hope"; he was not overcome by resignation or despondency. One might also notice a certain irony in the fact that in 1956, the same year Müller wrote his somber epigram, the GDR Germanist Hans Jürgen Geerdts published a novel about Büchner which bore the rosy title *Hoffnung hinterm Horizont* ("Hope beyond the Horizon"). I mention this book for its curiosity value only, since Müller's imputation of pessimism can be effectively refuted simply on the basis of a careful reading of Büchner's works and letters. Even after being forced into exile, the young writer professed (as we have heard) that he would always "hope for the best." And he underscored that point repeatedly.[15]

While Müller's epigram renders itself somewhat marginal through its misreading of Büchner's outlook, his play occupies a central position—all the more so because it serves as a bridge between the literary reception of Büchner in the German-speaking countries and the corresponding process in France. Although this parallel development beyond the Rhine began as early as the 1920s, it was not until the early 1950s that Büchner found an enthusiastic, indeed passionate, admirer in the person of Arthur Adamov, the Russian émigré who, before his death by suicide in 1970, became one of the major figures of postwar French drama. In his notebooks we read that *Woyzeck*, besides being "une très grande pièce," represents the first modern German drama ever. Adamov even went so far as to elevate Büchner above his other idol, August Strindberg, describing the young German as the only outstanding dramatist produced by Europe since the Elizabethan flowering around 1600! Or, as I like to declare in order to shock my colleagues in English and Drama: Had Büchner lived longer, he would have become the Shakespeare of the modern era—an opinion, indeed an insight, which was expressed as early as 1851 by Wilhelm Schulz.[16]

While the elective Frenchman remained true to Büchner to the very end, he eventually abandoned Strindberg and, in his stead, embraced Bertolt Brecht. Adamov has left a number of statements indicating that during the mid-1950s he and the inventor of epic theater spent an entire afternoon discussing Büchner.[17] This is no coincidence, for Brecht's work evidently represents a fruitful continuation of the Büchnerian heritage. However, if we really are to appreciate the nature and extent of these connections, we must keep in mind that Adamov was an ardent admirer not only of Büchner but also of Antonin Artaud—and this from the very beginning. Moreover, it is not at all improbable that it was Artaud who first introduced him to Büchner. As early as the 1920s, this ecstatic of the stage, who went on to develop his "theater of cruelty," was able to recognize—or, perhaps, intuitively to grasp—the full importance of Georg Büchner and his work.

But if Adamov gazed up at Büchner with open-mouthed admiration, Artaud viewed him as a co-equal with whom he was united in fraternal alliance. All the same, his support of Büchner went beyond mere statements—we should not allow ourselves to be fooled by his insistence that *Woyzeck* was included in the program of his theater of cruelty solely "out of a spirit of contradiction" (*par esprit de réaction contre nos principes*).[18] That the discovery of this play was a true "illumination" for him has been conclusively established by French scholars such as Alain Virmaux.[19] In a letter to Louis Jouvet, Artaud announced that "nothing" in the entire corpus of dramatic literature, indeed in all of written literature, was more deserving of being staged than *Woyzeck*. He even recommended to Jouvet Büchner's comedy, *Leonce and Lena!*[20] However much Artaud was attracted by Büchner's works, he was even more fascinated by the writer himself, the man whose overpowering presence he perceived in them. Virmaux points out that the spiritual and intellectual bonds linking Artaud to Büchner were so intense that they would provide sufficient grounds for associating the two writers even if the French visionary had never actually discovered his German "kinsman" (*frère de race*).[21]

I am in agreement with Virmaux, at least in regard to his basic thesis. This relationship is indeed extraordinarily important—or, more precisely, this fabric of relationships. For over and above the conclusions reached by the French scholar, we must remember that what we have here are connections between Artaud and Büchner *and* Brecht and Büchner—as well as connections between the two great heirs of the Hessian writer. These links need to be investigated, particularly if Brecht's epic theater of alienation and Artaud's theater of cruelty can rightly be said to constitute the two main forces which, working simultaneously *with* and *against* each other, have shaped modern world drama and theater during the past decades.[22] But then we must also confront a crucial question the relevance of which is hardly limited to historians of the theater: Is not this same dialectical unity of tendencies already present, however embryonically, in the works of Georg Büchner himself? As has been demonstrated before, this hypothesis, regardless of how startling it may seem at first glance, proves to be far more promising than the stale thesis which holds that Büchner anticipated the theater of the absurdists. Is there really anything to be gained from the tedious attempts to define his work as a prefiguration of, say, Eugène Ionesco's *La Cantatrice chauve* (*The Bald Soprano*) and the writer himself as having been a "chronicler of the absurd"?[23] I think not. Instead, let us turn our attention elsewhere. Works such as Müller's "The Mission" and Weiss's *Marat/Sade*, which directly or indirectly seek to continue as well as sublate Büchner's accomplishments, are indeed "chronicles." They are not, however, chronicles of the absurd, but rather of the ongoing process of revolution which began with the storming of the Bastille, and of the genre of the drama of revolution which, beginning with *Danton's Death*, has sought to accomplish an artistic representation (and perhaps a sublation) of this central category of our modern world. Müller and Weiss are both successful insofar as each effects an exemplary, though highly precarious and quite possibly inimitable, fusion of Brecht's rational and critical theater of the mind and Artaud's irrational and mythic theater of the body— a fusion in which these two contradictory and apparently irreconcilable elements serve to heighten and intensify each other. And in recognizing this, we are led to yet another observation: Instead of "rational and critical" I might have said "Socratic"; instead of "irrational and mythic," simply "Dionysian." For it cannot be denied that Friedrich Nietzsche, that most important (and most disruptive) mediator between Büchner's era and the present day, must also be taken into consideration when we deal with these issues. I am thinking, of course, of his *Birth of Tragedy*, first published in 1872. The very possibility that connections might exist between Büchner and Nietzsche is something which has been scrupulously ignored by the scholarly establishment. But the fact that Nietzsche apparently never concerned himself with Büchner—in any case, he never made any statements about him—does not force us to declare the matter closed. After all, Büchner scholarship, always ready to give (as well as to take) offense, has come up with philosophical (or pseudophilosophical) propositions far more dubious than this. At the moment, I do not want to speculate any further about the specific conclusions that might eventually be reached by such investigations; I merely want to emphasize that they are not only legitimate but entirely necessary. Indeed they are, as we have seen, unavoidable. Müller, for one, not only followed Weiss's lead in acknowledging a debt to *both* Brecht and Artaud, but also, in the same programmatic statement, referred explicitly to Nietzsche.[24] Compared with these truly epic connections, the various isolated links and echoes that can be located are of secondary importance. For example, if we turn our attention to literature written in English, we note that Rubashov, the protagonist of Arthur Koestler's novel *Darkness at Noon*, betrays a striking similarity to Büchner's Danton, extending even to specific thoughts and ideas.[25] But there is no need to engage here in a detailed discussion of Koestler's novel of 1940 or of any of the other "extramural" (i.e., nonacademic) contributions. I only wish to emphasize once again that they should not be overlooked. True, some of these texts possess only minimal importance; others, however, are extremely significant. And all of them must be regarded as "noteworthy" documents of a fascinating process of literary reception and interaction.

This last assessment, as general as it is inarguable, can be found in Hans Mayer's aforementioned *Georg Büchner und seine Zeit.*[26] It refers specifically to the speeches given by the recipients of the annual Georg Büchner Prize, speeches which Mayer justly regards as part of the "literature" on Büchner. Before proceeding any further, I feel that a few remarks concerning this prize are necessary.

Recently, the awarding of the Büchner Prize was described somewhat condescendingly as an "attempt at reparation" (*Wiedergutmachungsversuch*) staged yearly in Darmstadt.[27] To such an allegation, one can only reply that, in Germany, it is highly significant that this award (which the same critic had to acknowledge as "the most prestigious German literary prize") doesn't bear the name of Goethe or Schiller, but rather that of Georg Büchner. It is perhaps also useful to recall the obvious, though often overlooked, fact that as long as Hesse was ruled by its grand dukes there could be no overly vociferous acclamation of the revolutionary conspirator who had identified the prince as the "head of the leech" crawling over the Hessian people.[28] After all, this same people, having freed itself from the authority of the princes, established and funded a prize in the name of Büchner as early as 1923—and did so, it might be added, in a time of extreme economic misery. With that gesture, the author of *The Hessian Messenger* was finally "discovered . . . as the literary patron saint of his homeland," to quote Ernst Johann's somewhat pathos-laden, but by no means inaccurate, formulation.[29] This first Büchner Prize, unlike the present-day award, was neither purely literary nor were its recipients drawn from the entire German-speaking community. Instead, all varieties of artists were eligible—as long as they hailed from Hesse. Revived in 1945, the prize was continued in its original format until 1951, when an agreement between the Hessian Ministry of Culture, the city authorities of Darmstadt, and the German Academy for Language and Literature (*Deutsche Akademie für Sprache und Dichtung*) transferred control of it to the last-named institution. The prize was then redefined as an honor which could be bestowed on writers only, but at the same time the clause excluding non-Hessians was dropped. Anyone writing in the German language became eligible. The first recipient of the new award was the poet and essayist Gottfried Benn.

Admittedly, there have been instances in which certain elements or classes of the citizenry of Hesse (or, on occasion, Darmstadt alone) have voiced their outrage concerning specific awards; the most extreme example of this occurred when the recipient was Günter Grass. And, as became evident when Hans Magnus Enzensberger was given the prize, there can be bitter controversy even within the academy itself as to the wisdom of its selection. But then, such differences of opinion are not only understandable but, quite probably, unavoidable. (Let me add that, when I delivered an earlier version of these remarks in Darmstadt in 1981, I warmly greeted the awarding of that year's prize to the playwright and novelist, Martin Walser; at the same time, however, I vehemently argued that Peter Weiss had long deserved to be a recipient, and that the failure to admit him to the ranks of the honored was a grievous oversight which needed to be remedied as soon as possible. As it turned out, the 1982 prize was awarded to Weiss, who accepted it on his deathbed—although in a letter written only a few weeks earlier he had declared: "Since the mid-1960s, I have indeed always been on the verge of receiving the Büchner Prize, but it has been withheld from me for political reasons. I really don't know if I could even accept it now."[30] Thus it would seem that occasionally the critic is able to go beyond the mere writing of literary history, and actually help influence its course.)

So much for the supposed "attempt at reparation" as well as

for Büchner's reception at large. As for the scholarly study of Büchner and his works, it, too, began on a large scale in the 1920s and then recommenced after 1945. The first of these phases produced the so-called Bergemann edition, a textual foundation which for decades was regarded as reliable. The second phase was, to a great extent, initiated by the monographs of Hans Mayer and Karl Viëtor,[31] studies which at the time seemed so innovative that a number of critics were prepared to regard them as definitive. This was premature; the degree to which the two books were tied to (and shaped by) the era in which they were written has become evident with the passage of time, as has their inability to satisfy fully our desire to understand their tremendously complex subject. All of which in no way diminishes the achievement and historical importance of Mayer's and Viëtor's pioneering works. The former, for example, is guilty of studied modesty when he suggests that he has contributed just "a little" to Büchner scholarship; Mayer has done much more than that. As early as 1959, he himself observed that "with the end of the Second World War a new phase of the reception of Büchner" had begun. For only then did "that Hessian literary phenomenon" achieve recognition as a "world literary phenomenon"; only then did Büchner and his works become, "in a multitude of ways," the object of "interest in the entire world." And it must be added that this interest was by no means exclusively "artistic" in nature but rather—indeed, above all— scholarly.[32]

Today we can truly speak of an international body of Büchner scholarship. Not only is France (the homeland of Artaud and adopted homeland of Adamov) well represented in it, thanks to numerous essays and articles as well as the books that have been produced by Richard Thieberger and Jean Auger-Duvignaud,[33] but there are also various contributions by Anglo-American scholars, whose work has distinguished itself in terms of both quantity and quality. For a time, their contingent actually formed the vanguard of Büchner studies. And let us not forget the Italians and the Scandinavians. The latter, to be sure, have produced only the isolated—but all the more welcome—study by Bo Ullmann.[34] In Italy, however, as well as in the English-speaking countries, there has emerged a much wider interest in Büchner, producing, in both cases, a body of scholarship more than comparable to the Büchner literature which might be called "indigenous." South of the Alps, for instance, the process was in no way terminated by the appearance of Giorgio Dolfini's slim book.[35] On the contrary, the important journal *Studi tedeschi* devoted an entire issue to Büchner,[36] an issue which was, in every sense of the word, extremely weighty. (It should be noted that this periodical, like its sister-journal, *Studi germanici*, has shown an admirable willingness to provide non-Italian scholars with an opportunity to report their findings and present their theses. The same cosmopolitan spirit is beginning to manifest itself elsewhere, notably in Scandinavia: not long ago, a Danish journal published a brief but most insightful essay by a German literary historian.)[37]

When I spoke of a kind of leading role played by Anglo-American Büchner scholarship, I was of course referring to the book from which we took our initial cue in chapter 1: Maurice B. Benn's *The Drama of Revolt*.[38] (Benn, who died shortly before the publication of his study, was a native of England who lived and taught in Australia.) Exhibiting a rare degree of unanimity, scholars and critics alike, both in Germany and abroad, have agreed that this volume could lead to a "real revision" of previous views; it might even, if only "for the time being," replace "the obsolete standard works" by Viëtor and Mayer—and hence should be translated into German as quickly as possible. I wholeheartedly concur; indeed I was among the very first to acknowledge and praise Benn's achievement.[39] For the sake of balance, though, I noted then and shall now repeat that Anglo-American scholarship has also produced one of the most dubious books ever written about Büchner, the arrogant and obtuse study of A. H. J. Knight.[40] Between these two extremes one finds a great, even remarkable, number of publications—far too many for me to discuss each one individually. Once more, however, I wish to single out and mention the American comparatist Herbert Lindenberger, the author of the best English-language monograph before, and even along with, Benn; for, after having written a preliminary essay on *Danton's Death*, he produced another pertinent monograph entitled *The Historical Drama* where he again devotes a good deal of attention to Büchner.[41] Also, as is the case with German scholarship, we encounter studies which, although concerned with other questions and issues, nevertheless contain insights that are of value in dealing with Büchner. An example of this is Benjamin Bennett's *Modern Drama and German Classicism*, a daring and provocative study which covers the entire period extending from Gotthold Ephraim Lessing to Brecht (and to which we will return in chapter 4).[42] Having hardly begun my sketch of the history and current state of the critical literature on Büchner, I shall abruptly break it off. Surely it is not my task to offer a detailed description and assessment of all the accomplishments as well as blunders of Büchner scholarship around the world, complete with names, dates, and facts. Instead, the question must be posed whether, in addition to the emergence of an international interest in Büchner, which is presumably irreversible, and the culmination of certain long-standing trends and traditions, we can indeed discern the glimmering of a new beginning in Büchner scholarship. Furthermore, one must ask to what extent there exist—as intimated previously—points of contact between these scholarly endeavors and that current of "creative reception" here uncovered. Doubtless, a number of milestones have already been set in place. There is, first of all, Werner R. Lehmann's "historical-critical edition with commentary," an ambitious project which, unfortunately, has hung fire after having brought forth two volumes. Then, too, there are a number of separate editions and bold attempts to deal with the entirety of Büchner's life and work. What is more, scholars have produced a wide array of more limited investigations and have sought to increase our knowledge of the various sources Büchner utilized in writing his works. Finally, there is Thomas Michael Mayer's monumental and sensational thirty-six volume collection of documents relating to Büchner's life and time, a collection which provided the basis for the first of two special issues the influential journal *Text + Kritik*, devoted to our author.[43] In its review of this issue, the prestigious West German weekly *Die Zeit* bluntly declared that the volume—and a sizable one it was—had knocked existing Büchner scholarship into a cocked hat and rendered it obsolete. Overnight, the readers were told, "thousands of pages" had been reduced to "waste paper."[44]

Is that really so? I submit that, in a certain sense, nothing has changed—though, of course, the new situation is quite different from the status quo in other ways. Let me briefly explain and support this contention. Or, to return to an image I have already

used, let me add a few concluding strokes to my sketch, in order
to delineate some crucial contours and sharpen some basic con-
trasts. (And I hope I shall be permitted to pursue my aim in a
manner somewhat less heavy-handed than the approaches common among the all too earnest practitioners of literary history
and criticism.)

In the case of Büchner, I am, and intend to remain, more of an
aficionado than a sword-swinging participant in the bloody me-
lees which for years have swirled around the questions: Who
was Georg Büchner? and what was his literary and/or political
accomplishment? To say the least, there has never been any
shortage of polemical thrust and counterthrust within Büchner
scholarship—although, on occasion, admonition and correction
are dispensed in a friendly and even charming manner. For instance, I have received a message from a colleague concerning
the intentionally provocative emendation in the text of *Woyzeck*
which I suggest at the end of chapter 2. A German version of this
chapter had come out in 1979, said emendation amounting, as
will be recalled, to the simple and sobering claim that Woyzeck's
"doggy" was not "sniffing" at a "big hat [*Hut*]," but rather at a
"big dog [*Hund*]," which would indeed explain the doggy's distress at not being able to "get up."[45] My correspondent related
that he had carefully scrutinized the relevant Büchner manuscript in Weimar, and then went on to enlighten me: "Very clearly,
it was a hat. A veterinary-psychiatrist told me that dogs, particularly small ones, are often felt fetishists." A nice bit of information! And, I trust, the learned "veterinary-psychiatrist" is phe-
nomenally correct. It appears to me, however, that this actually
strengthens, rather than undermines, my fundamental thesis
that Büchner was interested in, and strove to portray, "love in all
its forms";[46] and while we have long known that in his *Lenz* he
managed a brilliant anticipation of modern insights into the
nature of schizophrenia, it would now seem that in *Woyzeck* he
achieved the same feat in the realm of animal psychology—or,
more precisely, the psychology of small dogs.

But let us not lose sight of the serious problem at hand: What
has remained the same in Büchner scholarship? And what is new?

In my opinion, present-day academic efforts to come to grips
with Georg Büchner and his work are still, with dismaying frequency, marred by one or more of three interrelated and equally
regrettable tendencies—this despite the fact that such tenden-

cies have been virtually endemic to the study of Büchner over the past fifty years. First, there is the seemingly unbreakable addiction to "monocausal explanations,"[47] a dogged determination to define Büchner's exceedingly complex oeuvre in terms of a single, simplistically unified concept. While critics who are given to this approach have never been able to agree *which* concept should be utilized, they nevertheless have closely resembled one another in the monomaniacal—and monotonous—intensity with which they have pursued their individual projects. The second tendency, closely tied to the first, is an anemic, but nonetheless unquenchable, desire to view Büchner's life and work solely in terms of abstract categories and ideas, be they existential or political in nature. As a result of that propensity, there has been an almost obsessive preoccupation with questions of ideology, philosophy, and religion—a situation that led no less a worthy than Hans Mayer to lament in 1959 that the study of Büchner had become preeminently "a problem of world views" (a pronouncement which also referred, at least in part, to the two German states and their conflicting systems and ideologies, and which, moreover, is nearly as valid today as when it was first voiced).[48] The third tendency is the inevitable by-product, as it were, of the preceding two, for discourse among Büchner scholars almost always degenerates into a bitter confrontation of opposing positions marred by the kind of stubborn inflexibility that grows out of unwavering commitment to a single, both limited and limiting, approach. Having convinced themselves of the absolute validity of their respective "standpoints," such scholars devote much—at times, even most—of their energy to trumpeting forth their own views, and castigating one another for failing to acknowledge their irrefutable correctness. With a self-confidence free from even the slightest twinge of doubt, they loudly announce that they have once and for all discovered, seized, and mastered the basic "unity" or "identity" of Büchner's life and work. Apart from their blatant arrogance, all of these supposed solutions have little or nothing to do with one another—as is aptly demonstrated by the fact that the two terms I just quoted come from a pair of studies which are completely at odds with each other: one is a radically political attempt to present Büchner as a *Robespierre redivivus*, the other, a radically apolitical effort to portray him as a raving pietist.[49]

Granted, scholars have not been entirely blind to these problems, although it has mostly been a case of noticing the mote in a neighbor's eye while remaining oblivious to the beam that is obscuring one's own vision. Thus, if I may be allowed to offer a brief montage of quotes, we encounter highly laudable warnings regarding the dangers of a "reductionist outlook" which would conceive of Büchner in terms of "a formula"; it has even been noted that when an exegete begins with a single concept and, "in a sense he himself has defined," seeks, "come what may," to "set [it] up as an 'absolute,'" he will "completely" fail to recognize the true nature of this writer. Such a procedure is said, not to illuminate Büchner's works, but rather to "obscure," indeed to distort and falsify them.[50] What should be cultivated instead is a "sense of the complexity" of Büchner's oeuvre—which, it must again be admitted, is an admirable realization and an even more admirable intention.[51] Alas, it is easier to proclaim than to fulfill. A few lines later, this same champion of complexity declares that Büchner "must [!] have" gained the foundation for the "unity . . . of the multifarious contradictions" present in his work through a "study of philosophy"—a contention which carries with it, however, the odd disclaimer that it is "not so important" whether Büchner actually read "the philosophers in question." It all depends, we are blithely assured, "how one views Büchner and his text."[52] Whose text? What is of primary importance here is clearly not what Büchner himself wrote, but rather the predetermined conclusions that are being forced upon his text by the one who is doing the "interpreting."

The real victim of all these tendencies is Georg Büchner. For the most disastrous result of the "monocausal" approach to interpretation is the critics' belief that the author is himself at fault if his life and works cannot be fitted into the various procrustean beds which they have so diligently constructed. They work hard to stretch, amputate, or—if all else fails—ignore those aspects and elements which do not fit; but should there remain an unresolved contradiction, then clearly the problem does not lie with their method, but rather with some artistic inadequacy, intellectual shortcoming, or even out-and-out failure on the part of the writer. Even Thomas Michael Mayer has complained, however mildly, that *Danton's Death* is "not entirely free from conceptual inconsistencies."[53] This understated critique, which quickly evoked the reproach that Mayer was attempting to project an unconvincing "one-dimensional meaning" (*Einsinnigkeit*) into Büchner's works,[54] pales beside the attitude that has been widespread ever since 1937, when Georg Lukács announced that he had found "a significant lack of clarity"—not in himself, but rather in Büchner. To this day, critics who are disciples of the relentless Hungarian, or at least share his basic temperament, have not hesitated to speak of the young writer's "insufficient insight" into reality.[55]

The obsession with abstract thought, the supposition that Büchner was an author who always wrote "in terms of ideas"[56] has other, no less deleterious, effects. For one thing, the mountain of "meaning" which has been heaped up by generations of scholars, and continues to grow at an ever-quickening pace, has actually begun to block our access to Büchner's works—to such an extent, in fact, that one is forced to recall, and reformulate, the words of Camille Desmoulins: "These people forget the poet in favor of his thoughts [assuming, of course, that they are indeed his thoughts and not ideas that have been thrust upon him by the hordes of zealous interpreters]. They see nothing of the poetic creation which renews itself every moment in and around them, glowing, rushing, luminous." Or, as it has been put so succinctly: "When one reduces what Büchner presents us with to a . . . presentation of his 'views,' one fails to do justice to the text."[57] Another problem which results from the obsession with ideas in Büchner scholarship is the tendency to overemphasize the writer's (actual or ostensible) sources, that is to say, the impulses and inspirations he supposedly received, the large—nay, immense—number of books he supposedly read and assimilated. When considering the lengthy list of such "probable" or "possible" sources, a list, moreover, which is constantly being expanded, one would do well to keep in mind an extremely simple but, for this very reason, most telling, point: "Büchner lived . . . only a few years, and the reading of those source texts which have already been definitely established . . . , along with his phenomenal activity and productivity in the areas of literature, natural science, and politics, filled those years to the very brim." Thus the perceptive observation offered by Thomas Michael Mayer.[58] But his own huge and most impressive collection of "secondary documents" has in turn caused an otherwise quite sympathetic reviewer to raise the "uneasy question" of the apparent imbalance—in terms of sheer size—that exists between it and Büchner's "slim oeuvre."[59]

And yet I do think that if one takes a close look at recent critical writing on Büchner, one must conclude that at least some of the negative traditions, having attained their culmination, are now dying out while new, positive traditions are coming into being. There is indeed reason to believe that we are witnessing a new beginning. Two points ought to be emphasized. First, one notes a growing realization that there is little to be gained by reducing Büchner to an abstract—and, in the final analysis, imaginary—definition, regardless of its specific ideological coloration. Instead, critics are beginning to see that what is necessary and truly useful is a willingness to recognize (and sustain) that extraordinarily complex host of correspondences and, above all, contradictions which we encounter in Büchner's life and work. The new Büchner scholarship is prepared to admit that it is dealing with a "distinctly 'unsystematic'" oeuvre, one which is "constantly . . . checking itself against concrete reality," marked as it is by a "realistic approach to perception, thinking, and writing which is 'anti-ideological' in the sense that it concentrates on the development of contradictions *within* things."[60] Critics are now able to pose the question: "Why should it be impossible for Büchner to have demonstrated his conviction that in a revolution the voice of the masses is the determining factor, to have involved himself in early communist political action, and yet at the same time to have also expressed in his drama [*Danton's Death*] horror over the implications of violence, including revolutionary violence?"[61] Drawing on one of Hans Magnus Enzensberger's earnest jests, we could even go on to ask whether all of us are not secretly obsessed with the *idée fixe* of a "correct interpretation" and with its necessary premise, the "delusion" that a work of art can be fully encompassed by a coherent definition.[62] And if we were in a sacrilegious—or, perhaps, merely realistic—mood, we might wish to reply with Büchner: "But what entitles us to make this definition?" (*Was berechtigt uns aber, dieße Definition zu machen?*)[63] For the time being, Büchner's bare rhetorical question will have to suffice as a response to those qualms; its grave repercussions in his life and work will occupy us in chapter 5.

The second—and final—observation I should like to make is the following: Büchner scholarship seems to be increasingly evidencing an unprecedented and highly commendable willingness to engage in both international and interdisciplinary communication and cooperation. It even appears as if the blood-smeared polemical combatants may drop their sharp-edged weapons and—at long last—extend their hands in friendship to one another. In any case, hopeful signs abound. With growing frequency, one encounters a lively and fruitful exchange of information and ideas—truly a welcome change from the brutal and, more often than not, sterile duels of academic one-upmanship, mutual denunciation, and ideological finger-pointing. Today many of those who are interested in Büchner are actually working together; there has been significant contact between the long-separated domains of philology and creative literature, scholarship and art, textual criticism and the theater, historical understanding and literary interpretation, even aesthetic hermeneutics. In particular, the creative and critical currents of Büchner reception have flowed together, producing something that indeed deserves the name "productive reception." The discoveries of the scholars aid the writers and artists in their endeavors; in return, the latter's insights and visions enrich the sensibilities of the former.

The concrete manifestations of these new tendencies are as numerous and varied as they are heartening. Let me list but a few. The meritorious historian, Walter Grab of Tel-Aviv, has brought to light a central document relating to Büchner, an essay-review written in 1851 by Wilhelm Schulz, one of the writer's closest friends.[64] In discovering this text, Grab has done a great service for the discipline of *Germanistik*, and not only of *Germanistik*. And the Germanists have returned the favor: the voluminous array of documents which Thomas Michael Mayer of Marburg has located and collected will be of great use to historians who study the *Vormärz* period.[65] Then there is Ivan Nagel, a major figure in the field of dramatic production and the former director (*Intendant*) of the Hamburg Staatstheater. Suddenly, he has shown a scholarly interest in Büchner's sources and, in an article in the *Frankfurter Allgemeine Zeitung* dealing with the speech given by St. Just in *Danton's Death*, has contributed substantially to our understanding of Büchner's concept of revolution.[66] Furthermore, when one of the most progressive theaters in Germany, the Frankfurt Schauspiel, put on *Danton's Death* in

1980, its production was in part shaped by the scholarly thesis that Büchner placed equal emphasis on love and revolution, a thesis first advanced in the abovementioned special issue of *Text + Kritik*. Here, too, the interaction between the stage and scholarship was reciprocal, for the Frankfurt project also involved the publication of a volume[67] containing analytical writings on Büchner as well as a critical assessment of that most noteworthy example of creative Büchner reception, Heiner Müller's *Der Auftrag*.[68]

Already, then, one can point to a respectable, even impressive, collection of events and developments. Which is not to say that I am entirely in agreement with everything that has been put forward. For instance, both Nagel's article and, to a still greater extent, the book from Frankfurt are, I believe, in need of modification and correction. In the latter, which bears the modish title, *Trauerarbeit im Schönen* ("The Labor of Mourning in the Realm of Beauty"), I find the hectic effort to lay bare pathological aberrations in *Danton's Death* unconvincing, even misleading;[69] moreover, the contention that this play is "the bourgeois end game *par excellence*"[70] is, to say the least, one-sided; even the illuminating comparison of Büchner's first drama and Müller's piece needs to be expanded and developed. The very fact that *Der Auftrag* has been influenced by *Danton's Death* should help us realize that Büchner's drama of revolution likewise draws on an important predecessor: namely, Goethe's famous tragedy of 1788, *Egmont*. Thus it is plainly wrong to say that Müller (who, like Enzensberger before him, seeks to confront the Hessian revolutionary—and through him, ourselves—with the Third World's struggles for liberation) "assembled . . . a collage of literary material," while the author of *Danton's Death* constructed one exclusively out of "historical material."[71] Instead, Büchner proceeded in a manner quite similar to Müller's approach in that he consciously established connections between his own play about the French Revolution and a classical drama which, in however indirect a way, deals with the wars of liberation in the Netherlands of the sixteenth century. In other words, what we have here is a double set of connections and relationships, as will become abundantly clear in chapter 4.

Having recognized this, we can proceed to establish the true historical location and significance of Büchner's supposed "bourgeois end game." Suffice it to say, at this juncture, that it reveals itself as an extraordinary, indeed unique, drama of revolution, a work which has managed to anticipate the entire direction and fundamental development of the century and a half that separates it from the present day. Decidedly, it is *Danton's Death* (and not Müller's "remembrance of a revolution," for all its importance) which can be said—to modify a slogan first coined in regard to *Ulysses*—to be "a revolutionary play to end all revolutionary plays." This work of Shakespearean stature, which simultaneously conveys the relevance of Büchner's life and oeuvre as a whole, stands as the dominant centerpiece of a German triptych of plays which extends from 1788 to 1979 and which possesses both world-literary and world-historical dimensions as it represents the thrust and progress of modern revolution in its totality.

"Georg Büchner will continue to be discussed. His relevance is greater than ever." This is how Hans Mayer chose to end the 1959 edition of his seminal book.[72] Now as then his remark could serve as a fitting conclusion to a survey of the state of Büchner reception and research. However, I prefer to close by quoting Büchner's friend, Wilhelm Schulz. I can think of no better summary or motto for the future endeavors of writers, artists, and scholars than the laudatory words which Schulz penned in 1851, words which are even more valid and useful today. They can be synthesized as follows:

Büchner was a socialist, not in the sense that he adhered to "any doctrinaire system," but rather through his radical rejection of, and struggle against, "the unequal distribution of material and intellectual goods." Büchner's "thoroughly skeptical nature even made him doubt his own doubts"; it "guarded him" against the "arrogance" of the dogmatists and their "pretensions to infallibility." With Büchner, one "never [encounters] a single one of the catchwords and clichés current during that era." Indeed, "he wrote just like he spoke." Büchner, once and for all, was "a poet through and through."[75]

Part 3

4 *Danton's Death*

A *"Counterconception"* to Goethe's Egmont?

Mit einem Wort, ich halte viel auf Goethe oder Shakespeare.
—Georg Büchner

"On the twentieth *Lenz* went through the mountains." Thus begins Georg Büchner's famous story of the same title. Although the name of the month is missing, it is accepted practice to insert "January."[1] Likewise under the twentieth of January, in another famous work of German literature, we encounter the following passage:

> Not a heartfelt moment, not a blissful hour—nothing . . . nothing. Sometimes I feel as if I were standing in front of a peep show. I can see tiny men and horses maneuvering in front of me, and I ask myself if it is not an optical illusion. I join in the games, or rather, I should say that I let myself be manipulated like a puppet, and sometimes I touch my neighbor's wooden hand and withdraw mine in horror. . . . I don't know why I get up or why I go to bed.[2]

"And so I reel with dread," we read earlier in the same work, "surrounded by the heavens and the earth and the powerful web they weave between them: I can see nothing but an eternally devouring, eternally regurgitating monster."[3]

These lines are taken from Goethe's first novel, *Die Leiden des jungen Werthers* (*The Sorrows of Young Werther*), initially published in 1774. Yet could they not just as well have been written two generations later by Büchner? Could they not be uttered by his Lenz or his Danton or even—with the addition of a slight Hes-

139

sian twang, which surely would have posed no problem to the author—by Woyzeck? But let us remain with Lenz; for there is scarcely a statement that would sound more authentic coming from him than Werther's declaration: "I have so much, yet . . . without her [the woman he loves] all of it is nothing."[4]

Still, despite this oft-repeated "nothing," Werther, shortly before his death, reaches a point where he is able to announce with the blissfulness of one who has been redeemed: "No, Lotte, no. How could I possibly perish? How could you pass away? You and I . . . we *are*! . . . I am not dreaming, I am not deluding myself! Close to the grave all grows lighter. We shall be! We shall see each other again!"[5] These words of farewell which treat death as a mere hurrying ahead to a "Father" who also awaits those left behind, words which—even on the verge of suicide—are certain of the mercy of the "Infinite": they could not by any stretch of the imagination be spoken by one of Büchner's characters, especially not by his theologian, Lenz. Even when we do encounter passages that are somewhat similar (e.g., in exchanges between Danton and Julie), they transfigure the shared death of the lovers and perhaps even the notion of nothingness, but not death itself or the chaos of existence.[6]

Here Goethe and Büchner, for all their points of contact, appear to be worlds apart from each other. And yet, decades later when he was in his sixties, the author of *Werther* wrote a letter to his friend Zelter after the latter's stepson had committed suicide, a letter in which he remarked:

> When the individual is seized by the *taedium vitae*, he is only to be pitied, not rebuked. That all the symptoms of this strange malady—as natural as it is unnatural—have at one time raged within me is something that cannot be doubted by anyone familiar with *Werther*. I know full well what determination and exertion it then cost me to escape from the waves of death, just as I have laboriously saved myself and slowly recovered from many a later ship wreck. . . . I am convinced I could write a new *Werther* that would cause the public's hair to stand on end even more than the first one did.[7]

These lines were penned on December 3, 1812, less than a year before the birth of the writer who, figuratively speaking, pro-

duced that "new *Werther*" which Goethe himself decided to
leave unwritten. Or phrased in a more general manner: In many
respects, Büchner's literary accomplishment represents a continuation as well as a heightening, indeed an exaggeration, of
what is clearly present and, quite often, even preformulated in
the works of the young Goethe. Moreover, this can be seen not
only in Goethe's worldwide bestseller of 1774, the work most fre-
quently cited as evidence of a connection between the two writers,[8] but also in his tragedy (*Trauerspiel*) *Egmont*, which was completed in 1788. As has been pointed out, one *can* read Büchner's
Lenz as "a radicalization of *Werther*";[9] one *must*, however, read
Danton's Death as a new and intensified *Egmont*. Indeed it may be
that what this play offers is not just a radicalization but instead a
radical inversion. In any event, Büchner's drama could well be a
sort of "counterconception" (*Gegenentwurf*), to use a term favored by Brecht.[10]

    That the young Büchner was familiar with Goethe's oeuvre has
already been established in some detail. In 1829–30, he encoun-
tered some of it in his Gymnasium curriculum;[11] and the great
man's collected works in the *Vollständige Ausgabe letzter Hand*
were "perhaps" even available in Büchner's own home.[12] Certainly the boy busied himself with these texts; and it has been
observed that the intensity of his preoccupation with Goethe
"cannot be overestimated."[13] Büchner himself, in a letter of July
28, 1835, forthrightly declared that he "greatly valued" both
Shakespeare (which is obvious and has never been overlooked)
and Goethe.[14] The author of the first—and to this day un-
equaled—drama of revolution "emphatically" aligned himself
with the tradition of his countryman: that of the "promethean
Goethe" as well as that of Goethe the "realist."[15] Despite the relative lateness of its completion—which came, so to speak, on the
eve of the French Revolution—*Egmont*, the tragedy set in the
Netherlands, belongs to both categories. The close relationship
between *Egmont* and *Danton's Death* is clear. Indeed, could not
the former carry the title *Egmont's Death*, just as the latter is often
referred to simply as *Danton*?

    Thus it is all the more odd that virtually no attention has been
paid to these connections. Here I am referring not just to the ties
between the two plays but to those linking Büchner to Goethe in
general. As far as I can tell, only a single contribution has been
devoted to this topic: an essay written in Japanese by Hideo

Nakamura and published in 1963 in Tokyo.[16] In the same year, Hans Mayer had the temerity to develop a sizable essay out of the *aperçu*: "Prince Leonce . . . comports himself . . . in a rather shameless manner, as if he were secretly parodying the ecstasies and crises of Goethe's Faust."[17] Yet, apart from a comparison of Goethe's and Büchner's scientific writings,[18] until recently there existed no truly substantial, easily available and thus—at least potentially—fruitful investigation of the relationship between the two authors. It is only of late, particularly with a chapter in a small volume published in 1980 by Hans-Jürgen Schings, that this regrettable situation has begun to be remedied.[19]

Schings, to whom we shall return later, discusses the "poetics of pity" (*Mitleidspoetik*) from Lessing to Büchner, and thus does not deal specifically with the question we have chosen to examine. Concerning it, there are, aside from an occasional fleeting remark,[20] really only two contributions to which one can refer: those provided by Wolfgang Wittkowski and Benjamin Bennett, which date from 1978 and 1979, respectively. Both function as elements of larger studies, neither is entirely satisfactory. Though Wittkowski is concerned with an altogether different set of problems, he is led to speak, if only in a footnote, of Büchner's "ties . . . to the figures, forms, images, and motifs of Goethe." Becoming somewhat more specific, he goes on to state:

> The so-called passive protagonist, his confrontation with opponents and a tribunal, his philosophical meditation in prison, the compression and expansion of space and time— we find all this also in *Götz* and *Egmont*. The latter is teeming with images which recur in *Danton*: the sky hangs so low that one almost knocks against it; Alba has fingers like a spider; our conscience is a mirror that flatters; the daily putting on and taking off, of deadly boredom. The individual is led by spirits; he kills out of envy and with pleasure, etc. The last motif also in *Götz*.[21]

This is certainly correct as far as it goes; however, it is extremely general (after all, we likewise encounter a "confrontation with opponents and a tribunal" in Schiller's *Maria Stuart*) and quite fragmentary (take, for instance, Alba's spiderlike fingers—an image which in actuality is present neither in Goethe's play nor in Büchner's, but instead results from the description of Alba as a spider, "one of the long-legged kind with small bodies" that spin "very fine threads," being blended with Robespierre's "thin fingers, twitching on the tribune").[22] Moreover, Wittkowski contents himself with mere enumeration; he offers neither an analysis nor conclusions.

Bennett, although he deals not only with *Egmont* and *Danton's Death*, devotes a number of pages to these works and thus provides the most detailed comparison presently available. His discussion oscillates between an avoidance of conclusions which recalls Wittkowski's approach and an eagerness to draw all kinds of inferences—unfortunately, rather one-sided ones—from the text. He, too, limits himself to setting up a list of similarities which connect the two plays, but he then proceeds to examine these connections in terms of his "paradox of the theater," a thesis which his entire book systematically strives to support. "Let it suffice to say," Bennett concludes, "that in *Danton*, as in *Egmont*, the hero's posturing at the end is related to the question of the nature and usefulness of theatrical performance. . . . In both plays, therefore, it appears that the question of why the hero bothers to rouse and delude himself at the end is related to the question of why we bother to go to the theater, and this question is vital to the whole modern dramatic tradition from Lessing on."[23] The almost imploring use of repetition betrays the forced nature of this comparison—and indeed, is it not, to say the least, somewhat audacious to describe Egmont's stance at the end of the play as one of "knowing self-delusion"? The most recent study of Goethe's play, Hartmut Reinhardt's essay of 1980, takes a very different view.[24] Moreover, it is quite evident that role-playing in *Danton's Death* has a much more complex and important function than that attributed to it by Bennett; for, in addition to illuminating the psyches of various figures, it possesses significant historical and historical-philosophical implications.[25]

Nevertheless, I do not mean to obscure the credit that is due Wittkowski as well as Bennett for having been the first to notice the links between the two works. Bennett in particular offers a wealth of concrete insights. For example, he observes: "The basic atmosphere of *Egmont*, especially the sense of aimlessness and futility in dialogue, is reproduced and magnified in Büchner's play. The inconclusiveness of *Danton's* conversations with friends and associates, the pointlessness of his talking directly to Robespierre, the intellectual confusion of the citizens in the street and the deputies at the National Convention, all have precedents in *Egmont*, although these are not developed so far toward the grotesque." [26] What is especially useful here is the perception, mentioned merely in passing, that Büchner's play not only echoes elements of *Egmont* but also intensifies and alters them. Bennett does not pursue this line of thought. Instead, he declares that both works are dominated by "an excessive or strained self-consciousness," and then goes on to state:

> Egmont and Danton also have much in common as characters. Both are fatalists; neither believes that any fundamental change can occur, either in the world at large or in his own personal condition. Egmont insists that "things will go their course as always" (*Eg.*, p. 223), despite the efforts of any Spanish official, and for Danton it is the self-determining history of the Revolution that mocks any individual's attempt at significant action: "We are puppets on strings held by unknown powers" (*DT*, p. 41). For both Egmont and Danton, however, this fatalism has a positive aspect; it is the basis of Egmont's belief in the eventual fulfillment of his destiny, or at least his belief in his own safety, which is paralleled by Danton's repeated insistence that he has become too integral a part of the scheme of things to be done away with (*DT*, pp. 25, 33, 39). Life is a "habit" (*Eg.*, p. 299; *DT*, p. 61) which appears unbreakable, "a feeling of permanence" (*DT*, p. 39) on the basis of which both Egmont and Danton are willing to risk playing with deadly political realities as though they were a game. [27]

With this, Bennett has provided himself with a springboard for a detailed development of the abovementioned interpretation in terms of theatrical psychology, an approach which leads him to speak of the "deep connection" between *Egmont* and *Danton's Death*. [28] At the same time, he does not hesitate to concede that "numerous other parallels in detail can be cited":

> Julie's and Klärchen's suicides, by poison, in order to accompany their executed lovers; Camille's desertion of Robespierre for Danton, as Ferdinand deserts Alba for Egmont.

The motif of Egmont's clothing, which occurs visually in the scene with Klärchen, also occurs verbally, when his fine Spanish attire moves Jetter to blurt out, "His neck would be a real temptation for the headsman" (*Eg.*, p. 212); thus Egmont, like Danton (who is doomed finally by the words, "Danton has nice clothes" *DT*, p. 64), is too well-dressed for his own good. Or we think of Egmont's metaphor of the Horses of the Sun and Danton's dream of riding on a runaway world (*DT*, p. 41), or of the significant claustrophobic images that crop up in both plays (*Eg.*, pp. 245, 281; *DT*, pp. 61, 66). And when we hear Danton say to Lacroix, "they had warned me" (*DT*, p. 49), we recall Egmont's admission to Ferdinand, "I was warned" (*Eg.*, p. 301).[29]

This is an impressive list, one longer as well as more differentiated than that offered by Wittkowski. And yet anyone familiar with the texts of both Goethe and Büchner will recognize that Bennett's inventory of similarities is by no means complete and, what is more, contains a number of items which are less than convincing, if not actually inaccurate. Aside from these lapses, however, there is no denying that Bennett and also Wittkowski are entirely correct *as far as they go*. What is surprising is the fact that there is not a greater degree of intersection between their studies. But then, what could better serve to establish the deep and extensive bond connecting the two plays than precisely this dearth of scholarly duplication?

Thus, when Bennett is forced to state that "there is no extrinsic evidence for a direct connection between *Danton* and *Egmont*" yet dares to proclaim that "there can be no doubt about the direct influences of *Egmont* on *Danton*," I can only voice my full and unqualified agreement. "In any case, the internal evidence in the two texts is conclusive."[30] Büchner's *Danton's Death* was influenced by, and is closely related to, Goethe's *Egmont*— even though we possess absolutely no documentation of this fact, except for the text of Büchner's play. Nonetheless, the connections are inarguable; indeed, they are obvious. Hence it is all the more important that their function and purpose be established.

First of all, I would like to reiterate that Büchner repeatedly and very conspicuously drew upon *Egmont* as a source of material that he then used for his own purposes. The work into which he integrated his gleanings was primarily—though not exclusively—*Danton's Death*. Second, it was not always one of his *works* which was affected by the process. Both of these theses, that of Büchner's large-scale borrowing from *Egmont* as well as the notion that its effects were not confined to his creative writings, can and must be elaborated on by means of additional, or at least thoroughly examined, examples.

Goethe's crowd scene (*Volksszene*) at the beginning of the second act (II/1: "Square in Brussels") is especially illuminating in regard to the first contention. After a "brawl" and a farcical tumult has erupted among the citizens, the play's protagonist appears and, thanks to his authority and popularity, is able to calm the excited crowd with a few words:

> (*Enter Egmont with retinue.*)
> EGMONT. Steady, steady now, all of you. What's going on? Silence! Separate them!
> CARPENTER. Your lordship, you come like an angel from heaven. Quiet, all of you! Can't you see it's Count Egmont? Pay your respects to Count Egmont![31]

In Act One of *Danton's Death* (I/2: "A street") we encounter a remarkably similar crowd scene. It develops out of the quarrel between the drunken prompter Simon and his "virtuous spouse," and culminates, with a comic anticlimax, in the noisy tumult around the Young Man who, because he possesses "a handkerchief," is to be hung from a lamp post. In this instance it is not the character after whom the play is named but rather his opponent Robespierre who unexpectedly enters the scene and in short order manages to quiet the mob:

> (*Robespierre enters, accompanied by women and sans-culottes.*)
> ROBESPIERRE. What's the matter, citizen? . . . In the name of the law!
> A WOMAN. Listen to the Messiah, who has been sent to choose and to judge. . . . His eyes are the eyes of choice, his hands are the hands of judgment.[32]

The structure and function of these two sudden entrances, the relationship between the crowd and a charismatic leader who is spoken of in terms of divine authority: all this reflects an amazing degree of similarity, even when one takes into account the replacement of the protagonist by the antagonist. There is, however, one tiny difference which, particularly since it is accompanied by so many precise correspondences, might give the reader pause. While Egmont *appears* to come to the people *like* "an angel from Heaven," Robespierre *is* without any reservation *the* "Messiah."

This by no means exhausts the fund of similarities. In Goethe's play, after "the great crowd" has dispersed, there occurs an exchange between a carpenter and the citizens Jetter and Soest. The subject of their conversation is—how could it be otherwise—the much-admired Egmont:

> JETTER. Did you notice his dress? It was in the latest fashion, the Spanish cut.
> CARPENTER. A handsome gentleman.
> JETTER. His neck would be a real feast to the executioner.
> SOEST. Are you mad? What's got into your head?
> JETTER. Yes, it's silly enough, the things that get into one's head. It's just what I happen to feel. When I see a fine, long neck, I can't help thinking at once: that's a good one for the axe. . . . All these cursed executions! One can't get them out of one's mind.[33]

This passage with Jetter's strange but prescient—and, in any case, hardly everyday—notion finds in Büchner's play a twofold, indeed, if one includes Bennett's reference to Danton's "nice clothes," a threefold echo. In the nocturnal scene (I/6) in which St. Just provides Robespierre with a list of the Dantonists who must be eliminated, the first individual he mentions is Hérault-Séchelles. Robespierre's response is as laconic as that of Goethe's carpenter: "A handsome head." And St. Just replies: "He was the nicely painted capital letter of the Constitutional Acts. We have no further need of such ornaments. He will be erased."[34] However, the most striking correspondence, one which in terms of structure is astoundingly exact, is found neither in this scene nor in the clothing motif emphasized by Bennett, but rather in yet another crowd scene or, more precisely, an exchange which follows a popular spectacle, namely, the execution of Danton and his friends. The play's penultimate scene (IV/8: "A Street") contains, along with the lamentations of the now-crazed Lucile, the following conversation among a troop of women returning home from the Square of the Revolution:

> FIRST WOMAN. A good-looking man, that Hérault.
> SECOND WOMAN. When he stood at the Arch of Triumph during the Constitutional Celebration, I thought, "he'll look good next to the guillotine, he will." That was sort of a hunch.
> THIRD WOMAN. Yes, you've got to see people in all kinds of situations. It's good that dying's being made public now.[35]

Any commentary would seem to be superfluous. Here, more than anywhere else, it appears that we are dealing, *mutatis mutandis*, with a case of direct appropriation.

Or are appearances deceiving? Is it, once again, precisely a divergence, however slight, in the midst of widespread agreement that needs to be noted and underscored? The divergence in question is not so much the fact that Goethe's scene occurs *before* the event that is discussed while Büchner's takes place *afterwards*; this difference is purely external and of relatively little importance. Instead, what has to be considered is the fundamentally different attitudes exhibited by the two groups of people toward public executions. In *Egmont* the citizens curse the killing and would like to avoid the very thought of it; in *Danton's Death* the women enjoy the guillotining and explicitly say that it is good. The Büchnerian populace does not perceive the falling of the blade as an oppressive threat, something to be feared and, as much as possible, forgotten. On the contrary, the executions are welcomed and boisterously celebrated as a kind of popular festival. "*Men and women sing and dance to the carmagnole*"—thus the stage direction for the previous scene (IV/7: "The Square of the Revolution"); indeed, the guillotine even serves as cynical compensation for the poverty and misery of the masses. "Make room! Make room!" shouts one of the women, "The children are crying, they're hungry. I have to let them look, so they'll be quiet. Make room!"[36] Danton is also familiar with this bleak situation. Addressing the suffering multitudes in the final speech he gives in his own defense (III/9: "The Revolutionary Tribunal"), he declares in regard to the Jacobin Terror: "You want bread and they throw you heads. You are thirsty and they make you lick the blood from the steps of the guillotine."[37]

Could one imagine such language and imagery in Goethe's play? And yet, as Wittkowski has correctly pointed out, *Egmont* positively swarms with images and formulations that recur in *Danton's Death*. Very few, however, are taken over by Büchner entirely unchanged. Most notably, this applies to the unusual phrase "evil genius," which Alba utters when Silva brings him the portentous news of Oranien's refusal to come to Brussels. Mercier uses the same words to describe the character and actions of Danton:

> ALBA. My evil genius speaks in you.[38]
>
> MERCIER. . . . He's the evil genius of the Revolution.[39]

A second correspondence, one that is almost equally exact, involves the lines in which Egmont poses—and answers—the calming question, "Who would dare to lay hands on us? . . . No, they do not dare to raise the banner of tyranny so high." These two sentences are spoken during the meeting with Oranien in the second act, and it is no accident that Egmont caps them off with the disarming admission "I don't believe it."[40] They are echoed by Danton no fewer than three times—first in a conversation with his friends (II/1: "A Room") and then in a monologue (II/4: "Open field"): ". . . they won't dare. (*To Camille.*) Come, my boy, I tell you, they won't dare. . . . It's all a lot of empty noise. They want to scare me. They won't dare."[41] It is important to note that the naive confidence expressed by Egmont is in no way affirmed by Büchner, but rather subjected to a radical negation. In the first of the two scenes in question, Danton's departure is followed by an illuminating and thoroughly unambiguous exchange:

> PHILIPPEAU. There he goes.
>
> LACROIX. And he doesn't believe a word he's said.[42]

Bennett's phrase, "knowing self-delusion," is indeed an apt description of the confidence evidenced by Danton; Egmont's attitude, on the other hand, is very clearly the exact opposite of this.

There are other striking correspondences which result less from the repetition of specific words than from the achievement of a remarkable duplication of meaning. Placed in a tense situation, Alba and Robespierre react with the same rhetorical (and rhythmic) gesture, impatiently responding:

> ALBA. Quickly, therefore . . .
> ROBESPIERRE. Then quickly. . . !

In both instances, this reply is preceded by a situation report: in *Egmont*, it is Silva's account of the "conduct" of the Flemish nobility; in *Danton's Death*, St. Just's description of the Dantonists' activities.[43] And then there is again the Spanish duke, Alba, who regards the citizens as nothing more than unruly subjects and declares that it is necessary to "hedge them in, to treat them like children, so that one can lead them to their own welfare like children." For, as he assures Egmont, "a people does not grow up, or grow wise; a people remains perpetually childish."[44] Essentially the same low opinion of the citizenry, or masses, is held by Danton, although he expresses it in a somewhat less arrogant manner. "The people are like children," he states, "they have to break everything open to see what's inside."[45]

If Alba and Robespierre and even Alba and Danton have their moments of congruence, this is also true of Danton and Egmont. The latter utters the lapidary statement: "I am tired of hangings." The former declares no less tersely: "I'm sick of it." Even if there were some way to save himself, Danton admits to his friends, he would "rather be guillotined than guillotine others." Once again, however, the similarities are accompanied by a significant divergence: While Egmont is responding directly to his secretary's query whether six belatedly arrested church-wreckers should be "hanged like the others," Danton is absorbed in general philosophical speculations and self-sufficient musings. But almost as if to balance this discrepancy, his words contain a Goethe quote, though one which is taken from an entirely unexpected source:

> Why should we human beings fight each other? We should sit down with each other in peace. A mistake was made when we were created—something is missing. I have no

name for it. We won't rip it out of each other's intestines, so why should we break open each other's bodies? Oh, we are miserable alchemists.[46]

"I have no name / For it" (*Ich habe keinen Namen / Dafür*): this is precisely what Faust says to Gretchen when she catechizes him regarding his religious faith. He is trying to convey his sense of the all-encompassing pantheistic totality whose omnipresence he so acutely perceives, yet he remains convinced that any attempt to name it would be nothing more than "noise and smoke."[47] And Danton? He very clearly transforms Faust's "feeling" into its direct antipode, a piercing awareness of something which is *not* present, something which is completely—and most painfully— absent. As before, we are confronted with a vivid example of the procedure so characteristic of Büchner's approach: his tendency to borrow and, at the same time, radically to modify. Indeed, in view of our basic thesis, are we not justified in speaking of an almost Brechtian process of redefinition (*Umfunktionierung*)?

Thus it seems as if the author of *Danton's Death* drew not only upon *Egmont* but from other works by Goethe as sources of raw material for his own literary endeavors. This cautious formulation is necessary, for the objection could of course be raised that the passages from *Faust* were, in Büchner's day, so well known as to be part of the "public domain." What is more, I lay no claim to providing an exhaustive list of such (potential) borrowings. The same cautiousness and the same disclaimer must therefore accompany the following observations. They concern, as mentioned previously, lines from *Egmont* which perhaps indicate that the influence of Goethe's tragedy on Büchner extends not only beyond *Danton's Death*, but even beyond the young writer's poetic works. In any event, the monologue delivered by Goethe's Regent, Margaret of Parma, in the second scene of the first act culminates in an image the recurrence of which in Büchner's most famous letter is, after all we have seen thus far, very difficult to dismiss as being purely coincidental. On the contrary, one could say that it takes us to the very heart of the ideas and imagery shared by these two writers. Having established how distressed the Regent is by the "terrible happenings" in her realm, Goethe has her cry: "Oh, what are the great, we the crests on the surge of humanity? We think that we rule its fury, but it bears us up and down, to and fro."[48] Büchner, in that much-discussed "fatalism letter" he wrote to his fiancée, develops both the image and the thought contained in this passage. He confirms, so to speak, the Regent's insight: "The individual [is] merely foam on the waves, greatness sheer chance, the mastery of genius a puppet play, a ludicrous struggle against an iron law: to recognize it is our utmost achievement, to control it is impossible."[49] Does it not seem as if Büchner were responding to her lament? There is no denying that his vivid image as well as the awful realization it conveys are present in embryonic form in the lines penned by Goethe. However, the change that has been implemented is not an inversion, let alone a redefinition, but rather an intensification. Danton's statement to Camille can be applied to the playwright himself: "You are a strong echo."[50] Strong and also multifarious, for the reference to a "puppet play" is clearly reminiscent of the passage from *Werther* quoted in the beginning—and, once more, it is hard to believe that the correspondence should be purely accidental.

But it is not enough simply to locate a neat series of parallels, an approach which even Bennett fails to transcend. We have established that Egmont is echoed not only by Danton, Alba not only by Robespierre; also, the connections between the two texts are not only manifold but manifoldly entangled in a manner which vitiates all attempts at schematic definition. And what is true of the male characters is equally true of the women: specifically, of Klärchen in *Egmont* and of Julie and Lucile in *Danton's Death* (though, it should be added, not of the Regent or of Büchner's Marion).[51] Bennett is quite correct when he points out that Julie, like Klärchen, intentionally poisons herself so that she can die along with her beloved; indeed, these two women exhibit a similarity to one another that extends to specific details.[52] Yet Lucile, too, has been endowed with a number of features which tie her to Klärchen. Goethe himself helps us to become aware of this connection when, in his *Italienische Reise* (*The Italian Journey*), he notes regarding his "heroine" that he located "her love" above all else "in the concept of the beloved's perfection" and "her ecstasy . . . in the pleasure of the incomprehensible fact that *this* man belongs to her."[53] For isn't this a startlingly precise description of Lucile's attitude of loving self-abnegation toward Camille? Let us recall, for example, the scene called "A Room" (II/3) and the words spoken by this couple:

> CAMILLE. What do you think, Lucile?
> LUCILE. Nothing, I like to watch you talk.
> CAMILLE. Do you listen to what I say, too?
> LUCILE. Yes, of course.
> CAMILLE. Was I right? Did you understand what I said?
> LUCILE. No—not at all.[54]

Even the motif of madness, which tends to be associated solely with Büchner's Lucile, is already present in Goethe's play. In the first scene of the fifth act ("Street at Dusk"), Klärchen asks her suitor Brackenburg: "Do you take me for a child, or a madwoman?"[55] The key word (i.e., the adjective *wahnsinnig*, "crazy," in the original) is also uttered by Lucile—long before she is actually seized by madness—and once again we encounter a Büchnerian inversion of the sort we have almost come to expect. Significantly enough, Lucile's question is phrased as follows: "Camille! That's nonsense, right? Am I crazy [*wahnsinnig*] to think of it?"[56] But this is not all. Even the reference to being childlike, a reproach Klärchen attributes to Brackenburg and vehemently rejects along with the notion that she is mad, recurs in *Danton's Death* both in a comparable manner and in a comparable context: "What a beautiful child she has borne of insanity. Why must I leave now? We would have laughed with it, cradled it, kissed it."[57] Here we have Camille speaking of Lucile near the end of the play (IV/5: "The Conciergerie"). As is the case in Klärchen's speech, the motifs of madness and childlikeness are woven together—and yet, they are also subjected to a radical revaluation.

Büchner is constantly borrowing. But only rarely does he do so without placing his stamp on the material by means of a—sometimes tiny, sometimes major, and almost always significant—addition and/or modification. Parallels in the strict sense of the word are very infrequent although, of course, there do remain sufficient similarities extending even into the macrostructures of the two plays. Once more, this can be seen most clearly in the male figures, especially in the two title characters and their friends, supporters, and opponents. There can be no doubt that Danton and Camille (along with the rest of the Dantonists) correspond to Egmont and Oranien,[58] just as Robespierre and St. Just (as well as the Jacobins and their other followers) correspond to the Spanish Duke and his various helpers and hangmen. The similarities of these character constellations are echoed in the structure and function of entire scenes. For example, it must be obvious that the nocturnal meeting between Danton and Robespierre (I/6: "A Room") corresponds precisely to the encounter between Egmont and Alba (IV/2: "Culenburg Palace. The Duke of Alba's Residence"), just as it ultimately generates very similar consequences.

One could adduce many such correspondences, but most of them have already been mentioned, in however brief and sketchy a manner, by Wittkowski and Bennett. I should like to add, however, that Büchner apparently drew on Goethe even in purely practical matters of dramaturgical technique. We need only recall the two crowd scenes with Egmont and Robespierre, for it is in these scenes that Goethe's protagonist and Büchner's antagonist put in their *first* appearances. Could a playwright possibly come up with a better—or, as Goethe would put it, a more "stage-worthy"[59]—solution to the problem? Both are, so to speak, entrances with a drum roll. There simply is no more theatrically effective way of introducing Egmont and Robespierre, no device that would better suit the possibilities of the stage and have such a strong impact on the audience.

I will halt here, and merely supplement my condensed and necessarily incomplete overview with a discussion of three specific correspondences which seem to me particularly revealing. They are: the "claustrophobic images" mentioned by Bennett (and, to a lesser extent, by Wittkowski); the connection, touched on only by Bennett, between the "horses of the sun" and Danton's supposed "riding" on a globe which is plunging ahead like a frightened horse (it is important to note that "riding" does not accurately describe Danton's situation); and, finally, the image of sleepwalking which, though mentioned neither by Wittkowski nor Bennett, is by no means unknown to Goethe specialists. As Brecht once remarked: There is much that is useful, but comparison is the most useful thing of all.

The phenomenon of claustrophobia is repeatedly referred to,

or even presented on stage, not only in Büchner's drama but also in Goethe's tragedy. In the fourth act of *Egmont* (IV/1: "A Street") the tailor Jetter whispers to the carpenter that since the entry of the Spanish occupation force he feels "as though the sky were covered with black crepe and hung down so low that one has to bend down to avoid knocking one's head against it"; Egmont himself in a monologue in Act Five (V/2: "Prison") not only describes his cell as "prefiguring the grave," but even admits in retrospect that when he was "between the gloomy walls of a great hall . . . the beams of the ceiling" always seemed to "throttle" him.[60] Danton, who is also a prisoner (III/7: "The Conciergerie"), declares that all mankind is "buried alive" and scratches "for fifty years . . . on the lid of the coffin"; not long afterwards, still in the Conciergerie (IV/3), he soliloquizes: "Why doesn't the clock stop? With every tick it moves the walls closer around me until they're as tight as a coffin. I once read a story like that as a child; my hair stood on end."[61] However, the most vivid and overwhelming evocation of such experiences occurs a bit later in the same scene when Camille describes his nightmare. Apart from a lyrical ritardando it most jarringly interrupts, this description follows directly the monologue by Danton the opening lines of which I just quoted:

> CAMILLE. Oh! (*He has gotten up and is reaching toward the ceiling.*)
> DANTON. What's the matter, Camille?
> CAMILLE. Oh, oh!
> DANTON. (*Shakes him.*) Do you want to tear down the ceiling?
> CAMILLE. Oh, you, you . . . oh, hold me—say something, Danton!
> DANTON. You're trembling all over, there's sweat on your brow.
> CAMILLE. That's you—this is me—there! This is my hand! Yes, now I remember. Oh, Danton, that was terrifying.
> DANTON. What was?
> CAMILLE. I was half dreaming, half awake. The ceiling disappeared and the moon sank down very near, very close, my hand seized it. The sky with its lights had

come down, I beat against it, I touched the stars, I
reeled like a man drowning under a layer of ice. That
was terrifying, Danton.[62]

It is obvious what these four passages have in common; yet the
differences that emerge are no less evident. Goethe's images—
we must remember that he is speaking figuratively even when
this does not appear to be the case—are bounded in terms of
time and space insofar as they refer to specific political oppression or to an individual's psychological constraint. In contrast,
Büchner's images or, rather, experiences—for this is what they
are for the most part—reveal themselves as limitless, as it were,
since they implicitly lay claim to being universally valid for all
mankind. In Goethe's play we have a specific "as if," or figurative, diction, while the passage from Büchner evokes a basic existential feeling as well as moments of terror which are either real
(like the nightmare) or experienced as real (as when children
read frightening stories).

How do things stand in our second example, that of the horses
of the sun and Danton's supposed ride? Here, too, one need only
juxtapose the two texts. Goethe's powerful evocation of the Greek
myth (II/2: "Egmont's House") is one of the most famous and
significant of all his images; these splendid lines were so dear to
him that, decades later, he used them to top off and crown his
autobiography, *Dichtung und Wahrheit* (*Poetry and Truth*).[63] In the
play, Egmont responds almost blithely to the timid objection of
his secretary who claims that "it makes the pedestrian dizzy to
watch a traveller rush past him with such speed":

> EGMONT. . . . As though whipped by invisible spirits, the
> horses of the sun, Time's horses, run away with the
> light chariot of our destinies; and we have no choice
> but to grip the reins with resolute courage and, now
> to the right, now to the left, avert the wheels from a
> stone here, a precipice there. As for the end of the
> journey, who knows what it is? When we hardly re-
> member where it began.[64]

The corresponding passage in Büchner's play contains no trace
of blitheness. Like Camille, Danton groans under the weight of a
terrifying nightmare or vision. His wife Julie seeks to quiet him:

JULIE. You were dreaming, Danton. Get hold of yourself.
DANTON. Dreaming? Yes, I was dreaming—but it was different—I'll tell you right away, my poor head is weak—
right away! There—now I've got it! Beneath me the
globe was panting in its flight, I had seized it like a wild
horse, with immense limbs I rooted in its mane and
pressed its ribs, with my head bent down, my hair
streaming out over the abyss. I was being dragged
along. I screamed in fear and awoke.[65]

Once again, comparison of the passages reveals similarities
along with significant differences. Büchner's text, rather than
being a simple expansion of the Goethean model, offers a thoroughgoing modification—indeed to the point of direct inversion.
In spite of everything, Egmont grips the reins "with resolute
courage" and is able to steer his "chariot" away from danger;
Danton, however, screaming in "fear," is "dragged along" helplessly by his cosmic "horse." There is absolutely no indication
that he is in control; at the most, he clings to the "mane" and
"ribs" out of sheer desperation, in order to avoid being thrown
into the "abyss." If Goethe's image expresses a sense of fate and
the individual's inner demon so intensely as to be reminiscent of
the ancient Greeks, Büchner's counterimage is marked by an almost demonic grotesqueness of the most modern variety.[66] It is
not by chance that at the end of the scene Danton, crying out
in utter despair, surpasses Egmont's "*As though* whipped by in-
visible spirits": "We are nothing but puppets, our strings are
pulled by unknown forces, we ourselves are nothing, nothing!
Swords that spirits fight with—you just don't see any hands, as
in a fairy tale."[67] In short, Goethe's lines evince "trust in fate"
(Reinhardt)[68] while Büchner's contain a sense of being totally at
the mercy of unchained powers. Here again, the latter speaks
quite concretely while the former speaks only in a figurative
sense.

All these findings are fully confirmed by the motif of sleepwalking and the images associated with it. In *Egmont*, it appears
in the same scene as the mythological allusion we have just discussed, the scene in which the protagonist and his secretary react to Count Oliva's letter of warning; in *Danton's Death*, sleepwalking is an element of the highly revealing monologue which
Robespierre delivers in Act One, after his embarrassing encoun-

ter with Danton and before the arrival of St. Just. One last time, let us compare:

> EGMONT. And yet he [Count Oliva] always touches this same string. He has long known how I hate these incessant admonitions. They serve only to unnerve me, never to help. And if I were a sleepwalker, balanced on the knife-edge of a roof top, would it be a friendly act to call out my name to warn me, wake me, and kill me? Let every man go his own way. . . .[69]

> ROBESPIERRE. (*Alone.*) . . . Night snores over the earth and wallows in wild dreams. Thoughts, hardly perceived wishes, confused and formless, having crept shyly from daylight, now take shape and steal into the silent house of dreams. They open doors, they look out of windows, they become almost flesh, their limbs stretch out in sleep, their lips murmur. . . . And isn't our waking a more lucid dream? Aren't we sleepwalkers? Aren't our actions dreamlike, only clearer, more certain, more complete? Who can reproach us for that?[70]

While Egmont and Robespierre make use of the same basic idea, their speeches are anything but identical; once again, we find an important divergence occurring amidst a basic correspondence. With respect to Goethe's protagonist, this divergence has been accurately summed up as follows: "The image of sleepwalking . . . testifies . . . to a happy confidence in life and fate *without* the fatalistic valence that it receives, for example, in Büchner's work."[71] Egmont, unswervingly true to his innermost being, believes himself to be safe in what is commonly referred to as "the certainty of a sleepwalker." Robespierre, in contrast, is deeply uncertain, seeking to comfort himself by dwelling on the sleepwalkers' unwitting compulsion—and with it, their total freedom from responsibility. Indeed, he applies this excuse not only to himself but to all human activity. There is no happy trust in fate carrying him through life; instead, he feels himself—even as the "Messiah of Blood"[72]—in the grip of a dark determinism. Might it not be argued that what we have in Goethe's tragedy is merely a hypothesis, which is then transformed in Büchner's drama into a plain rhetorical question (leaving aside the specific context and similar instances of expansion, intensification, and inversion)? But my question, too, is of course rhetorical. Just as the connections between *Egmont* and *Danton's Death* are becoming increasingly clear, so, too, are the differences which separate the two plays emerging with growing clarity.

Which is a rather abstract conclusion, granted. Should it be all our investigation is able to yield? Or might there be more? To recall and restate the thesis broached at the outset: Are we really justified in regarding *Danton's Death* as a counterconception to Goethe's *Egmont*?

Without a doubt, Büchner was thoroughly familiar with Goethe's work. Not only was he impressed and influenced by it, but his drama also contains numerous passages which refer in a variety of ways to his predecessor's play. Much of the material he appropriated and shaped for his own purposes has been intensified or inverted, indeed appears to have been subjected to a Brechtian type of redefinition, although there are a few instances in which one has the impression that Büchner simply used Goethe's text(s) as a source of useful raw material. In any event, is it conceivable that the creator of so dense and complicated a network of connections was entirely unaware of what he had done? I think not. Of course, the author of *Danton's Death* was still far removed from Brecht's irreverent concept of "material value" (*Materialwert*), according to which established masterpieces can be cheerfully demolished and vandalized for whatever they contain that might be useful;[73] clearly, we cannot judge with certainty whether he approached Goethe's tragedy with the same degree of conscious intent manifested by the Marxist playwright in countless instances. One may suspect that he did, but such things can be neither proven nor disproven. (In view of what we do know about Büchner, it is by no means inconceivable.) Be that as it may, *Danton's Death* both echoes and contradicts *Egmont*. The way these two works are so closely bound together, while at the same time being different in so many respects, even diametrically opposed to each other, not only allows us but almost forces us to apply Brecht's concept to Büchner's drama. If the essence of this concept is that the writer, "after reading" a given work, appropriates "several elements and characters," but "on the whole" effects a fundamental change, then—as long as we are willing to accept a certain terminological largesse or, to use a more Brechtian term, "laxness"—we can indeed speak of *Danton's Death* as "a kind of counterconception" to Goethe's *Egmont*.[74]

It may well be that there is yet another, wider sense in which Brecht's term can be applied to Büchner's play. The Goethean tragedy, dating from 1788, was completed before the outbreak of the French Revolution and stands as the final and, perhaps, purest drama of liberty and the *old* law. Büchner's work, which dates from 1835, was written decades after the collapse of the French Revolution, on the eve, as it were, of *The Communist Manifesto*; it is the first and greatest modern drama of revolution and the *new* law. In *Egmont*, as in England's Glorious Revolution and, to a great extent, in the North American War of Independence, the primary emphasis is on the reestablishment of a traditional rule of law which has been suspended by despotism. In *Danton's Death*, on the other hand, as in the French Revolution and, later, in the Russian October Revolution, indeed in all revolutions that are truly modern, the emphasis is on a totally "new beginning" which involves a complete break with the past, including the law previously in force.[75] "The Revolution is like the daughters of Pelias," declares St. Just in his speech to the National Convention at the end of Act Two (II/7); "it cuts humanity in pieces to rejuvenate it." And, intoxicated by his own icy—though, at the same time, dubious—logic, he continues in a distinctly visionary vein:

> Humanity will rise up with mighty limbs out of this cauldron of blood, like the earth out of the waters of the Flood, as if it had been newly created. (*Long, sustained applause. Several Deputies rise with enthusiasm.*) We summon all the secret enemies of tyranny, who in Europe and in the entire world carry the dagger of Brutus beneath their cloaks to share with us this sublime hour! (*The spectators and the Deputies begin the Marseillaise.*)[76]

This is an extraordinarily impressive conclusion to a scene and an act. Egmont, facing the execution which he views as his sacrifice "for freedom," delivers lines that are quite similar to St. Just's in their sublime enthusiasm and absolute confidence in the future. Yet the basic thrust of his statement is fundamentally different from that of the French revolutionary. "Brave people!"— these are the words of Goethe's hero in his visionary soliloquy: "The goddess of Victory leads you. And as the sea bursts through the dikes you build, so you shall burst and tumble down the mound of tyranny and, flooding all, wash it away from the dear site it has usurped." Egmont is a hero of the people who dies for the old law, rather than killing—or even murdering—for a new one. "Swords are flashing," he exclaims—

> Courage, friends, more courage! Behind you parents, wives, and children wait! (*Pointing at the guards.*) And these, the ruler's hollow words impel, not their true feelings. Protect your property! And to preserve your dearest ones, willingly, gladly fall as my example shows you. (*Drumbeats. As he walks towards the guards, towards the back exit, the curtain falls; the music strikes up and concludes in a victory symphony.*)[77]

In spite of their various points of similarity, the ideological contrast between these two texts and the scenes from which they are taken could hardly be more pronounced.

Their divergence derives not only from the fact that Egmont speaks of hearth and home, of possessions and family, while St. Just refers to "humanity" and "the entire world." Nor does it stem from the fact that the Flemish patriot calls for resistance and the defense of historically established—and historically specific—"property" against the violent encroachments of an arbitrary and illegitimate authority, while the French revolutionary advocates a great offensive in order to achieve, by means of violence, the realization of the "Rights of Man" and thus of a general concept unlimited to a specific time or place. The difference cuts deeper than all this. Büchner, always the unflinching realist, even goes so far as to undermine, as it were, the very idea of revolution to which he gives poetic substance in his play, and which his St. Just proclaims with such rousing pathos. For what exactly is the revealing breach of logic that slips into the revolutionary's cascading rhetoric? To answer this question we need only remember that the bloody attempt at rejuvenating Pelias was a terrible failure: After being dismembered by his daughters, he did not come back to life; all that remained was the blood bath, the hecatomb of mangled flesh. The words of Büchner's revolutionary reveal themselves as being no less "hollow" than those of Goethe's "ruler," whose "tyranny" St. Just would smash to pieces and, like an angry flood, wash away from the site it has dared to usurp. (I say flood, and not "the Flood," for the longer one considers St. Just's use of that term, the more dubious it becomes.) Conversely, in Goethe's play there is not the slightest hint of any attempt at relativizing either the established concept of law or its advocate, Egmont.

Nor can it be denied that the last scene of *Danton's Death*, while properly corresponding to the finale of Egmont, is yet completely different. Here we have what may well be the most vivid and moving manifestation of Büchner's tendency to both radicalize and radically invert what he found in Goethe. However famous this ending may be, let me point out that it contains, among other things, a final, tersely evoked collision between the old law and the new, between tradition and revolution:

> LUCILE. Long live the King!
> CITIZEN. In the name of the Republic! (*She is surrounded by the watch and led off.*)[78]

Despite the important differences that separate this scene from its counterpart in Goethe's tragedy, the two remain connected by a series of shared motifs. At the end of *Egmont*, a group of guards appear before the hero. He advances to meet them, self-possessed and filled with lofty joy; indeed his departure is accompanied by the triumphant strains of a "victory symphony"! Lucile, on the other hand, once the final words have been spoken, is silently surrounded and led off by the watch. True, her final appearance is also associated with a musical motif; but by the time of her arrest it has already faded away—although its echoes may linger on. Moreover, this motif could scarcely be more different from that of Egmont. Against the caterwauling of the executioners who, in the background, "close up shop" and depart, Lucile, crouching on the steps of the guillotine, sings a pair of verses from an old folk song:

I know a reaper, Death's his name,
His might is from the Lord God's flame.

   . . .

A hundred thousand, big and small,
His sickle always makes them fall.[79]

More than in any other scene, death casts its shadow over
Büchner's finale; in comparison, Goethe's finale is flooded by the
radiant light of life. Egmont, though he is "surrounded on all
sides by the threat of death," is able "to feel brave life" flowing
through him "with redoubled speed"—thus the wording chosen
by the playwright who clearly sought to underscore the anti-
thetical nature of both the line and the situation.[80] Goethe's work
is open in a way that implies hope for the future and, as a result,
ends on an almost buoyant note; Büchner's play is, in this sense,
utterly closed. Also, it is important to remember that *Egmont*
ends before the successful revolt even begins, while *Danton's
Death* begins at a point when the self-destruction of the revolution is in full swing and its end is clearly in sight. These op-
positions are profound; pat phrases such as "perspective" or
"optimism" and "pessimism"—I am aware that I am simplify-
ing—can hardly be avoided. In any case, Goethe's luminous conclusion is all the more dazzling when viewed against the gather-
ing darkness that marks the end of Büchner's play. Does not even
the oft-cited "*salto mortale* into an opera-world" that Schiller felt
compelled to criticize[81] form an integral part of this radiance and
overflowing luminosity, this fanfare-like, indeed (and not merely
in a figurative sense) Beethoven-like quality that fills Goethe's
play? Viewed in this way, Schiller's concept reveals itself to be a
grievous misconception. In *Egmont*, Goethe presents quite the
opposite of a death leap. Thus my playful suggestion at the outset that one could rechristen this work *Egmont's Death* turns out
to be not such a good idea after all, whereas the appropriateness
of Büchner's title becomes all the more apparent. For all the ambiguities and complexities in *Danton's Death* as a whole—and in
its closing scene in particular—in this regard the play is entirely
unequivocal.[82]

    That Lucile and Julie follow their men in death seals the fact
that love and revolution are inseparably intertwined in Büchner's

drama,[83] just as love and liberty are woven together in Goethe's tragedy. But in Büchner, death and defeat are also one and the same; it is only Egmont's death that, in a wondrous manner reminiscent of an opera or an oratorio, is "swallowed up in victory." How else can one put it? Would it not be possible for Goethe's protagonist virtually to echo the Apostle: "O death, where is thy sting? O grave, where is thy victory?"[84] Egmont, who openly declares that he "offer[s] up himself,"[85] is a martyr for liberty who overcomes and triumphs; he is able to deliver himself to the tyrant's hirelings with such courage and serenity because he is certain of his own transfiguration. The notion of victory in (and through) death so basic to the Baroque martyr drama possesses central importance in Goethe's play—along with several other components of that subgenre. For example, there is the obviously intentional juxtaposition of "fate" and "good fortune,"[86] terms which inevitably recall the Baroque concepts of *fatum* and *fortuna*. The correctness of this association is indicated by Klärchen's remarks concerning the "unreliability" of the "world" and its "inconstancy,"[87] as well as by a letter written by the playwright to Madame von Stein in which he implicitly defines both the incalculability of fate and the transitoriness of good fortune as the objects of drama. His work on *Egmont* was not the least of the factors that led him to observe "how the mighty *play* with men and the gods *play* with the mighty."[88] His tragedy of 1788 has roots which extend all the way to the source of the German *Trauerspiel*, that is, Andreas Gryphius and his plays.[89] Likewise, if from *Egmont* one can look back to the seventeenth century, then from *Danton's Death* one can look ahead to the twentieth century, indeed right up to the present day. While Goethe's work recalls the Baroque period and the Christian martyr drama, Büchner's is a thoroughly modern and thoroughly secularized "remembrance of a revolution"—to quote once more the programmatic subtitle of that closely related work, *Der Auftrag* by Heiner Müller. I know of no other play that draws so explicitly and thought-provokingly on *Danton's Death* and Büchner's presentation of events of the French Revolution as does this fascinating, though, admittedly, problematical and enigmatic text of 1979.[90]

It is hard to resist developing these literary-historical connections a little further. One could (and, if only in passing, must) point out that midway between *Egmont* and *Danton's Death* there stands, surprisingly yet logically enough, Schiller's play of 1804, *Wilhelm Tell*, a work that is simultaneously a drama of the old law and a drama of revolution—and even manages, in a unique manner, to unite these contradictory views.[91] But earlier I mentioned an additional aspect of Büchner which, in a twofold sense, can be seen in terms of Brecht's concept of a counterproposal. In order to illustrate it I must deal briefly with something already alluded to very generally with the word "pessimism," but which is more precisely denoted by terms such as "nihilism" and "atheism." That the latter concepts have nothing to do with the death and life of Egmont is obvious, and it is equally obvious that they are of central importance to the life and death of Danton and his friends. While I do not wish to exaggerate the Christian element in Goethe's tragedy, nor the deistic element in his oeuvre at large, it must be repeated that even Werther, who in his despair perceives the world as an "eternally devouring, eternally regurgitating monster," ultimately comes to entrust himself with total confidence to the "Father," the "all-loving Father" referred to in Goethe's poem "Ganymede."[92] This returning to the fold, this recovery of a faith once lost is not even remotely possible in Büchner's works: neither in his narrative *Lenz*, in which Werther is both echoed and radicalized, nor in *Danton's Death*, that intensified, radicalized (one might even say perverted) version of *Egmont*.

The cue to Büchner's second counterproposal is again provided by Goethe's heroic martyr. Facing imminent and ignominious death, he is able to declare with radiant serenity: "Unobstructed flows the circle of inner harmonies."[93] What is true of the inner harmonies is also true of the outer: microcosm and macrocosm form a harmonious unity, pure and complete, capable of flooding the individual with the highest joy. In regard to this "a priori of a doctrine of metaphysical harmony and sympathy," the young Goethe's "concept of art" (*Kunstlehre*) has been compared with what Büchner's Lenz experiences and, in the much-discussed "conversation on art" (*Kunstgespräch*), articulates. The conclusion arrived at could not be any more clear-cut: "Lenz *literally embodies* the crisis and collapse of that view of the world."[94] We need only add that by the same token he—and with him the entire company, as it were, of Büchner's characters—embodies the experience of atheism and nihilism.

Not infrequently, characters in Büchner's work openly express these concepts. "Lenz laughed loudly," we are told, "and with that laugh *atheism* [my emphasis] took hold of him surely and calmly and firmly."[95] And what is the only word Büchner chose to emphasize in his story? What is the only sentence or half sentence underscored in his drama of revolution? Near the end of *Lenz*, one finds the blunt and evocative statement: "He had *nothing*" (the fact that a name is also italicized is of little import).[96] In a central passage from *Danton's Death* contained in Act Three, Payne announces: "*There is no God*";[97] he then goes on to develop this thought, spinning—like St. Just—a series of merciless, annihilating "phrases."[98] Furthermore, what Payne elaborates with his icy and flawless logic is, in the fifth scene of the final act, translated into grandiose imagery, as powerful as it is moving. The way this sudden eruption of ever more striking images draws on Egmont's statement about the flowing harmonies and on Goethe's concept of a harmonious cosmos makes it yet another outstanding example of Büchner's technique of inversion. How does the pious Philippeau seek to comfort his comrades in misery, these desperate men whose reactions to approaching death run the gamut from lamentation to blasphemy, from the grossest obscenity to the most melancholy of witticisms? How does he try to persuade them of the existence of God and of the sanctity of existence? Precisely by telling them of a "divine . . . ear for which cacophony and deafening outcries are a *stream of harmonies*"![99] "But we are the poor musicians and our bodies the instruments," Danton retorts sarcastically, utilizing Philippeau's—and also Egmont's—image. The inversion that he accomplishes clearly transforms these figurative instruments into instruments of torture:

> DANTON. . . . Are those horrible sounds they scratch out only there to rise up higher and higher and finally die away as a sensual breath in heavenly ears?
>
> HERAULT. Are we like young pigs who are beaten to death with rods for royal dinners so that their meat is tastier?
>
> DANTON. Are we children who are roasted in the glowing Moloch arms of this world and are tickled with light

rays so that the gods amuse themselves with the children's laughter?

CAMILLE. Is the ether with its golden eyes a bowl of golden carp, which stands at the table of the blessed gods, and the blessed gods laugh eternally and the fish die eternally and the gods eternally enjoy the iridescence of the death battle? [100]

This massive, indeed "choric" rejection of the world view once embraced by Goethe reveals itself as a fourfold counterproposal to his and every other metaphysical concept of cosmic harmony and sympathy. However, what emanates from Büchner's lines is no longer promethean defiance but rather utter desperation. Turning away, Danton proceeds to draw the only conclusion that remains: "The world is *chaos*. *Nothingness* is the world-god yet to be born." [101]

Georg Büchner died in 1837. Exactly fifty years later, the man commonly regarded as having been the first to diagnose the rise of nihilism (I am referring, of course, to Friedrich Nietzsche) noted: "The greatest recent event—that 'God is dead' . . . is already beginning to cast its first shadows over Europe." [102] This observation—which, in retrospect, can surely be termed astounding—is contained in the expanded second version (published in 1887) of *Die fröhliche Wissenschaft* (*The Gay Science*). However, its most decisive expression can already be found in the original version of 1882. It is the famous aphorism number 125, entitled "The Madman." Speaking through this figure who carries a lighted lantern in the middle of the day, Nietzsche informs mankind as to the fate of God:

We have killed him—you and I. All of us are his murderers. But how did we do this? How could we drink up the sea? Who gave us the sponge to wipe away the entire horizon? What were we doing when we unchained this earth from its sun? Whither is it moving now? Whither are we moving? Away from all suns? Are we not plunging continually? Backward, sideward, forward, in all directions? Is there still any up or down? Are we not straying as through an infinite *nothing*? Do we not feel the breath of empty space? Has it not become colder? Is not night continually closing in on us? Do we not need to light lanterns in the morning?[103]

These words of the philosopher who was born in 1844, seven years after Büchner's death, aptly demonstrate how presciently Büchner anticipated the future with his proclamations of nothingness and the death of God. It would be easy to adduce additional passages from Nietzsche's works to reinforce this connection. On the other hand, Büchner also drew on the recent past, a past so recent, in fact, that it still formed a part of the present in which he lived. This can be seen with particular clarity if we examine lines penned by Jean Paul, a writer who, though his birth antedates Büchner's by a full half century, had been dead for only twelve years when the latter died. The relationship, not of *Danton's Death* or of *Lenz*, but rather of *Woyzeck*, to these lines offers in a nutshell a precise analogue to the all-encompassing counterconception to Goethe's *Egmont* provided by Büchner's drama of revolution.

The passage in question is Jean Paul's "Rede des todten Christus vom Weltgebäude herab, daß kein Gott sei" ("Speech of the Dead Christ Down from the Edifice of the Universe That There Is No God") included in his novel *Blumen-, Frucht- und Dornenstücke; oder Ehestand, Tod und Hochzeit des Armenadvokaten F. St. Siebenkäs* (*Flower, Fruit, and Thorn Pieces: or the Married Life, Death, and Marriage of the Attorney of the Poor, F. St. Siebenkäs*), a book which was written in 1795–96, published in 1796–97, and then reissued in revised form in 1818. It has been demonstrated that Büchner was influenced by the writings of Jean Paul,[104] and there can be no doubt that he was familiar with this speech. What is perhaps less well-known is that Nietzsche, too, may well have read it at an early age and, what is more, found it to his liking.[105] In any case, in the speech's "Introduction" (*Vorbericht*) we find— as in "The Madman" and other Nietzsche texts[106]—a reference to God as "the sun" of the "world"; also, in images that are remarkably similar to Nietzsche's, we are informed that the "entire spiritual universe" is being "exploded and smashed by the hand of atheism into countless mercurial points of individual egos that gleam, run, lose themselves, flowing together and apart, without unity or stability."[107] Even when Jean Paul adds "that to a belief in atheism, there can be added without contradiction a belief in immortality," we cannot help noting an uncanny anticipation of Nietzsche. For, in keeping with the latter's views though using different imagery, the "Introduction" goes on to explain: "The same Necessity that in this life flung my shining dew-drop of self in the goblet of a flower and under a sun, can do the same in a second life;—indeed the second time through it can render me incarnate with even greater ease than the first time." [108] In its essence, what is this other than the Nietzschean concept of Eternal Recurrence, which was given its first fully developed expression precisely in *The Gay Science* of 1882 (compare the aphorism "The Greatest Weight")? [109] The crucial difference is that Nietzsche, although at first deeply disturbed by this thought, came to view it in an increasingly positive light and ultimately arrived at a point where he unreservedly, indeed rapturously, affirmed it. Even his seemingly sober and detached statement that nihilism was beginning to make its presence felt in Europe bears the—at first glance, startlingly incongruous—title: "The Meaning of Our Cheerfulness." [110]

In Jean Paul there is not the slightest trace of such "cheerfulness," not to mention the neo-pagan faith in fate which was so important to Nietzsche (who repeatedly declared *amor fati* to be his "innermost nature"). [111] That which the author of *Siebenkäs* experienced was "cosmic terror"; [112] what he portrayed, using to the fullest his impressive powers of language, was man's absolute abandonment in a world stripped of God. A vision of apocalyptic horror unfolds in Jean Paul's nocturnal "flower piece" or *Blumenstück* (thus the strange and seemingly inappropriate term he chose to label the category of this text). After a brief introduction, the author begins:

> I . . . awoke in the graveyard and sought the sun in the empty night sky, for I thought that an eclipse had covered it with the moon. All the graves were open and the iron doors of the charnel house kept opening and shutting, moved by invisible hands. On the walls flitted shadows cast by no one, and other shadows moved upright in thin air. In the open coffins only the children were still asleep. Across the heavens there hung in great folds a sultry grey fog that a giant shadow was pulling in like a net, ever nearer, tighter and hotter. Above me I heard the roar of dis-

tant avalanches, under me the first rumblings of an immense earthquake. The church was shaken up and down by two unceasing dissonances that were battling with one another within, vainly trying to flow together into a harmony. Now and then a grey glimmer hopped up to the church's windows and wherever the glimmer appeared the lead and iron flowed down, melted.[113]

Driven into the church by the "net" of the "fog" and the trembling of the earth, the poet describes how "all the shadows" were assembled "around the altar"; how "instead of their hearts" their "breasts" were throbbing and quivering; how they all were gazing at the "clock face of *eternity*" up on the vault, a face on which "only a black finger was pointing." Only after this preparation, itself not lacking in grandiosity, does Jean Paul's "Speech of the Dead Christ" actually begin:

Now a lofty, noble figure bearing the impress of eternal sorrow descended from on high down to the altar, and all the dead cried, "Christ! Is there no God?"

He answered, "There is none."

The entire shadow of each of the dead trembled, not just its breast, and the quivering ran all through the shadows, so that one by one the shudder shook them apart.

Christ continued, "I passed among the planets, I climbed up to the suns and flew with the Milky Way through the deserts of heaven; but there is no God. I descended as far as Existence casts its shadow, and peered into the abyss and cried: "Father, where are you?" but I heard only the eternal storm which rages on, controlled by no one, and the shimmering rainbow of Being stood—without the sun that created it—over the abyss and trickled down. And when I looked up at the immense universe, searching for the Divine *eye*, it was staring at me with an empty, bottomless *eye socket*, and Eternity lay on Chaos and gnawed away at it and regurgitated and rechewed what it had already eaten.—Scream on, you dissonances, scream the shadows to shreds; for He does not exist!"

The pale shadows vanished, as a frosty mist melts away with a warm breath; and everything became empty. Then—

terrible for the heart—there appeared the dead children
who had awakened in the graveyard; they prostrated themselves before the lofty figure at the altar and said: "Jesus!
Have we no Father?"—And he answered with streaming
tears: "We are all orphans, I and you, we have no Father."
Then the dissonances shrieked louder—the trembling
walls of the temple split asunder—and the temple and the
children sank down—and the earth and the sun sank
down after them—and the entire edifice of the universe
sank down before us in its immensity—and up on the pinnacle of immense Nature Christ stood and gazed down
into the edifice of the universe that was fretted with a thousand suns, down as it were into a mine tunneled into eternal night in which the suns were like miner's lamps and the
Milky Way like veins of silver.[114]

One hesitates to interrupt Jean Paul's vision with commentary:
to point out, for example, its connection to both *Werther* ("eternity . . . regurgitated and rechewed what it had already eaten")
and Danton's last outburst, as well as to the Goethe text so radically inverted by Büchner (the "dissonances" that were "vainly
trying to flow together into a harmony"). Likewise, one is reluctant to condense and shorten this brilliantly conceived and mas-
terfully executed text that unfolds before us in a steadily building crescendo of intensity. But neither the commentary nor the
condensation can be avoided. In any case, it is evident that for
Jean Paul, too, the experience of atheism, of the Nietzschean
death or the Büchnerian *nonexistence* of God, leads to the experience of nihilism and of a world which is utterly chaotic. For him,
as for Büchner, these views belong together. "The loftiest of the
finite beings," Jean Paul's Christ, "raises his eyes up toward
nothingness and the empty immensity" and cries: "Motionless,
mute *nothingness*! cold, eternal necessity! Mad randomness! . . .
When will you smash this edifice and me?"[115] This outburst is
followed by the lament, "How *alone* is each of us in the broad
charnel-house of the world!"[116] That the experience of isolation,
of existential as well as cosmic loneliness, possesses central importance not only in Büchner's oeuvre but also in his life, has
long become obvious (and it will occupy us again in chapter 5).
Nor is it a secret that Jean Paul's "flower piece" ends by com-

pletely inverting itself, and thereby fully justifies this designation which at first seemed so ill-chosen. The text concludes—after even the dead Christ has fallen silent—with a second climax as well as a total reversal. "And as I fell down and looked into the glowing edifice of the universe," the narrator recounts,

> I saw the raised-up coils of the giant serpent of Eternity which had wrapped itself around the cosmos—and the coils fell and the snake doubled its hold—then it wound itself a thousand times around Nature—and squeezed the planets together—and crushed the infinite temple into a graveyard-church—and everything became narrow, dark, and fearful—and an immense bell-clapper was about to toll the final hour of Time and shatter the edifice of the universe . . . and then I awoke.
>
> My soul wept with joy that it could once again pray to God—and my joy and my weeping and my belief in Him were the prayer. And as I rose, the sun gleamed low in the west, behind the ripe purple ears of grain, and tranquilly cast its last glowing toward the little moon that was rising in the east without an aurora; and between heaven and earth a happy transitory world spread its short wings and lived, like myself, in the eternal Father's sight; and from all of Nature around me there flowed tranquil tones, as if from distant vesper-bells.[117]

The supposed awakening with which the apocalyptic vision of cosmic horror began was in reality the beginning of the dream, while at the end we have a real awakening, a return not only to consciousness but also to the truth. What the poet is left with is certainly not the *new* "cheerfulness" described by Nietzsche, but rather the *old* "joy," the blissful tears which are diametrically opposed to the Nietzschean state of mind. It would be hard to imagine a more complete inversion of an inversion than that accomplished by Jean Paul—or, for that matter, a wider gulf than the one separating him from Nietzsche. In its "Introduction"— indeed, in its first sentence—the author of the "Speech of the Dead Christ" seeks to mollify the reader with the assurance: "The goal of this fiction excuses its audacity."[118] Jean Paul has even tried to head off any misconceptions that might arise re-

garding this goal, going so far as to provide his title with a footnote in which he declares: "If ever my heart were so unhappy
and dead that in it all the feelings that affirm the existence of God
were destroyed, then I would shock myself with this essay of
mine and—it would cure me and give me back my feelings." [119]
In the so-called fairy tale told by the grandmother in Büchner's
Woyzeck, a text which irrefutably draws on that of Jean Paul,
there is no salvation of any sort, no refuge or joy—let alone a
paradoxical cheerfulness—nor anything that resembles tears of
bliss; instead, there is only infinite sadness, the bitterest grief,
and ceaseless weeping. Dream and consciousness do not alter-
nate here, in however deceptive a manner; in fact, there is no
change at all, only the naked, bleak, immutable reality of a universe devoid of God, a cosmos turned into chaos and nothingness. One can scarcely conceive of a more marked divergence
accompanied by a more marked similarity—which is to say,
of a more profound counterconception. Like the dead Christ,
Büchner's "poor little child" [120] wanders through the entire universe only to find that it is indeed an orphan, completely alone
in this "charnel-house"; but unlike Jean Paul's "fiction," *Woyzeck*
offers no beatific reversal and recantation. On the contrary,
Büchner reiterates and heightens the sense of absolute abandonment. Twice he notes that "no one was left in the whole world,"
"nobody was left on the earth"; twice he repeats the phrases "all
alone" and "everything was dead"; twice, once at the beginning
and once at the end, he tells how the child "cried." It is precisely
the childlike, homely quality, the simplicity, in short, the fairy-
tale-like (or, rather, "anti-fairy-tale-like") language and tone of
the grandmother's story [121] that makes its message all the more
heartrending and all the more hopeless. While the figures in
Danton's Death are themselves the most eloquent exponents
of their universal desperation, the child in *Woyzeck* is nothing
but the mute incorporation of this world-grief, stripped of any
"speech" even in the sense of Jean Paul, which it so clearly contradicts. All that remains are his "streaming tears."

The stunning modernity of Büchner's works is by no means
limited to what we have discussed. Still, we have by now obtained an adequate sense of their historical situation. In particular, we are now able to understand the crucial position occupied by *Danton's Death* in its relationship to *Egmont*. For must it

not strike us as both fascinating and highly significant that the "Speech of the Dead Christ Down from the Edifice of the Universe That There Is No God" was preceded by an earlier version bearing the title "The Dead Shakespeare's Lament among Dead Listeners in a Church That There Is No God"—a version which was written in August 1789,[122] on the morning, as it were, after the storming of the Bastille, just as Goethe's play, also conceived very early in his career, finally attained completion in 1788, on the eve, as it were, of the French Revolution? Might not the latter, no less than the death of God, likewise be considered "the greatest recent event"? In the years separating *Egmont* and *Danton's Death*, we find the most important turning point of modern history: that is, the dual culmination of radical Enlightenment and radical Revolution, both concentrating in a mere decade and a half a "long plenitude and sequence of breakdown, destruction, ruin, and cataclysm."[123] Is it not remarkable again what multifarious if often ambiguous correspondences and manifestations the events of this era, the brief period extending from 1788–89 through the disorders and excesses of the 1790s up to Napoleon's coronation as emperor in 1804, evoked in German literature? That which erupted so mightily then has since become a world revolution and has also progressed to a nihilism that is no longer merely European in scope, but has taken on global dimensions. If there are some who felt—and perhaps still feel—"illumined as if by a new dawn" when watching these two developments, then there are others who, at least at times, have perceived them as a "gloom and eclipse of the sun whose like has probably never yet occurred on earth." Thus Nietzsche in his *Gay Science* of 1887,[124] and it must be admitted that this penetrating diagnosis of his has proven itself to be overwhelmingly correct.

Goethe's *Egmont* and Büchner's *Danton's Death*. The former is located before, the latter after, the great watershed of world history. On one side, a "divine"[125] drama of liberty concerned with the preservation of the old law and filled with unbroken certainty and joyfulness which, in their absolute self-confidence, are strongly reminiscent of the Christian martyr tradition; on the other side, a drama of revolution, deeply involved with the emergence not only of the new law but also of a fragile and fragmented attitude toward the world, an attitude filled with skepticism, resignation, and sadness, yet one so radical it even begins to call into question its own presuppositions. For what we see at work in Büchner is not only the dialectic of the Revolution but also that of Enlightenment. Indeed, might he not be termed the "prophet" as well as the first critic of "this monstrous logic of terror"?[126] It is as if he wanted to expose and examine in their full contradictoriness both the bloody logic of terror articulated by St. Just and the cold cheerfulness of the logic voiced by Payne. Does not the latter comport himself like a Nietzschean free thinker who is both "able and daring" enough to use his reason "consistently," in order to demonstrate that "the old God is dead"?[127] Yet Payne identifies as the "rock of atheism" precisely human suffering, declaring: "The smallest twinge of pain, and may it stir only a single atom, makes a rent in Creation from top to bottom."[128] This is the same Creation that Goethe's hero was allowed to experience as whole and harmonious even in his hour of death.

Egmont and *Danton's Death*. If ever there were two works that reflect and illuminate each other, then it is this splendid pair of plays.

5   A Dirge That Is a Paean

Paradox Once More

Le ciel est triste et beau.
—Charles Baudelaire

What I am submitting here in lieu of a conclusion is fragmentary; it will of necessity entail a number of repetitions. Nevertheless, I want to bring forth a grave methodological and theoretical problem hitherto merely hinted at. In Büchner's scenes and utterances, especially from his first play, the tragic abyss of life and history is inextricably intertwined with a strange, even crude serenity—no matter how heartrending the spectacle presented. Similarly intermixed are revolution and despair, revolt and resignation—not only in *Danton's Death* but in Büchner's life and work at large. As a result, the final mood he seems to convey is, ever so often, an unfathomable melancholy. Nowhere can this be felt more poignantly than in the grandmother's fairy tale—or "anti-fairy tale" (*Antimärchen*)—from *Woyzeck*. Let me quote it again:

> Once upon a time there was a poor little child with no father and no mother, everything was dead, and no one was left in the whole world. Everything was dead, and it went and cried day and night. And since nobody was left on the earth, it wanted to go up to the heavens, and the moon was looking at it so friendly, and when it finally got to the moon, the moon was a piece of rotten wood and then it went to the sun and when it got there, the sun was a wilted sunflower and when it got to the stars, they were little golden flies stuck up there like the shrike sticks 'em

176

on the blackthorn; and when it wanted to go back down to
the earth, the earth was an upset pot and it was all alone
and it sat down and cried and there it sits to this day, all
alone.[1]

When analyzing this consummate myth of man's forlorn condition in a merciless universe, Maurice B. Benn first calls it an
"expression of profound metaphysical revolt," and, at a later
stage, "the most powerful" of such expressions in Büchner's entire writings.[2] This latter judgment is, of course, patently wrong.
Benn himself cannot but realize, and does in fact acknowledge,
that this fairy tale is "an expression of the melancholy view of
the world which is basic to Büchner's play."[3] He justly holds, however, that Woyzeck must be seen as a work both "of universal human passion" and "of social protest."[4] But neither revolution nor
metaphysical revolt are present in the story of the grandmother.
Rather, they are to be found in passages such as Woyzeck's replies
to the captain:

The likes of us are unhappy in this world and in the next.
I guess if we ever got to Heaven, we'd have to help with the
thunder.[5]

Look: such a beautiful, hard, rough sky—you'd almost feel
like pounding a block of wood into it and hanging yourself
on it.[6]

These are clear images of either social or metaphysical revolt
and, in part, of a combination of both. To make sure, Woyzeck
prefaces his vision of thundering with an unmistakable "Us
poor people" (Wir arme Leut).

Admittedly, there is an element of "poverty" in the grandmother's fairy tale, too. Yet it should not be overestimated. Büchner, it is true, expressly makes the child "a poor child" and,
moreover, has his story told by a poor old woman to the children
of the poor. That by this token we are reminded of the social implications inherent in man's misery cannot be denied. However,
is it permissible to conclude that a "rich child" would have fared
better?[7] After all, Büchner's child is both fatherless and mother-
less. In addition, everything around him is dead; no one is left in

the entire world. Under such circumstances, it must be obvious that the connotation "pitiful" (*bemitleidenswert*) of the epithet "poor" cannot be denied, either. Quite to the contrary, Büchner's metaphysical melancholy, in his "anti-fairy tale," far outweighs all social implications—not to mention social criticism or revolution. No revolt whatsoever is at work here, not even the metaphysical one advocated by Benn, who, though emphasizing the social protest put forth by the play as a whole, wisely refrains from imputing it to the old woman's story.

Instead, by drawing a parallel with Jean Paul's deeply moving "Speech of the Dead Christ," Benn again corroborates, unwittingly or not, a different interpretation. This speech is permeated by the same mood, the same boundless melancholy as is the fairy tale in *Woyzeck*. Not only is it one of the earliest documents of European nihilism;[8] it is also more than likely to have directly influenced Büchner. As we have seen in chapter 4, Jean Paul had painted quite a similar picture: "There it is Christ who visits the sun and the stars in a fruitless quest for God; there Christ as well as the children are 'without a father,' and 'each one is so alone in the broad charnel-house of the world' (*Wie ist jeder so allein in der weiten Leichengruft des All!*)."[9] Tears are the sole answer, as for Büchner's poor little child; they are streaming down Christ's cheeks when he has to tell the dead children: "All of us are orphans, both you and I" (*Wir sind alle Waisen, ich und ihr*). According to Benn's cautious contention, the similarities between the two texts are so striking "that one may wonder if Büchner was not perhaps thinking of Jean Paul when he wrote his *Antimärchen*."[10]

No further comment is necessary, except that we might be inclined to draw yet another parallel—but this time, to a text composed roughly a century after Büchner's. What I have in mind is a piece by the German poet Gottfried Benn. First published in 1925, it is entitled "Theogonien" ("Theogonies"), and it begins with the following strophe:

> Theogonies—
> from the things of the world,
> melancholies move
> toward the firmament,
> weaving gods and dragons,

singing blazes and Baal,
to endow with meaning
bondage and pain.[11]

The title and the opening line allude to Hesiod's epic, *Theogony*, whose subject, the origin of the gods, is unfolded in the course of the poem. Yet its author, by using the Greek term in the plural, extends his gaze beyond that cradle of Western culture, Mediterranean antiquity, to include all peoples of the earth and their manifold myths, represented specifically, as will be seen from the last strophe, by the American Indians (though there are plenty of other mythologies represented, such as Persian, Semitic, Polynesian).[12] In close relation to the ideas of Büchner's contemporary, the philosopher Ludwig Feuerbach, Gottfried Benn develops his lyrical thesis that religion has been born out of human misery and grief, that men of all ages and races have tried to give life a meaning by projecting in the heavens divine and mythical figures filled with superhuman power and strength, as foils to their own existence. In fact, the Marxian "opiate of the people," the old battle cry of the socialists, is not too far away either, despite Benn's disgust with Marxism. More important, however, his poem—although highly learned, to be sure, and at times quite cryptical—is a modern as well as adult version, as it were, of the fairy tale from *Woyzeck*. Even the social implications ("bondage") are present in Benn's verse—though they are, to be sure, as faint as in Büchner's story. Both authors describe the same futile quest, the same movement from this world to those heavens which stand for an afterworld that proves to be nonexistent, and both their texts impart the same infinite sadness and melancholy that only tears can answer yet never soothe. Accordingly, Benn's poem, explicitly naming the Algonquin, culminates in these lines:

How must they all have suffered
to flee thus to the dream,
and be the pastureland of grief,
as here the Algonquin!
Also to other beasts, to stones
their death they did entrust,

and went abroad to weep,
the peoples white and red.[13]

It is not just a lone child who sits down to weep, but all peoples from all over the world that gather to bewail their hopeless misery. In this poem the pastures of Heaven, those beatitudes of a Paradise long lost, are irrevocably replaced by eternal pastures of grief. Indeed the metaphor itself has been reversed, since Benn's "pastureland of grief" (des Kummers Weiden) makes suffering mankind the pastureland on which the personified affliction feeds.[14] Neither here nor in the fairy tale of the grandmother is there anything comparable to the surprise solution in Jean Paul's "Speech of the Dead Christ"—whose author, in spite of his dreadful vision, reveals his experience as "only a dream from which one may and must awaken to a renewed faith in God," as Maurice Benn summarizes. "For Büchner," he continues, "there is no awakening. And if our love and compassion for the solitary child must be all the more intense for that fact, our revulsion from the pitiless universe must be all the more passionate."[15] But we should look for meaning in the play as a whole; Woyzeck being what it is, namely a tragedy, can evoke a cathartic effect as well. Nevertheless, Benn is basically right. To Büchner, "bondage and pain" are devoid of meaning unless they incite, ever anew, to revolt and rebellion. This is part of his "extraordinary paradox"[16]—whereas Gottfried Benn demonstrates the marvelous capability (too easily exercised, I am afraid) of sublating all misery and injustice in the flawless sphere of aesthetic form and consummate beauty. An eager disciple, not so much of Nietzsche the philosopher as of Nietzsche the artist, Benn contends that "bondage and pain" must be accepted, yet at the same time asserts that they can be endowed with a novel meaning— made sinnvoll—by being transformed into art. They are justified by the statues, the verse, and the music born out of the very sufferings of mankind.[17] In place of an afterworld that is irretrievably gone, and against a reality he continuously questions, Benn construes a new world of pure aesthetic "expression": his beloved Ausdruckswelt, or world of art, where nothing is said to reign but "tranquil form and perfection" (formstille Vollendung), as he succinctly phrased it in a poem of 1936.[18] This world, for good reason, is equated by him with the Nietzschean "Olympus of appearances" (*Olymp des Scheins*).[19]

Yet, with regard to Büchner, it would appear to be even more fitting to quote from a very different source—the works of Shakespeare. Büchner's indebtedness to him is well known; it has been demonstrated at length. The young playwright was intimately familiar with that most important of all influences upon the development of German drama. But are we as critics equally aware of *how* it affected him and, in particular, in what way he tried to appropriate, and perhaps managed to transcend, his great model? It is Büchner's fairy tale again, his *Antimärchen* or antimyth, which provides a gripping example. All we have to do is compare his image of the stars, which are "little golden flies stuck up there like the shrike sticks them on the blackthorn," with these famous lines from *King Lear*:

> As flies to wanton boys, are we to the gods;
> They kill us for their sport.

Shakespeare stays within the human domain, picturing man as the helpless victim of cruel gods, whose existence is taken for granted. Büchner, though making use of the same basic metaphor, not only imbues it with the unfeeling cruelty of beasts but expands it to embrace the entire universe, simultaneously belying the notion of a divine order and characterizing this world as a senseless torture chamber and charnel house. Thus, on the one hand, the Shakespearean image is raised to cosmic dimensions; on the other hand, the very existence of the gods themselves is negated because the stars, their most sacred, most venerable symbol and manifestation, have been victimized by some unknown power. (Or rather, the universe as such is turned into a dark, self-devouring process, as is also evinced by the analogous treatment of sun and moon.) This kind of creative response to Shakespeare is anything but plain imitation. Conversely, when Büchner does adhere to the traditional concept of a Supreme Being, if only figuratively, God is reduced to pitiful human dimensions because man's own weakness, suffering, and helplessness are attributed to Him. Compare, for instance, what Danton has to say when looking at that Kantian "starred sky" (*gestirnter Himmel*) which used to instill such profound consolation: "The stars are scattered over the sky like shimmering tears. There must be deep sorrow in the eye from which they trickled."[20] I can see nothing "grotesque" or "ironical" in these words (as does a recent *Forschungsbericht*)[21] but solely an immense sadness and sorrow, a universal melancholy and grief. Not only Büchner's desolate orphan but even his deity—or the fading concept thereof, present as a mere figure of speech—is left with streaming eyes. Child and God alike suffer from the same boundless affliction.

And so does the Son of Man. It is this experience, not the miraculous awakening, which actually remains of Jean Paul's "Speech of the Dead Christ," at least as far as Büchner is concerned. In fact, the solidarity of suffering that unites man and God, indeed the whole universe, may also explain those much-disputed "last words" of his: "We have not too much pain, we have too little, for through pain we enter into God!—We are death, dust, ashes, what right have we to complain?"[22] Unless Büchner yielded, on his deathbed, to a fit of ghastly, of grotesque and macabre irony, this equality in suffering is the only valid explanation of a confession that otherwise would belie nearly everything he had previously written. Or else, the dying man who spoke his words with an unnaturally "calm, elevated, solemn voice" (*mit ruhiger, erhobener, feierlicher Stimme*)[23] was really no longer in full possession of his mental faculties—which is the usual (and simplest) refutation of eager Christian rescuers (it is Benn's, too).[24] Yet, would it not make more sense to recognize, by acknowledging Büchner's metaphysical solidarity,[25] at least a flicker of his former ideas in those words? Must we not conclude that, rather than viewing himself in sackcloth and ashes, like a latter-day pietist,[26] he saw in God or "the gods"— that is, in the entire creation—the same "death, dust, ashes" which he saw in man? (Truly, what right then would we have to complain?) Isn't all this confirmed in abundance by the author of *Danton's Death*, who wrote that "the Son of Man is crucified in each of us," that "we all struggle in bloody sweat in the Garden of Gethsemane, but not one of us redeems the other with his wounds"?[27] These are the words of Robespierre, granted. But his theological image is superseded by a most pertinent one from the lips of Danton, an image both ontological and cosmological:

"Nothingness has killed itself, Creation is its wound, we are its drops of blood, the world is the grave in which it rots."[28] To be sure, Danton adds: "That sounds crazy." Still, he also insists that "there's some truth to it."[29] What is this truth other than a variation on the self-devouring universe, conjured up so overpoweringly in the tale from *Woyzeck*? As anyone versed in Büchner well knows, there exist many similar passages.[30]

On the other hand, he who is familiar with Expressionism will probably point out that the image of Christ in the way used by Robespierre became a leitmotif of that entire movement. But then, had not Nietzsche already portrayed himself not only as the *Antichrist* but precisely as an *Ecce homo*, according to his last and most personal works? Have we not observed, since the turn of the century, a whole variety of such repercussions and parallels? Wherever one approaches Büchner one is bound to stir up, in a widening gyre, the deepest and most universal concerns of modern man. Nevertheless, there is one decisive aspect that, to my knowledge, has barely been touched upon in Büchner criticism—an aspect, I hasten to add, which also brings up the grave methodological question I mentioned earlier. Maurice Benn, as we saw in chapter 1, elaborated on Albert Camus in order to distinguish between an aesthetic, a social, and a metaphysical revolt, and thus to arrive at what he thought was Büchner's coherent ideology. In many ways this three-dimensional construct has proved to be a fair and satisfactory critical tool.[31] But if we wish to grasp Büchner's message in full, we shall have to allow (as I suggested in chapter 2) for a fourth dimension, although it may now appear to be flatly contradicted by almost everything adduced so far in these concluding deliberations. On closer scrutiny, however, it will reveal itself as less complicated though more complex—in sum, as complementary as well as contradictory.

Let us recall that the same man who wrote the fairy tale of the grandmother, that heartrending testimony of somber despair, also testified in his fragmentary novella, *Lenz*, to a strange and totally unexpected serenity. "Only one thing remains," he has the poet-hero of his story profess: "an endless beauty moving from one form to another, eternally unfolding, changing."[32] If this is a hymn to life uttered from the verge of madness, Camille Desmoulin's corresponding utterance in *Danton's Death* resounds virtually from the steps of the guillotine. Instead of denouncing the world as a torture chamber and charnel house, and of dwelling on man's utterly forlorn lot in a senseless universe, the friend of Danton speaks of a "Creation which renews itself every moment," and he lovingly praises it as "glowing, rushing, [and] luminous."[33] Danton himself goes even further. "Don't expect me to be serious," he urges Camille when gleefully observing the crowd, the teeming life in the city of Paris. Both exuberantly and sardonically, he exclaims: "Isn't that funny, isn't that a laugh?" (*Geht das nicht lustig?*—note the double entendre in Danton's *lustig*, the allusion to both *Lustigkeit*, "merriment," and *Lust* or *Wollust*, "lust" or "concupiscence.")[34] The very sun which in Büchner's *Antimärchen* is likened to something dead—a "wilted sunflower" (*verwelkt Sonneblum*) or, according to the critical edition, a "croaked sunflower" (*verreckt Sonneblum*)[35]—is pictured here, with equal audacity, as the absolute opposite thereof. For that is what the alleged nihilist or pietist, Georg Büchner, makes Danton say: "I sense something in the atmosphere. It's as if the sun were hatching out lechery. Don't you feel like jumping into the middle of it, tearing off your pants and copulating over someone's ass like dogs in the streets?"[36]

Such coarse, vulgar boisterousness would seem to be the ultimate expression of Danton's *Lustigkeit*, but it is merely one half of his crude serenity, for Büchner goes further. Just as, on a truly cosmic scale, obscene death is replaced by obscene life, so the cosmic outcry and bitter tears of the grandmother's fairy tale are replaced by a frantic, frenetic merriment and cosmic laughter: "I can't understand why people don't stop on the street and laugh in each other's faces. I'd think they'd have to laugh out of the windows and out of the graves, and the heavens would burst and the earth would be convulsed with laughter."[37] Universal lust and lechery and laughter are insolubly fused in this scene— by the selfsame author who, in his *Antimärchen* as elsewhere, evokes a universal grief and melancholy. Again, other pertinent examples could be supplied by anyone well-read in Büchner.

Let us not forget that Woyzeck, too, falls back upon the image employed by Danton. This occurs when he is watching Marie, his unfaithful woman, dance with the drum major. To be sure, in his case cosmic "lechery" (*Unzucht*, as he expressly says) is paired with a cosmic catastrophe which he invokes, rather than with any laughter or merriment. "Why doesn't God blow out the sun so that everything can roll around in lust, man and woman, man and beast," Woyzeck groans in helpless wrath and disgust, and he adds: "They'll do it in broad daylight, they'll do it on our hands, like flies."[38] What emanates from the pages of this fragment is not only utter melancholy, not only grief over man's condition, but also utter loathing of life and the entire world. Woyzeck is virtually "choking," according to the accompanying stage direction. Still, such devastating experiences—in *Woyzeck* as well as in the remainder of Büchner's oeuvre—appear side by side with a boundless lust for life, a naive and childlike joy in the world's beauty and eternal creativeness. Marie, for instance, though caught again in the net of traditional morality, is full of such lust, as is Marion, the "grisette" in *Danton's Death* who has freed herself forever from any repressive bonds. Similarly, Julie and Lucile, the wives of Danton and his friend, bear witness to the world's loveliness even when dying, or crushed by the onslaught of insanity. The same applies to Lenz who, for all his suffering, is able to perceive an "endless beauty" around him; let alone Camille's delight in the everlasting "Creation" he enjoys and extols.

Solely poor Woyzeck, then, abused and downtrodden, seems wholly bereft of all joy, love, and lust. He is condemned to nothing but misery and exploitation, injustice and hatred, imputed sinfulness and impending doom. And yet, while it is true that he is the most wretched of Büchner's figures, it should also be remembered that he has in fact had his modest share, not just of joy and love but precisely of lust. He continues in no uncertain terms, with regard to Marie's and the drum major's lewd, lecherous dancing: "That woman is hot, hot! On and on, on and on. . . . The bastard! Look how he's grabbing her, grabbing her body! He—he's got her now, *like I used to have her!*"[39] Which is to say, in short, that not even Woyzeck is completely shut off from the great chain of lustful life extending through Büchner's endlessly self-procreating universe—a universe conjured up in no less overwhelming and variegated a way than the endlessly self-devouring one it so vehemently contradicts. Both worlds, whether viewed negatively or positively, manifest themselves with equal intensity. Indeed, the very imagery and observations Büchner uses (compare, for example, the flies in the grandmother's fairy tale and the flies in Woyzeck's outburst quoted above)[40] can be shown to contribute to this ferocious contradictoriness.

The scene in which Büchner's vision of a universal promiscuity reaches its climax is that great if much-debated love scene from *Danton's Death* (I/5). Here, once and for all, Danton and Marion are brought together. Their scene consists mainly of Marion's story of her life and description of her world and world view, framed by a few bits of dialogue before she begins and after she has finished. Yet this tale, in its terseness, constitutes a masterful poetic utterance rightly as famous as the *Antimärchen* from *Woyzeck*. Nowhere can the strange, even crude serenity that marks Büchner's fourth dimension be felt more poignantly than in Marion's calm and sober report which is, at one and the same time, a tender and cruel lyric rhapsody.

Marion first relates, it will be remembered, her youth and upbringing and how she met that handsome young man who "often said crazy things" which caused her "to laugh," until "finally," as she puts it, "we couldn't see why we might not just as well lie together between two sheets as sit next to each other in two chairs." Indeed, "I enjoyed that more than our conversations," she explains with disarming directness, almost cheerfully. Then, in a somewhat more somber vein, she goes on: "But I became like an ocean, swallowing everything and swirling deeper and deeper. For me there was only one opposite: all men melted into one body."[41] Unmoved, Marion ascribes this to her "nature" and proceeds to tell how the young man, when at last he realized what was happening, committed suicide by drowning himself. As callously as she had stated, "I had to laugh," so she now states, with unchanged straightforwardness and impassivity: "I had to cry." While Danton is impatiently waiting to kiss and embrace her, she concludes her tale with an account, both serene and serious, simple and sophisticated, of what has been termed Büchner's philosophy of pleasure:[42]

> Other people have Sundays and working days, they work for six days and pray on the seventh; once a year, on their birthdays, they get sentimental, and every year on New Year's Day they reflect. I don't understand all that. For me, there is no stopping, no changing. I'm always the same, an

endless longing and seizing, a fire, a torrent. My mother died of grief, people point at me. That's silly. It's all the same, whatever we enjoy: bodies, icons, flowers, or toys, it's all the same feeling. Whoever enjoys the most prays the most.

The sole response of Danton, who is ever more enraptured, is a passionate appeal to Marion's "beauty" and that "beautiful body" of hers he so fervently desires. "Why," he implores her, "can't I contain your beauty in me completely, surround it entirely?" As in the scene with Camille, he invokes a cosmic notion, but this time it is one of sheer grandeur, without any sardonic overtones: "I wish I were a part of the atmosphere so that I could bathe you in my flood and break on every wave of your beautiful body."[43] Danton seems virtually to stammer out these words, nearly breathless with lust and wantonness. Or should we rather say that he groans them out, near choking, not unlike Woyzeck while watching Marie?

Anyhow, the correspondences ought to be clear. A startling similarity can be shown to exist between Büchner's love scene and all those manifestations of his self-procreating universe I have cited, be they affirmed or negated by his characters. Some correspondences go even further, touching upon his self-devouring universe. They span the entire gamut of Büchner's world view, extending from his philosophy of pleasure straight to his philosophy of pain,[44] even to his very deathbed. That Marion's dynamic imagery of "fire" and "torrent," for example, bears a close resemblance to Camille's ecstatic epithets, "glowing" and "rushing," can hardly be overlooked; nor is this affinity merely literal (*Gluth/glühend*). Indeed, might not his whole "Creation, which renews itself every moment," be compared to her "endless longing and seizing"? Moreover, isn't that creation "always the same," as Marion proclaims of herself? The original here is still more instructive. *Ich bin immer nur Eins*, says Marion—an almost biblical formulation most intimately related to that of Lenz who professes: *Nur eins bleibt*. As before, this analogy far transcends a merely verbal or technical correspondence. "Only one thing remains," according to Lenz: "an endless beauty moving from one form to another, eternally unfolding, changing." Conversely yet concomitantly, Marion prefaces her self-proclamation with the words: "For me there is no stopping, no changing." Whereas Lenz stresses the eternal change in oneness, Marion emphasizes the oneness of eternal change. Both are aiming at "one and the same," and it is Camille whose vision best summarizes what each of them (and through them, the author) wants to express. Not despite her "endless" (*ununterbrochen*) promiscuity, but by virtue of it, Marion is *immer nur Eins*, just as the "endless [*unendlich*] beauty" perceived by Lenz remains *nur eins*, not although but because it is eternally changing. Similarly, it is by constant change and renewal that Camille's *Schöpfung, die . . . sich jeden Augenblick neu gebiert* reveals itself as identical and maintains its oneness in all eternity.

Every value is being reevaluated in Büchner's love scene; for hasn't his prostitute been accorded the splendor and dignity otherwise reserved, even by Büchner himself, for nothing less than divine creation? Perhaps, after all we have heard, this is not so surprising, especially when we reconsider Danton's blunt and totally undignified judgment, uttered at a crucial point toward the end of the play: "Life's a whore, it fornicates with the whole world."[45] If indeed all life is prostitution, why shouldn't a prostitute stand for all life, and be endowed with cosmic qualities and once divine attributes?

In addition to his central analogy, Büchner has established a host of further relations, a veritable web of subtly though tightly interwoven threads, in order to link this bold scene which is a picture of life and the world in general, to his portrayals of man and life in this world which culminate with cosmic visions and universal views. But lest I yield to the very fallacy I wish to controvert, I hasten to declare that such views and visions, while seemingly dominated by lust, lewdness, and lechery, are in fact permeated, to an equal extent, by loveliness, joy, and delight—as well as pervaded by cruelty, pain, and despair. Or rather, all these experiences are inextricably intertwined.

I have already hinted at possible connections (which would reveal a truly contradictory world) between Woyzeck's plight and Danton's rapture. Yet, not only are the lusts of the flesh, abhorred by the former in his misery, raised to a cosmic level by the latter, but Danton, in his hymn to Marion's body, actually praises them as something no less manifold and magnificent than the "beauty" contemplated by Lenz, nor less "luminous" and lovely than the "Creation" enjoyed so intensely by Camille. Besides, as "birth, copulation, and death" are "equated" in the images associated with Lucile and Julie,[46] so, too, are these loving, tender, faithful wives themselves associated, if not equated, with Büchner's cruel yet tender "whore." The same childlike "joy" that is embodied in Marion also characterizes Lucile, whether sane or insane, whether radiant with life and love in Camille's presence or wandering around in loneliness, anguish, and agony. In Julie's case, such similarities are even more pronounced. Quite aptly, she is seated side by side, as it were, with Marion who expressly tells Danton: "No, leave me like this. Here at your feet." This implicit stage direction corresponds nearly verbatim to an explicit one which assigns Danton a position "at Julie's feet" exactly like that afterwards occupied by the prostitute. That Büchner thus purposely wanted to indicate a hidden kinship between the two women—let alone Danton's attitude toward them—is as undeniable as is their serenity in the midst of destruction.

These are not the only ambiguities and equivalents that could be adduced. For instance, Marion, in her tale, describes how, on the evening of her young lover's suicide, she was sitting "at the window." Her comment is brief: "I'm very sensitive, and I relate to everything around me only through a feeling." Whereupon, equally curtly but significantly enough, she offers another highly ambiguous image: "I sank into the waves of the sunset." The weight of this image, in terms of equivalence as well as ambiguity, is borne out by Marion's next words, for they refer to her dead lover: "Then a group of people came down the street, children out in front, women looking out of their windows. I looked down— they were carrying him by in a basket, the moon shone on his pale forehead, his hair was damp. He had drowned himself."[47]

When combined with this ballad-like street scene, which almost amounts to a sad romantic prose poem, the meaning of Marion's image becomes transparent. While she observed the beautiful sunset, virtually sinking into its waves though glowing with life and lustful emotion, the young man, heartbroken and hopeless, sought his mournful death in the actual waves of some nearby river or pond. He underwent in gruesome reality what she, transported with delight, merely experienced figuratively. Once more it is clear that Büchner operated on purpose, creating

his paradoxical unity as a deliberate expression of his poetic
world view, all the more so since he again provided an equivalent in the figure, words, and actions of Julie. I am alluding to
her last scene, the one where she in turn commits suicide—
though surely not out of despair, for *want* of love, but, quite to
the contrary, out of an *abundance* of love and happiness. Without
Danton, Julie cannot go on living; therefore, she will be united
with him even in death. "Come, dearest priest, your amen makes
us go to sleep," she addresses the poisoned cup she is about to
drain. Yet before doing so, she, like Marion, "goes to the window" to enjoy both the beauty of the sunset and the feelings it
arouses in her:

> Parting is so pleasant; I just have to close the door behind
> me. (*She drinks.*) I'd like to stand here like this forever. The
> sun has set. The lines of the earth were so sharply drawn in
> its light, but now her face is as still and serious as that of a
> dying person. How beautifully the evening light plays on
> her forehead and cheeks. She's becoming ever paler; she's
> sinking like a corpse into the flood of the ether. Isn't there
> an arm to catch her by her golden locks and pull her from
> the stream and bury her? I'll leave her quietly. I won't kiss
> her, so that no breath, no sigh will wake her from her
> slumber. Sleep, sleep. (*She dies.*)[48]

More than anything else in *Danton's Death*, including the "ballad" of Marion, Julie's monologue can justly be called a touching
prose poem. The correspondences between the devoted wife
who dies out of love and the unwitting prostitute who drives her
lover to kill himself couldn't be more striking. I trust I do not
have to enumerate them: Büchner's imagery in its telling ambiguity, his motifs in their gripping similarity all speak for themselves.[49] The "flood of the ether," for example, which washes
around the beautiful corpse of the sinking sun, indeed "bathes"
it, to borrow Danton's phrase, needs must recall the latter's wish
to become "ether" whose "waves" break on the beautiful body of
Marion, indeed want to sink her in their "flood."[50] Such analo-
gies and almost musical variations, ambiguous as they are, can
hardly be missed. Nor can one ignore the blatantly sexual overtones in Julie's suicide, this romantic "love-death" which so dif-

fers from that related by Marion yet closely resembles it. The naming of the "priest" who sends the newly wedded couple to the bridal bed ought to suffice. Here, as elsewhere in Büchner's Baudelairean "Harmonie du soir" ("Evening Harmony," as one of the poems in *Les Fleurs du mal* is entitled), the ecstasy of life and love and the finality of death and decay are welded together.

And so, in paradoxical unity, are seriousness and serenity, sadness and beauty. Like Charles Baudelaire in *The Flowers of Evil*, Büchner might have written:

> The sky is sad and beautiful like an immense altar;
> The sun has drowned in his blood which congeals.[51]

Or, like Friedrich Hölderlin when facing the advance of the night, he might have coined the oxymoron, "sad and splendid" (*traurig und prächtig*),[52] in order to grasp the paradox of being, the contradictions of a world and a life that both rend the heart so that it can never be fully healed, and charm it so that it can never be fully rent.[53] Is not Büchner's entire oeuvre, despite its fragmentariness, a poetic universe of such dualism in oneness, both sad and serene, and thus an "extraordinary paradox" of vast dimensions,[54] uniting in its cosmos, as does the microcosm around Marion, life with death, laughter with tears, endless bliss and joy with boundless cruelty and suffering? Must we not infer that this, if anything, is the final mood and message, the ultimate, all-embracing philosophy Büchner meant to convey? As he has Marion, from the core of lustful life, inflict death and destruction on others, so he himself extricates pleasure and beauty from the very midst of pain and decomposition. The fragments of a dirge Büchner left are the fragments of a paean as well. Like the themes of a dissonant fugue, their broken stanzas are stated separately and contrasted with each other, but also strangely developed according to the ruthless counterpoint of his brief, hectic existence. His self-procreating universe eliciting ecstatic exuberance and his self-devouring one evoking unfathomable melancholy are juxtaposed though seldom balanced, despite the harmony in Julie's farewell—rather, as often as not, they are insolubly interwoven and intertwined.

None of Büchner's utterances and scenes can be isolated; they must be perceived together in all their polyphonic dissonance, their irreconcilable contradictoriness. This applies in particular to what is imparted by the grandmother's fairy tale, and to what can be gleaned from the tale of Marion. For if the former strikes us as the consummate myth of the forlorn lot to which man is condemned in an absurd universe, then the latter may rightly be said to be the intimate yet bold legend of grace and redemption allotted us in a benign universe thriving "in and around [us]."[55] The pleasure Marion experiences and expresses, her unique delight in life, conforms exactly to the singular pain crushing the lone child in a world not only devoid of consolation but virtually dead. Büchner's universal promiscuity is nothing less than the reverse of his universal suffering. To be sure, Marion's conclusion that "Whoever enjoys the most prays the most" seems far removed from the "last words" of the dying poet, "We have not too much pain, we have too little, for through pain we enter into God"; yet her words may be viewed as the exact counterpart of that cryptic legacy. We "enter into God," so Büchner learned and taught,[56] either through limitless suffering or through unlimited lust—or, rather, through lust as well as suffering. His philosophy of pain and his philosophy of pleasure merge, and his world view, once again, culminates in a paradoxical unity.

Such a yoking of devotion and prostitution, where deathbed and brothel become interchangeable,[57] will be as repulsive to certain critics as is Marion's indiscriminate sequence of "bodies, icons [Christusbilder], flowers, or toys." It might be as shocking as the "last words" of Büchner have been to other critics—words which, as we know, arrive at the rhetorical conclusion: "We are death, dust, ashes [Tod, Staub, Asche], what right have we to complain?" The same words and ideas occur almost literally in the grotesque and incoherent speech of the drunken barber in Woyzeck, where they are combined with Camille's and Lenz's concepts of beauty—concepts pertaining, it must be repeated, not to any atheistic universe but, expressly, to divine creation![58] "What is man?" and "What is nature?" asks the barber, twice answering up: "Dust, sand, dirt. . . . Dust, sand, dirt" (Staub, Sand, Dreck. . . . Staub, Sand, Dreck). Man is but "bones," he exclaims. "But," he muses cryptically, "those stupid people, those stupid people."[59] Then the barber points to his limbs, again asking and answering in one breath: "What's this? A leg, an arm, flesh, bones, veins? What's this? Dirt [*Dreck*]?" "Should it really be dirt," he muses once more, "which is the solution?" (*Was steckt's im Dreck?*)[60] He adds yet another rhetorical question, albeit, this time, to the opposite effect: "So should I cut my arm off?" (His answer is an emphatic "No.") This drunken philosophizing rambles on and on until, at the end, it exceeds any and all apprehensions. The barber produces a whole series of ambiguous and paradoxical statements juxtaposed abruptly, which finally culminates in a wildly funny yet, even from the barber's mouth, completely unexpected image. Nevertheless, it is reminiscent of the cosmic destruction and misery in the grandmother's fairy tale:

> Man is egoistic, but he hits, shoots, stabs, goes whoring. (*He sobs.*) We must. Friends, I'm touched. Look, I wish our noses were two bottles and we could pour them down each other's throats. Oh, how beautiful the world is! Friend! A friend! The world! (*Moved.*) Look how the sun's coming out of the clouds, like a chamberpot emptying out. (*He cries.*)

As the grandmother pictures the earth as an "upset pot" (*umgestürzter Hafen* or *Topf*) and has the child cry, so the crying barber likens the sun to a "chamberpot" (*potchambre* or *Nachttopf*).[61] The *Antimärchen* and the drunkard's speech both offer visions of utter grotesqueness, be they weird and demonic or ludicrous and ribald. If this is a somewhat covert connection, others are all the more plain and evident. Examples include the barber's kinsmen in *Woyzeck*,[62] as well as that Shakespearean fool in Büchner's comedy, Valerio, who indulges not only in bawdy jokes but also in grotesque images.

Such correspondences also occur in one of the most tragic scenes in *Danton's Death*, indeed one of the most personal and piercing utterances of the author himself. "I studied the history of the revolution," Büchner wrote to his fiancée almost immediately before preparing the draft of *The Hessian Messenger*, his passionate revolutionary pamphlet. Yet what he confided in this famous letter was anything but revolutionary faith, or belief in historical progress. In its entirety, his confession reads as follows:

I felt as if I were crushed under the terrible fatalism of history. I find in human nature a horrifying sameness, in the human condition an inescapable force, granted to all and to no one. The individual merely foam on the waves, greatness sheer chance, the mastery of genius a puppet play, a ludicrous struggle against an iron law: to recognize it is our utmost achievement, to control it is impossible. I no longer intend to bow down to the parade horses and cornerstones of history. I have accustomed myself to the sight of blood. But I am no guillotine blade. The word *must* is one of the curses with which man has been baptized. The dictum, "It must needs be that offense come; but woe to that man by whom the offense cometh," is terrifying. What is it within us that lies, murders, steals? I no longer care to pursue the thought.[63]

However, this very thought kept haunting Büchner throughout his brief life, as has been observed by many a critic.[64]

Also, much attention has been paid to the biblical origin of the dictum (see Matthew 18:7).[65] But something else is at least equally noteworthy, although it seems to be less conspicuous. For isn't man, according to Büchner's "fatalism letter," literally "baptized" with "curses" ([*mit*] *Verdammungsworten . . . getauft*)? Isn't this yet another oxymoron apt to remind us of Büchner's contradictory experience and view of the world? Even in Christian terms, man is seen to be condemned and redeemed simultaneously, his fate an extraordinary paradox. Still, it is a mundane, not a religious, condemnation, much like the mundane and human redemption Büchner advocates. His stunning phrase corresponds to the barber's senseless (or seemingly senseless) oxymoron, "Man is egoistic, *but* he hits, shoots, stabs." The dictum by which it was prompted is repeated by Danton, who leaves no doubt as to where it originated, nor, for that matter, about his attitude toward Christ. In what is perhaps the most telling scene between Julie and her husband, Danton confesses:

The Man on the Cross made it easy for Himself: "It must needs be that offense come, but woe to that man by whom the offense cometh." It must—it was this "must." Who would curse the hand on which the curse of "must" has fallen? Who has determined this "must," who? What is it in us that whores, lies, steals, and murders? We are nothing but puppets, our strings are pulled by unknown forces, we ourselves are nothing, nothing! Swords that spirits fight with—you just don't see any hands, as in a fairy tale.[66]

In spite of all appearances, that which Danton is made to experience, in his life as well as his death, is not an *Antimärchen* but a true fairy tale of sorts. Or to be more precise, it is an inextricable combination thereof, a paradox he is both granted to enjoy and compelled to undergo. Just as the tortured poet sought and found refuge "at the bosom" of his fiancée, so, too, is the haunted revolutionary being comforted by his loving wife. Büchner's letter continues not only with a sigh of profound yearning but with a blatant erotic fantasy,[67] and Danton's nightmare leads to a tender union with Julie, the sexual overtones of which are no less unmistakable. "Now I'm calm," he concludes his outburst, and the scene ends with those telling words:

JULIE: Completely calm, dear?
DANTON: Yes, Julie, come to bed.[68]

In either case, love and lust are the sole consolation left to man under the iron law of history as in the agony of all existence.

Could it be, then, that the ramblings of the staggering barber reveal themselves as another most remarkable piece of writing, comparable in weight and range not only to the grandmother's fairy tale but also to Marion's scene? Is it conceivable that Büchner entrusted a drunkard with his most essential philosophical message? I am tempted to answer in the affirmative, for this would surely not be the first instance of his making use of such an unusual device. Simon, the drunken prompter in *Danton's Death*, can be shown to fulfill a similar function, employed as he is as the grotesque mouthpiece for an important ideological message.[69] However, I shall refrain from any further digressions, and, instead, content myself with summarizing the meaning of the barber's speech.

All four dimensions of Büchner's poetic world and world view are present or hinted at here: the metaphysical and the aesthetic revolt, as well as the social one and, of course, that indispens-

able fourth dimension which I hope has been sufficiently revealed. Man and his fellows, the fate of nature and of the universe, the fatalism of history and of revolution: all are secretly
brought together, both in negation and affirmation. Like the
grandmother and the dying poet himself, the barber dismisses
life and the world as dust, sand, ashes, dirt, and death; like
Marion and the glutton Valerio, he strives for lustful life and
worldly enjoyment; and, like Lenz and Camille, he praises the
wonders of a creation which, however much pain it inflicts upon
man, endlessly overwhelms him with pleasure. "Oh, how beautiful the world is!" (*Ach was die Welt schön ist!*) The entire universe
is a benign, blissful home for human comfort and relief, a cosmos
indeed, and yet a cruel, evil torture chamber and charnel house,
an "abyss"—as is every single person, according to Büchner's relentless insight (*Jeder Mensch ist ein Abgrund, es schwindelt einem,
wenn man hinabsieht*).[70]

Although a grotesque caricature, the barber, like his author, is
virtually rent by these contradictions. Accordingly, his speech,
half jubilant and half morose, is reduced to abrupt, disjointed
exclamations. "A friend! The world!"—thus he rejoices, and we
know full well what these words imply. With equally momentous implications, he also sighs and sobs: "We must." In sum,
his is a rebellious acceptance of man's condition and the state of
the world, as was the young revolutionary's who, in his paradoxical attitude toward a rotten society he felt unable to change,
nevertheless inextricably combined rebellion and despair, revolt
and resignation. Actually, the barber starts with a sum total of
this kind, and a highly philosophical one to boot:

> What is it that God can't do, huh? Undo what's been done,
> that's what. Heh heh heh! But that's the way it is, and that's
> the way it should be [*und es ist gut, daß es so ist*]. But better
> is better.[71]

The reference to God is a broad hint. The barber grotesquely
parodies the Divine Creator Himself, harking back to His universal satisfaction in Genesis 1:31: "And God saw every thing he
had made, and, behold, it was very good [*es war sehr gut*]." As
can be inferred from the German text, Büchner's allusion is
really quite straightforward, in particular when linked to the

whole series of identical phrases (*Und Gott sah, daß es gut war*) leading up to that final pronouncement.[72] Should it be permissible, therefore, to read something similar into his own words of satisfaction, contained in a letter to his fiancée written just a few weeks before he died? On January 20, 1837, Büchner summed up his brief existence with the laconic expression: *Doch ist's gut.*[73] To be sure, this is a much more casual statement and, above all, far less complex; yet it has the same biblical ring. Its author, in writing it down, may well have thought of what he had couched in the mind and mouth of the barber. For those familiar words, seemingly modest and harmless, both hide and betray his most penetrating paradox in its extraordinary totality. Neither in person nor directly dared Büchner state his innermost feelings; rather, he relegated them to the whims of a drunkard, the wisdom of a fool, the willfullness of a child.[74] He was absolutely aware, though, of what he was doing. As he himself put it so succinctly: "Fools, children, and—well?—drunks speak the truth."[75] They speak the truth, we might add, either plainly or, as witness the barber's words, by willfully, incoherently, contradictorily mixing up tears with convulsive laughter, somber tragedy with comic and cosmic relief—indeed the universals of God, world, and existence, the mystery of all mankind, with the most ridiculous, petty, even sordid trivia of everyday life and its bodily functions. Such a disparate, fragmentary form perfectly renders and veils the contradictoriness, the insoluble paradoxicalness of that identity of pain and pleasure, melancholy and serenity, which distinguishes the works and life of Georg Büchner.

Granted, seen from a certain angle—say, for the purpose of fighting latter-day prudishness and bigotry—Büchner's fourth dimension appears to be lust and his fourth revolt, modern sexual revolt. Yet the erotic aspect in Büchner comprises, as became obvious in chapter 2, the whole realm of Eros as well as of Agape. And there are still minor aspects, such as that of nature, associated with this major one. Hence, as far as we can judge, the erotic realm was for Büchner what art was for Gottfried Benn, who claimed to despise love and lust as "cheap" (though, in truth, liberally practicing them). Büchner, for his part, scorned "Art with a capital A" (although, to be sure, he practiced art in an exemplary manner). At any rate, if Benn the artist was capable of sublating everything in the aesthetic sphere but hardly anything in nature, much less in love, then Büchner the man was capable of sublating everything—or nearly everything—precisely in love and, at least to some extent, in nature,[76] but hardly anything in art. However, not only did he produce great works, but he also recognized and amply revealed in his writings the dark side of that erotic realm he so cherished. The compelling manifestations of Büchner's fourfold revolt, which was an acceptance as well, incessantly complement *and* contradict each other in every possible way. His is one bold, extraordinary paradox expressed, with equal boldness, in an extraordinary mixture of the grotesque and the sublime.[77]

Little remains to be said. Implicitly, our methodological problem has been dealt with as we moved along in our considerations. By the same token, it has perhaps been solved to a reasonable degree. To tackle it in the abstract is difficult anyhow, since this problem, a grave theoretical question indeed, is nothing short of what might be termed *la terrible simplification idéologique.* Or, as Enzensberger has phrased it, "the *idée fixe* of correct interpretation." Contrary to his contention this is anything but a novel phenomenon—nor can it be cured, I hasten to object, by simply equating, saucily if provocatively, the act of reading with anarchism.[78] Nevertheless, we are in dire need of an antidote, especially in Büchner criticism, which over the decades has indulged (as I pointed out in chapter 3) in construing ideological or philosophical absolutes and dichotomies, the most recent of them being that of piety, indeed pietism, versus practically everything else. One critic, for example, who solemnly propagates the "outlines" of such a "new image of Büchner," prides himself without a pinch of irony on having succeeded, thanks to a special method he derives from Schopenhauer, "in divulgir.g the alleged atheist, Büchner, as one of the most religious writers."[79] I for one, humbly yet firmly, have to reply that this is crass reductionism, a critical—or rather, un-critical—approach or non-approach which, however awe-inspiring it wishes to be, cannot but plunge its champion headlong into a one-sidedness and, ultimately, one-dimensionality that is the very opposite of what Büchner experienced in life and saw fit to put forth in his work. Yet I further submit that to reject this pious straitjacket doesn't mean to belittle religion, nor, for that matter, to jump to unqualified atheistic or nihilistic allegations. He who rejects or, worse yet, refutes an ideology does not necessarily besmirch it, as many ideologues would have us believe. Also, to acknowledge the importance religious problems held for Büchner, which is indisputable, need hardly amount to dragging God in by the head and shoulders at any and each opportunity.

Other critics—and, luckily, there are those rare birds in Büchner research—have avoided the pitfalls of the ideological fallacy, and presented theses that are much sounder and decidedly more justifiable. Heinrich Anz belongs to them,[80] and so did Maurice Benn. But not even he was fully proof against that raging fallacy, as we have seen. Benn was unable to perceive that Büchner's "happiness and joy" are fused, intrinsically though paradoxically, not only with his concept of modern social, metaphysical, and aesthetic revolt but also with his age-old melancholy, indeed pessimism (certainly a paradox in itself). The playwright and revolutionary knew all this full well; yet his conscientious critic chose to maintain that "in Büchner's writings no adequate recognition is accorded it."[81] Unlike most of his colleagues, though, Benn was sober enough to realize his own limitations, and honest enough to admit them.

I wholeheartedly join the late British critic in his commendable frankness and skepticism. After all, our methodological problem is not restricted by any means to the confines of Büchner research. Nor is it restricted to criticism and literature as such. In life, as in art, we all seem to be obsessed with the notion of coherence and perfection in things, and of their correct and consistent interpretation; it is, in a way, an *idée fixe*. But, as Büchner asked,[82] what really forces us to operate under this tacit assumption? Is it not, ever so patently, a false premise?

When I still fancied one could come up with "original ideas," I once jotted down the ambitious maxim: "Alle Welterklärungen, die stimmen, sind falsch." All world views that are right, I proudly argued, are wrong; for how can any of them possibly be in order, in view of the world being what it is? Of course, this neat paradox or oxymoron belongs to the insights (but we might as well call them truisms) which one discusses and shares, not without irony, with intimate friends but rarely entrusts to the printed page. Thus let me conclude quickly and simply. Like Büchner and, I daresay, every great poet, we humble critics must be bold and modest enough to accept and endure—and, if need

be, to proffer—gaping incoherencies and insoluble inconsistencies, just as, in our inexplicable human condition, we are cursed
and blessed to face the extraordinary paradox of life and the
world at large. However, it also follows that only then shall we be
able to experience both to the very brim, in all their contradictoriness—before, sooner or later, we shall pass away. "What
more can we want than that? No man at all can be living forever,
and we must be satisfied." [83]

Postface

A few additional remarks must be appended. Namely, my contention—first voiced at the Internationales Georg Büchner Symposium in Darmstadt in 1981—that a "new beginning" seems to mark Büchner scholarship (cf. chapter 3) has already been borne out by two important publications. Not only has a new, fully revised edition of *Woyzeck* appeared in East Germany, but the Forschungsstelle Georg Büchner, which is affiliated with the West German University of Marburg, has also prepared and distributed a sizable report outlining the "premises and principles" of an entirely new historical-critical edition of the complete works and writings of Büchner—an edition, moreover, that will entail "fundamental changes" (cf. Georg Büchner, *Woyzeck*. Nach den Handschriften neu hergestellt und kommentiert von Henri Poschmann [Leipzig, 1984] and *Marburger Denkschrift über Voraussetzungen und Prinzipien einer Historisch-kritischen Ausgabe der Sämtlichen Werke und Schriften Georg Büchners* [Marburg, 1984; for the quotation, see p. vii]). I further wish to note that Thomas Michael Mayer, the driving force of the Forschungsstelle and chief author of the "Marburg Memoir," has twice confirmed my much-debated conjecture regarding *Woyzeck* (cf. chapter 2, p. 111), both in *GB III* (p. 289) and in said *Denkschrift* (p. 246). Finally, since I so often invoke the Gramscian maxim, "pessimism of the intellect, optimism of the will," I might do well to state that I am quite aware that it was originally derived from Romain Rolland . . . , who for his part had drawn on Pascal. What is de-

201

cisive, however, is Gramsci's thoroughgoing appropriation of this dictum, as witness pronouncements such as the following, which dates from 1921: "È aumentato il nostro pessimismo, ma è sempre viva e attuale la *nostra divisa*: pessimismo dell'intelligenza, ottimismo della volontà" (Antonio Gramsci, *Scritti politici*, ed. Paolo Spriano [Roma, 1967], p. 418; my emphasis). Doubtless, those words are at least as topical nowadays as they were then.

Notes

Introduction

1 See Karl Gutzkow, *Liberale Energie: Eine Sammlung seiner kritischen Schriften*, selected and introduced by Peter Demetz (Frankfurt, Berlin, and Wien, 1974), p. 188. This handy volume contains all of Gutzkow's writings pertaining to Büchner.

2 Friedrich Hebbel, *Tagebücher: Historisch-kritische Ausgabe*, ed. R. M. Werner (Berlin-Steglitz, n.d.), 1, 398.

3 Richard Gilman, *The Making of Modern Drama: A Study of Büchner, Ibsen, Strindberg, Chekhov, Pirandello, Brecht, Beckett, Handke* (New York, 1974), p. 14.

4 *CCW* 311; cf. *HA* 2, 434–35: "Sie werden . . . sich also nicht wundern, wie ich Ihre Thüre aufreiße, in Ihr Zimmer trete, Ihnen ein Manuscript auf die Brust setze und ein Allmosen abfordere. Ich bitte Sie nämlich, das Manuscript so schnell wie möglich zu durchlesen, es, im Fall Ihnen Ihr *Gewissen als Kritiker dies erlauben sollte*, dem Herrn Sauerländer zu empfehlen und sogleich zu antworten."

5 Ibid.

6 See *HA* 2, 449: "die Vogesen sind ein Gebirg, das ich liebe, wie eine Mutter, ich kenne jede Bergspitze und jedes Thal," etc.; also, compare *HA* 2, 418ff.

7 Gutzkow, p. 192.

8 *CCW* 111–12; cf. *HA* 1, 79–80: "Die Gipfel und die hohen Bergflächen im Schnee, die Thäler hinunter graues Gestein, grüne Flächen, Felsen und Tannen. Es war naßkalt, das Wasser rieselte die Felsen hinunter und sprang über den Weg. Die Äste der Tannen hingen schwer herab in die feuchte Luft. Am Himmel zogen graue Wolken, aber Alles so dicht, und dann dampfte der Nebel herauf und strich schwer und feucht durch das Gesträuch, so träg, so plump. Er ging gleichgültig weiter, es lag ihm nichts am Weg, bald auf- bald abwärts.

Müdigkeit spürte er keine, nur war es ihm manchmal unangenehm, daß er nicht auf dem Kopf gehn konnte. Anfangs drängte es ihm in der Brust, wenn das Gestein so wegsprang, der graue Wald sich unter ihm schüttelte, und der Nebel die Formen bald verschlang, bald die gewaltigen Glieder halb enthüllte; es drängte in ihm, er suchte nach etwas, wie nach verlornen Träumen, aber er fand nichts. Es war ihm alles so klein, so nahe, so naß, er hätte die Erde hinter den Ofen setzen mögen, er begriff nicht, daß er so viel Zeit brauchte, um einen Abhang hinter zu klimmen, einen fernen Punkt zu erreichen; er meinte, er müsse Alles mit ein Paar Schritten ausmessen können. Nur manchmal, wenn der Sturm das Gewölk in die Thäler warf, und es den Wald herauf dampfte, und die Stimmen an den Felsen wach wurden, bald wie fern verhallende Donner, und dann gewaltig heran brausten, in Tönen, als wollten sie in ihrem wilden Jubel die Erde besingen, und die Wolken wie wilde wiehernde Rosse heransprengten, und der Sonnenschein dazwischen durchging und kam und sein blitzendes Schwert an den Schneeflächen zog, so daß ein helles, blendendes Licht über die Gipfel in die Thäler schnitt; oder wenn der Sturm das Gewölk abwärts trieb und einen lichtblauen See hineinriß, und dann der Wind verhallte und tief unten aus den Schluchten, aus den Wipfeln der Tannen wie ein Wiegenlied und Glockengeläute heraufsummte, und am tiefen Blau ein leises Rot hinaufklomm, und kleine Wölkchen auf silbernen Flügeln durchzogen und alle Berggipfel scharf und fest, weit über das Land hin glänzten und blitzten, riß es ihm in der Brust, er stand, keuchend, den Leib vorwärts gebogen, Augen und Mund weit offen, er meinte, er müsse den Sturm in sich ziehen, Alles in sich fassen, er dehnte sich aus und lag über der Erde, er wühlte sich in das All hinein, es war eine Lust, die ihm wehe that; oder er stand still und legte das Haupt in's Moos und schloß die Augen halb, und dann zog es weit von ihm, die Erde wich unter ihm, sie wurde klein wie ein wandelnder Stern und tauchte sich in einen brausenden Strom, der seine klare Fluth unter ihm zog."

9 CCW 133–34. Compare HA 1, 100–101: "Er saß mit kalter Resignation im Wagen, wie sie das Thal hervor nach Westen fuhren. Es war ihm einerlei, wohin man ihn führte; mehrmals wo der Wagen bei dem schlechten Wege in Gefahr gerieth, blieb er ganz ruhig sitzen; er war vollkommen gleichgültig. In diesem Zustand legte er den Weg durch's Gebirg zurück. Gegen Abend waren sie im Rheintale. Sie entfernten sich allmählig vom Gebirg, das nun wie eine tiefblaue Krystallwelle sich in das Abendroth hob, und auf deren warmer Fluth die rothen Strahlen des Abends spielten; über die Ebene hin am Fuße des Gebirges lag ein schimmerndes bläuliches Gespinnst. Es wurde finster, je mehr sie sich Straßburg näherten; hoher Vollmond, alle fernen Gegenstände dunkel, nur der Berg neben bildete eine scharfe Linie, die Erde war wie ein goldner Pokal, über den schäumend die Goldwellen des Monds liefen. Lenz starrte ruhig hinaus, keine Ahnung, kein Drang; nur wuchs eine dumpfe Angst

in ihm, je mehr die Gegenstände sich in der Finsterniß verloren. Sie mußten einkehren; da machte er wieder mehre Versuche, Hand an sich zu legen, war aber zu scharf bewacht. Am folgenden Morgen bei trübem regnerischem Wetter traf er in Straßburg ein. Er schien ganz vernünftig, sprach mit den Leuten; er that Alles wie es die Anderen thaten, es war aber eine entsetzliche Leere in ihm, er fühlte keine Angst mehr, kein Verlangen; sein Dasein war ihm eine nothwendige Last.—So lebte er hin."

10 Unfortunately, Gerhard Irle's study of 1965, *Der psychiatrische Roman*, which contains a chapter on *Lenz*, was inaccessible to me; but compare the pertinent report by Gerhard P. Knapp, "Kommentierte Bibliographie zu Georg Büchner," in *GB I/II*, p. 447.

11 See Hartmut Dedert, Hubert Gersch, Stephan Oswald, Reinhard F. Spieß, "J.-F. Oberlin: *Herr L*.....: Edition des bisher unveröffentlichten Manuskripts. Ein Beitrag zur Lenz- und Büchner-Forschung," *Revue des langues vivantes / Tijdschrift voor levende talen* 42 (1976): 357–85.

12 Wilhelm Schulz as quoted by Walter Grab, "Der hessische Demokrat Wilhelm Schulz und seine Schriften über Georg Büchner und Friedrich Ludwig Weidig," *Georg Büchner Jahrbuch* 2 (1982): 227–48; here, p. 236.

13 Ibid.

14 For a comprehensive treatment, see Walter Grab, *Ein Mann der Marx Ideen gab: Wilhelm Schulz, Weggefährte Georg Büchners, Demokrat der Paulskirche. Eine politische Biographie* (Düsseldorf, 1979).

15 See *Lexikon der deutschen Geschichte: Personen / Ereignisse / Institutionen. Von der Zeitwende bis zum Ausgang des 2. Weltkrieges*, in cooperation with historians and archivists, edited by Gerhard Taddey (Stuttgart, 1979), p. 1265. Also, compare *Untersuchungsberichte zur republikanischen Bewegung in Hessen 1831–1834*, ed. Reinhard Görisch and Thomas Michael Mayer (Frankfurt, 1982), as well as Mayer's monographic study cited in note 17 below.

16 See Grab's title *Ein Mann der Marx Ideen gab*.

17 Compare Thomas Michael Mayer, "Büchner und Weidig—Frühkommunismus und revolutionäre Demokratie: Zur Textverteilung des *Hessischen Lanboten*," in *GB I/II*, pp. 16–298. These and other ideological implications are, however, still being debated; cf. esp. Heinz Wetzel, "Ein Büchnerbild der siebziger Jahre: Zu Thomas Michael Mayer: 'Büchner und Weidig—Frühkommunismus und revolutionäre Demokratie,'" in *GB III*, pp. 247–64.

18 Thus Gilman, p. xi.

19 See Wolfgang Hildesheimer, *Interpretationen: James Joyce / Georg Büchner. Zwei Frankfurter Vorlesungen* (Frankfurt, 1969), p. 35.

20 See the epigraph on page v of this book, and compare Simon's introduction to Georg Büchner, *Danton's Death*, trans. with notes and supplementary material by Henry J. Schmidt (New York, 1971), pp. 11–23; here, p. 11 (also in *Y/T*, pp. 35–44).

21 Compare also chapter 4, n. 123.

22 For these and all other biographical data, see Thomas Michael Mayer, "Georg Büchner: Eine kurze Chronik zu Leben und Werk," in *GB I/II*, pp. 357–425.

23 Schulz as quoted by Grab in *Georg Büchner Jahrbuch* 2 (1982): 228.

24 See note 2 above.

25 There are three entries altogether: (1) "Büchners *Danton*, von dem ich eben Proben im Phönix lese, ist herrlich. Warum *schreib'* ich solch einen Gemeinplatz hin? Um meinem Gefühl genug zu thun." (2) "Büchners Danton ist freilich ein Product der *Revolutions-Idee*, aber nur so, wie wir Alle Producte Gottes sind oder, wie alle Pflanzen und Bäume, trotz ihrer Verschiedenheit, von der Sonne zeugen." (3) "Grabbe und Büchner: der eine hat den Riß zur Schöpfung, der andere die Kraft." See Hebbel, *Tagebücher*, 1, pp. 398–99 (October 28, 1839); *Riß* is clearly ambiguous, meaning both "pattern" and "urge."

26 See *HA* 2, 422: "Die politischen Verhältnisse könnten mich rasend machen. Das arme Volk schleppt geduldig den Karren, worauf die Fürsten und Liberalen ihre Affenkomödie spielen. Ich bete jeden Abend zum Hanf und zu d[en] Laternen."

27 See *CCW* 23–24; cf. *HA* I, 14–15.

28 See *CCW* 254; cf. *HA* II, 425–26.

29 For more details see T. M. Mayer, "Büchner und Weidig"; also, compare Walter Grab, "Die revolutionäre Agitation und die Kerkerhaft Leopold Eichelbergs: Ein jüdischer Demokrat aus dem Umkreis Georg Büchners," *Jahrbuch des Instituts für Deutsche Geschichte* [Tel-Aviv], supplement 4 (1983): 137–73.

30 Georg Büchner, *Nachgelassene Schriften*, ed. Ludwig Büchner (Frankfurt, 1850).

31 The proverbial exception to the rule is constituted, and most brilliantly at that, by Wilhelm Schulz and his 1851 review, which actually amounts to a sizable, impassioned, and perspicacious essay. This important text was rediscovered and reprinted only very recently; see Grab, *Ein Mann der Marx Ideen gab.*

32 Georg Büchner, *Sämmtliche Werke und handschriftlicher Nachlaß: Erste kritische Gesammtausgabe*, introduced and edited by Karl Emil Franzos (Frankfurt, 1879).

33 Compare also Helmut Schanze, "Büchners Spätrezeption: Zum Problem des 'modernen' Dramas in der zweiten Hälfte des 19. Jahrhunderts," in *Gestaltungsgeschichte und Gesellschaftsgeschichte: Literatur-, kunst- und musikwissenschaftliche Studien*, in collaboration with Käte Hamburger, edited by Helmut Kreuzer (Stuttgart, 1969), pp. 338–51.

34 See Mayer, "Eine kurze Chronik," pp. 403–4.

35 Compare Gerhart Hauptmann's naturalistic *Bahnwärter Thiel* and *Der Apostel*, written in 1887 and 1889, respectively; as to expressionistic stories or novellas influenced by *Lenz*, compare Alfred Döblin's *Die Ermordung einer Butterblume* (1910) and Georg Heym's *Der Irre* (1913).

36 A brief discussion of Brecht's attitude toward Rilke can be found in my *Von der Armut und vom Regen: Rilkes Antwort auf die soziale Frage* (Königstein, 1981), pp. 41ff.

37 This is Schmidt's translation (see *CCW* 403). Though "into violence" (for *ins Gewaltige*) must be termed a rather free rendition of Rilke's letter, it surely does capture the spirit of Büchner's play.

38 The pertinent original in its entirety reads as follows: "Mich hat Hermann Keyserling beschäftigt, außerdem Strindberg (der Strindberg der wahrhaft unerhörten *Gespenstersonate*, die hier erschütternd gespielt worden ist), das bestimmteste Ereignis auf dem Theater neben dem *Wozzek* [sic] Georg Büchners, mit dem die Hoftheater, noch gerade vor den Ferien, großmütig hervorgekommen sind. Eine ungeheure Sache, vor mehr als achtzig Jahren geschrieben (G. Büchner war der jungverstorbene Bruder des bekannteren Ludwig B.), nichts als das Schicksal eines gemeinen Soldaten (um 1848 etwa), der seine ungetreue Geliebte ersticht, aber gewaltig darstellend, wie um die mindeste Existenz, für die selbst die Uniform eines gewöhnlichen Infanteristen zu weit und zu betont scheint, wie selbst um den Rekruten Wozzek [sic], alle Größe des Daseins steht, wie ers nicht hindern kann, daß bald da, bald dort, vor, hinter zu Seiten seiner dumpfen Seele die Horizonte ins Gewaltige, ins Ungeheure, ins Unendliche aufreißen, ein Schauspiel ohnegleichen, wie dieser mißbrauchte Mensch in seiner Stalljacke im Weltraum steht, malgré lui, im unendlichen Bezug der Sterne. Das ist Theater, so könnte Theater sein." See Rainer Maria Rilke, *Briefe* (Wiesbaden, 1950), 2, p. 26.

39 John Willett, *Brecht in Context: Comparative Approaches* (London and New York, 1984), p. 240.

40 Bertolt Brecht, *Arbeitsjournal*, ed. Werner Hecht (Frankfurt, 1973), 1, p. 452: "[Reinhardt] finde[t] WOYZECK das stärkste drama der deutschen literatur [sic]." Note that the superlative here used signifies, in German theater lingo, not only "most powerful" but also "best," or "greatest."

41 Bertolt Brecht, *Briefe*, edited with a commentary by Günter Glaeser (Frankfurt, 1981), 1, p. 685: "[*Die Mutter*] folgt . . . der klassischen deutschen Bauweise (vom *Götz* bis zum *Wozzek* [sic])."

42 For more details, see chapter 1.

43 As late as 1949, for example, Brecht seems to have pondered a production (with possible adaptation) of *Danton's Death* (see his letter to his wife, Helene Weigel, of March 6): "Wäre Engel [the director and friend of Brecht, Erich Engel] interessiert an Büchners *Dantons Tod* . . . ? Müßte ergänzt werden: Danton verrät Revolution tatsächlich, da er mit Aristokratie verkehrt, sie beschützt, bewundert, sich von ihr bewundern läßt, überhaupt ein Star wird usw. Ist so schuld an dem nötigen Terror (nötig gegen ihn), einem Terror, der dann auch Robespierre verschlingt." See Brecht, *Briefe*, 1, p. 591. That Brecht's plan did not materialize was perhaps due to his one-sided interpretation.

44 Compare again Brecht's entry in his *Arbeitsjournal*, 1, p. 452.
45 In a letter of December 1, 1952, Brecht told Leopold Infeld, who had
   sent him his book, *Whom the Gods Love: The Story of Evariste Galois*:
   "Das politische Schicksal dieses jungen Genius gewinnt seine Bedeutung hauptsächlich aus seiner wissenschaftlichen Größe. (Auf
   Schwierigkeiten der gleichen Gattung stößt man auch bei einer
   Dramatisierung des Lebens Georg Büchners, selbst bei einer Dramatisierung des Lebens von Karl Marx.)" Galois, a mathematician,
   was an almost exact contemporary of Büchner's; he lived from 1811
   to 1832. Infeld's book came out in 1948. See Brecht, *Briefe*, 1, p. 687;
   2, p. 1128.
46 This is the wrong spelling introduced by Franzos; as we have seen,
   it persists not only in the title of Berg's opera.
47 Other, and less important operatic treatments are listed by Gerhard
   P. Knapp in his *Georg Büchner* (Stuttgart, 1977), p. 104.
48 For its history and implications, see chapter 3.
49 See Elias Canetti, *Das Gewissen der Worte: Essays* (München, n.d.),
   p. 211.
50 Ibid.
51 Ibid., p. 220.
52 Ibid., p. 212.
53 Ibid., p. 54.
54 Ibid., p. 211.
55 Ibid., p. 221.
56 Gilbert Frederick Hartwig, "Georg Büchner: Nineteenth Century
   Avant-Garde," *The Southern Quarterly* 1 (1963): 98–128; here, p. 128.
57 Cf. Gottfried Benn, *Gesammelte Werke in vier Bänden*, ed. Dieter
   Wellershoff (Wiesbaden, 1958–61), 4, pp. 132–33: "Der Roman
   ist . . . *orangenförmig* gebaut. Eine Orange besteht aus zahlreichen
   Sektoren, den einzelnen Fruchtteilen, den Schnitten, alle gleich,
   alle nebeneinander, gleichwertig, die eine Schnitte enthält vielleicht einige Kerne mehr, die andere weniger, aber sie alle ten-
   dieren . . . in die Mitte, nach der weißen zähen Wurzel, die wir
   beim Auseinandernehmen aus der Frucht entfernen. Diese zähe
   Wurzel ist der Phänotyp, der Existenzielle, nichts wie er, nur er"
   (Benn's emphasis).
58 See William Burroughs, *Naked Lunch* (New York, 1959), pp. 224, 229.
59 Compare Marc Saporta, *Composition no I* (Paris, 1962), n.p.: "Chaque
   touche vit pour elle-même, contre les autres, et cela compose un
   monde qui tourne autour de son axe, pris dans un lacis de mété-
   ores, dans des liens d'étoiles filantes."
60 For a detailed analysis, compare my "Marc Saporta oder der Roman
   als Kartenspiel," *Sprache im technischen Zeitalter* 14 (April/June 1965):
   1172–84 (rev. English version: "Marc Saporta: The Novel as Card
   Game," *Contemporary Literature* 19 [1978]: 280–99).
61 As to Saporta in general, see Pietro Ferrua, *Eros chez Thanatos: Essai
   sur les romans de Marc Saporta* (Paris and Portland, 1979).
62 Compare Volker Klotz, *Geschlossene und offene Form im Drama* (Mün-

chen, 1960), p. 231: "Gegenspieler des Helden ist keine Person, sondern die Welt in der Fülle ihrer Einzelerscheinungen. Von allen Seiten auf ihn eindringend[,] macht sie den Helden zum 'Monagonisten' und unterwirft die Handlung meist einer afinalen Kreisbewegung. Entsprechend ist das vorwiegende Kompositionsprinzip das einer kreisenden Variation."

63 Compare Wilhelm Emrich, *Polemik: Streitschriften, Pressefehden und kritische Essays um Prinzipien, Methoden und Maßstäbe der Literaturkritik* (Frankfurt and Bonn, 1968), pp. 132–33: "Es gibt keine eigentliche Handlung mehr . . . Vielmehr ist die Katastrophe bereits vor Beginn des Dramas da." This may sound similar to, but is in fact very different from, Friedrich Schiller's observation regarding the structure of his *Maria Stuart* of 1800: namely, "daß man die Catastrophe gleich in den ersten Scenen sieht, und indem die Handlung des Stücks sich davon wegzubewegen scheint, ihr immer näher und näher geführt wird"; cf. *Schillers Briefe*, edited with annotations by Fritz Jonas (Stuttgart, Leipzig, Berlin, and Wien, 1892–96), p. 46.

64 Emrich, p. 131.

65 Schmidt, in *CCW*, p. 408.

66 Emrich, pp. 131–32.

67 Gilman, p. 22.

68 Canetti, pp. 220–21.

69 Eric Bentley, *The Life of the Drama* (New York, 1964), p. 76.

70 Gilman, p. 26.

71 Emrich, pp. 131ff.

72 Hildesheimer, p. 37.

73 Gilman, p. 29; compare also his essay, "Georg Büchner: History Redeemed," *Y/T*, pp. 8–34.

74 For more details, see n. 35 above.

75 Robert Brustein, "Büchner: Artist and Visionary," *Y/T*, pp. 4–7; here, p. 4.

76 Volker Braun, "Büchners Briefe," *Georg Büchner Jahrbuch* 1 (1981): 11–21; here, pp. 11–12.

77 From Seghers' *Über Kunst und Wirklichkeit*, as quoted by Henri Poschmann, "Probleme einer literarisch-historischen Ortsbestimmung Georg Büchners," *Georg Büchner Jahrbuch* 2 (1982): 133–43; here, p. 135.

78 Compare, for instance, the extensive listings supplied by Schmidt in *CCW*, pp. 408ff.; as to overshooting the mark, see Brustein, p. 6, especially his inclusion of the paintings of Max Ernst and the movies of G. W. Pabst.

79 Compare, in particular, *GB I/II, GB III, Y/T,* and *CCW*, as well as the first volumes of the newly founded *Georg Büchner Jahrbuch.*

80 David G. Richards, *Georg Büchner and the Birth of Modern Drama* (Albany, 1977), p. ix.

81 Ibid.

82 See Herbert Lindenberger, *Georg Büchner*, with a Preface by Harry T. Moore (Carbondale, 1964), pp. 115ff.

83 To give a certain idea of the range and complexity of at least one of those "connective threads" which, while anything but marginal as such, are relegated to the margin here: The development in question implies, among other things, the abolition of the *Ständeklausel*, that is, the normative rule which decreed that only persons of high station, such as kings, princes, or noblemen, are worthy of a tragic fate, whereas persons of lowly station, such as burghers, peasants, servants, or workers, are unworthy of tragedy, and therefore have to content themselves with a comic lot in the lowlands of comedy. This development extends from the early eighteenth century, with the simultaneous formation of the hybrid genres of "bourgeois tragedy" (*bürgerliches Trauerspiel*) and "tearful comedy" (*comédie larmoyante*) in England, France, and Germany, to the late nineteenth century, when it brought about plays such as Hauptmann's *Die Weber* (*The Weavers*) and Frank Wedekind's *Frühlings Erwachen* (*Spring's Awakening*), which contain even collective heroes of lowly station: the oppressed and suffering masses in the first case and a group of pubescent children and youngsters in the second. The interrelatedness of all this with some of the other phenomena here listed ought to be as obvious as is its continuation into the twentieth century (if we think of Brecht and his disciples) and, in fact, right down to the present day (if we think, for example, of Franz Xaver Kroetz).

84 See, for instance, Luc Lamberechts, "Zur Struktur von Büchners *Woyzeck*: Mit einer Darstellung des dramaturgischen Verhältnisses Büchner—Brecht," *Amsterdamer Beiträge zur Neueren Germanistik* 1 (1972): 119–48; Luciano Zagari, "Segni apocalittici e critica delle ideologie nel *Woyzeck* di Büchner," *Studi tedeschi* 19/2 (1976): 121–237, especially pp. 225ff. As to the "epicization" of drama in general, compare Peter Szondi, *Theorie des modernen Dramas* (Frankfurt, 1956), Marianne Kesting, *Das epische Theater: Zur Struktur des modernen Dramas* (Stuttgart, 1959), *Episches Theater*, ed. Reinhold Grimm (Köln, 1966), and Juliane Eckhardt, *Das epische Theater* (Darmstadt, 1983).

85 As an early representative of the grotesque, Büchner is joined not only by Victor Hugo (whose name, naturally, comes most readily to mind) but also by the Russian Gogol and the American Poe. While the latter connections are discernible only in retrospect, the former tie was evident at least to Gutzkow, who spoke of the "genuinely poetic kinship" (*echt dichterische Verwandtschaft*) between Büchner and Hugo (see Gutzkow, p. 188). Also compare Gerda Bell, "Traduttore—traditore? Some Remarks on Georg Büchner's Victor Hugo Translations," *Monatshefte* 63 (1971): 19–27. Concerning the successive development of the grotesque, whether influenced by Büchner or not, mention should be made of Alfred Jarry, Iwan Goll, and Friedrich Dürrenmatt as well as of the movements of Expressionism and Dadaism, Surrealism and Absurdism. Even the two Spanish playwrights, Ramón del Valle-Inclán and Federico García Lorca,

might qualify: the former, with his *esperpentos*, such as *Luces de Bohemia* ("Bohemian Lights," 1920) and *Los cuernos de Don Friolera* ("Don Friolera's Horns," 1921), the latter, with his *La zapatera prodigiosa* (*The Shoemaker's Prodigious Wife*, 1929 [subtitled, *farsa violenta*]) and his *Bodas de Sangre* (*Blood Wedding*, 1932). I am indebted here to my student, Belén Castañeda, who undertook a first investigation at my suggestion. For an interesting case of precursorship, see Wolfgang Proß, "Was wird er damit machen? oder 'Spero poder sfogar la doppia brama, / De saziar la mia fame, e la mia fama,'" *Georg Büchner Jahrbuch* 1 (1981): pp. 252–56; it is devoted to Büchner's cryptic and laconic "Vorrede" ("Preface") to *Leonce and Lena*.

86 Even now, there are hardly any pertinent studies, although I presented this thesis as early as 1974. The two most important contributions so far have appeared in Great Britain: Martin Swales, "Ontology, Politics, Sexuality: A Note on Georg Büchner's Drama *Danton's Tod*," *New German Studies* 3 (1975): 109–25; John Reddick, "Mosaic and Flux: Georg Büchner and the Marion Episode in *Dantons Tod*," *Oxford German Studies* 11 (1980): 40–67. In spite of its promising title, a third essay remains rather vague and general: Karl S. Guthke, "Evangelium des Sozialismus oder Evangelium der Liebe? Über Georg Büchners Gegenwärtigkeit," in his *Das Abenteuer der Literatur: Studien zum literarischen Leben der deutschsprachigen Länder von der Aufklärung bis zum Exil* (Bern and München, 1981), pp. 259–65. Finally, an amusing dogfight has been provoked by Heinz Wetzel, "Vom Filzfetischismus kleiner Hunde: Über eine Textstelle in Büchners *Woyzeck*," *Euphorion* 77 (1983): 226–29. See my rejoinder, "Woyzecks Hundele und Wetzels alter Hut: Eine (fast überflüssige) Erwiderung," *Georg Büchner Jahrbuch* 4 (1985).

87 None other than Carlyle, who was surely aware of what he was talking about, observed: "Without the French Revolution . . . one would not know what to make of an age like this at all"; see *The Works of Thomas Carlyle*, ed. H. D. Traill (London, 1899), 5, p. 201.

88 Regrettably, William H. Rey's most recent book, *Deutschland und die Revolution: Der Zerfall der humanistischen Utopie in Theorie und Drama* (Bern, 1983) devotes merely a few fleeting remarks to Büchner.

89 Regarding Nietzsche and Büchner, there seems to be only one contribution, which, moreover, is extremely limited in every respect: Gisela Benda, "Angst vor dem kommenden Chaos: Heine und Büchner als Vorgänger Nietzsches," *Germanic Notes* 8 (1979): 4–8.

90 As already indicated by its title, Arnaldo Momo's *Brecht, Artaud e le avanguardie teatrali: Teatro divertimento—teatro gioco* (Venezia, 1979) pursues aims entirely different from mine. Compare, however, Fernando Peixoto, *Georg Büchner: A Dramaturgia do Terror* (São Paolo, 1983). As far as I can see, Peixoto is the first Büchner critic to have assumed these theses. A writer who, while rooted in his own time, anticipates the future like the Hessian, he states, is a timeless writer: "Um escritor que, enraizado em seu tempo histórico, com febril e vertiginosa lucidez destaca-se de seus contemporâneos e

avança em direção ao futuro, costruindo novos valores, antecipando projetos e temas, é um escritor para sempre" (p. 10). I couldn't agree more.

91 Besides, Büchner criticism and research continue to proceed, nowadays more than ever. Thus I have been unable to consult and/or integrate the following five contributions: Cornelie Ueding, "*Dantons Tod*—Drama der unmenschlichen Geschichte," in *Geschichte als Schauspiel: Deutsche Geschichtsdramen, Interpretationen*, ed. Walter Hinck (Frankfurt, 1981), pp. 210–26; Dorothy James, *Georg Büchner's "Dantons Tod": A Reappraisal* (London, 1982); Henri Poschmann, *Georg Büchner: Dichtung der Revolution und Revolution der Dichtung* (Berlin and Weimar, 1983); Helmut Kreuzer, "Georg Büchner und seine Wirkung: Aus einem japanischen Seminar über *Dantons Tod*," *Siegerländer Hochschulblätter* 1 (1984): 38–54; Inge Stephan, "Ein Schatten, ein Traum—Lenz–Rezeption bei Büchner," in Inge Stephan and Hans Gerd-Winter, "*Ein vorübergehendes Meteor? J. M. R. Lenz und seine Rezeption in Deutschland* (Stuttgart, 1984), pp. 64–110. The same applies to some volumes of the *Georg Büchner Jahrbuch*.

Chapter 1

1 See Benn and introduction, n. 82. As to Knight, see chapter 3, n. 40.

2 See his Georg Büchner, *Woyzeck* (New York, 1969); *Danton's Death* (New York, 1971); and CCW.

3 See Benn, pp. 99–102.

4 For these as well as the following quotations, see ibid., p. 265.

5 Ernst Bloch, *Das Prinzip Hoffnung*, 3 vols. (Frankfurt, 1959).

6 Albert Camus, *The Rebel: An Essay on Man in Revolt*, trans. Anthony Bower, foreword by Sir Herbert Read (New York, 1967), p. 306; Albert Camus, *L'Homme révolté* (Paris, 1958), pp. 377–78.

7 Benn, p. 268.

8 Ibid., pp. 14, 70, 209, 262.

9 Albert Camus, *The Myth of Sisyphus*, trans. Justin O'Brien (London, 1955), p. 99; Albert Camus, *Le Mythe de Sisyphe*, new edition expanded with a study of Franz Kafka (Paris, 1958), p. 168.

10 CCW 50; cf. HA 1, 37: "die glühend, brausend und leuchtend, um und in [uns], sich jeden Augenblick neu gebiert."

11 CCW 119–20; cf. HA 1, 87: "eine unendliche Schönheit, die aus einer Form in die andre tritt, ewig aufgeblättert, verändert."

12 Benn, p. 194.

13 Ibid., p. 2.

14 Ibid., p. 3.

15 Ibid., pp. 33ff. et passim.

16 Gianni Vattimo, *Il soggetto e la maschera: Nietzsche e il problema della liberazione* (Milano, 1974).

17 Massimo Castri, *Per un teatro politico: Piscator Brecht Artaud* (Torino, 1973).

18 But note also the subsequent allusion to Castri in Giorgio Strehler's *Per un teatro umano: Pensieri scritti, parlati e attuati*, ed. Sinah Kessler (Milano, 1974).

19 For a more detailed discussion, see my essays "Dionysus and Socrates: Nietzsche and the Concept of a New Political Theater," *Neohelicon* [Budapest] 7/1 (1979): 147–69 and "A Pudding Without Proof: Notes on a Book on Modern Political Theater," *New German Critique* 16 (Winter 1979): 135–43.

20 For a preliminary survey, see my articles "Brecht, Artaud e il teatro contemporaneo," *Studi tedeschi* 19 (1976): 91–112 and "Bertolt Brecht and Antonin Artaud: Some Comparative Remarks," in *Perspectives and Personalities: Studies in Modern German Literature Honoring Claude Hill*, ed. Ralph Ley et al. (Heidelberg, 1978), pp. 118–24, as well as my book *Nach dem Naturalismus: Essays zur modernen Dramatik* (Kronberg, 1978), pp. 185ff.; also, compare Guy Scarpetta, "Brecht et Artaud," *La Nouvelle Critique*, n.s. 25 (June 1969): 60–68; Henri Gouhier, *Antonin Artaud et l'essence du théâtre* (Paris, 1974), pp. 191ff.; and Alain Virmaux, *Antonin Artaud et le théâtre* (Paris, 1970), p. 139 et passim.

21 For a fundamental if summary treatment, including a reevaluation of Nietzsche's own theory, see my essay "The Hidden Heritage: Repercussions of Nietzsche in Modern Theater and Its Theory," *Nietzsche-Studien* 12 (1983): 355–71. As to Brecht and Nietzsche, compare my *Brecht und Nietzsche oder Geständnisse eines Dichters: Fünf Essays und ein Bruchstück* (Frankfurt, 1979), pp. 156–245 et passim, as well as Christof Šubik, *Einverständnis, Verfremdung und Produktivität: Versuche über die Philosophie Bertolt Brechts* (Wien, 1982) and Hans-Thies Lehmann and Helmut Lethen, "Verworfenes Denken: Zu Reinhold Grimms Essay *Brecht und Nietzsche oder Geständnisse eines Dichters*," *Brecht-Jahrbuch 1980* (Frankfurt, 1981), pp. 149–71. As to Artaud and Nietzsche, compare Virmaux, pp. 113ff. (who tries to play it down) and Gouhier, pp. 179ff. (who offers a fairly balanced assessment although he still feels obliged to put "striking resemblances" [*ressemblances frappantes*] in ironic quotation marks).

22 *CCW* 254; cf. *HA* 2, 425–26.

23 Friedrich Nietzsche, *Kritische Gesamtausgabe*, ed. Giorgio Colli and Mazzino Montinari (Berlin and New York, 1967–77), 3/1, p. 79.

24 Compare Stefan S. Brecht's review of Richard Schechner's *Dionysus in 69*—a rather free adaptation of Euripides' play *The Bacchae*—in *The Drama Review* 13, no. 5 (1969): 156–69; also, compare his volume, *Nuovo teatro americano 1968–1973* (Roma, 1974), pp. 59ff. Brecht is the son of the playwright, incidentally.

25 See Bertolt Brecht, *Gesammelte Werke in 20 Bänden* (Frankfurt, 1967), 16, p. 662.

26 Benn, p. 264.

27 Ibid., p. 305; cf. Arthur Adamov, "Wozzeck [*sic*] ou la fatalité mise en cause," *Les Lettres françaises*, Nov. 28, 1963.

28 Brecht, 15, p. 95.
29 Ibid., 17, p. 1280: "zu einer eigentümlichen Gattung von Fragmenten, die nicht unvollkommen, sondern Meisterwerke sind, hingeworfen in einer wunderbaren Skizzenform."
30 Bertolt Brecht, *Tagebücher 1920–22 / Autobiographische Aufzeichnungen 1920–1954*, ed. Herta Ramthun (Frankfurt, 1975), p. 161.
31 See Brecht, 15, pp. 105–6.
32 Brecht, *Tagebücher*, p. 161.
33 Ibid.
34 Benn, pp. 262ff. et passim.
35 Apart from Herbert Reichert's collection, *Friedrich Nietzsche's Impact on Modern German Literature* (Chapel Hill, 1975), see especially Lia Secci, "Nietzsche e l'espressionismo," in *Il caso Nietzsche* [ed. Marino Freschi] (Cremona, 1973), pp. 85–117 and Gunter Martens, "Im Aufbruch das Ziel: Nietzsches Wirkung im Expressionismus," in *Nietzsche: Werk und Wirkungen*, ed. Hans Steffen (Göttingen, 1974), pp. 115–66.
36 See Brecht, 16, p. 939.
37 Ibid., p. 599: "Er war ein junger Mann, als der erste Weltkrieg zu Ende ging. Er studierte Medizin in Süddeutschland. Zwei Dichter . . . beeinflußten ihn am meisten. In diesen Jahren wurde der Dichter Büchner . . . zum erstenmal aufgeführt."
38 Ibid.
39 Benn, p. 264.
40 Interestingly, the term can already be found in the first great work of an author who was not exactly a favorite of Brecht's: in Thomas Mann's novel of 1901, *Buddenbrooks: Verfall einer Familie* (Berlin, 1955), p. 198.
41 Brecht, 16, p. 694.
42 Ibid., pp. 693–94.
43 Nietzsche, 6/3, p. 283.
44 Ibid., 3/1, p. 80.
45 Antonin Artaud, *Œuvres complètes* (Paris, 1956–74), 4, pp. 91, 93: "Shakespeare et ses imitateurs"; ". . . litéraires, c'est-à-dire fixés; et fixés en des formes qui ne répond plus aux besoins du temps." For the English versions of these and the following quotations, see Antonin Artaud, *The Theater and Its Double*, trans. Mary Caroline Richards (New York, 1958), pp. 13, 74ff.
46 Ibid., pp. 93–94: "On doit en finir avec cette superstition des textes et de la poésie *écrite*."
47 Ibid., p. 91: "grands mélodrames romantiques."
48 Ibid., p. 94: "Sous la poésie des textes, il y a la poésie tout court."
49 Ibid., p. 91: "conformisme bourgeois"; "idolâtrie des chefs-d'œuvre fixés."
50 Ibid., p. 18: "Briser le langage pour toucher la vie, c'est faire ou refaire le théâtre."
51 Ibid., p. 99.

52 Ibid., p. 120: "Il ne s'agit pas dans cette Cruauté ni de sadisme ni de sang, du moins pas de façon exclusive. / Je ne cultive pas systématiquement l'horreur. Ce mot de cruauté doit être pris dans un sens large. . . . Cette identification de la cruauté avec les supplices est un tout petit côté de la question. Il y a dans la cruauté qu'on exerce une sorte de déterminisme supérieur. . . . La cruauté est avant tout lucide, c'est une sorte de direction rigide, la soumission à la nécessité. Pas de cruauté sans conscience, sans une sorte de conscience appliquée."

53 Ibid., p. 122: "J'emploie le mot de cruauté dans le sens d'appétit de vie, de rigueur cosmique et de nécessité implacable, dans le sens gnostique de tourbillon de vie qui dévore les ténèbres, dans le sens de cette douleur hors de la nécessité inéluctable de laquelle la vie ne saurait s'exercer. . . . Le dieu caché quand il crée obéit à la nécessité cruelle de la création qui lui est imposée à lui-même . . . Et le théâtre dans le sens de création continue . . . obéit à cette nécessité. Une pièce où il n'y aurait pas cette volonté, cet appétit de vie aveugle, et capable de passer sur tout, visible dans chaque geste et dans chaque acte, et dans le côté transcendant de l'action, serait une pièce inutile et manquée."

54 Ibid.: "La cruauté n'est pas surajoutée à ma pensée; elle y a toujours vécu: mais il me fallait en prendre conscience."

55 Ibid., p. 124: "idées métaphysiques."

56 Ibid., pp. 123–24: "Eros est . . . cruauté . . . ; la mort est cruauté, la résurrection est cruauté, la transfiguration est cruauté. . . . C'est avec cruauté que se coagulent les choses, que se forment les plans du créé."

57 Ibid.: "un monde circulaire et clos"; ". . . [un] espace clos . . . nourri de vies, et . . . chaque vie plus forte passe à travers les autres, donc les mange dans un massacre qui est une transfiguration et un bien."

58 Artaud did know both Nietzsche's *Birth of Tragedy* and his *Götzendämmerung (Twilight of the Idols)*; see Gouhier, p. 242, n. 2. Gouhier, despite his previous reservations, has to state in no uncertain terms: "C'est . . . Dionysos qui rapproche Antonin Artaud de Nietzsche: entre eux, l'accord est, d'abord, métaphysique; il subsiste au niveau du théâtre dans la mésure où, ici et là, le théâtre participe à l'*esprit dionysien* . . . leur commune vision métaphysique de 'la cruauté cosmique' va même les conduire à porter sur le théâtre un jugement assez semblable." Cf. ibid., pp. 185–86.

59 Benn, p. 153.

60 See *Antonin Artaud Anthology*, ed. Jack Hirschman, 2d rev. ed. (San Francisco, 1965), p. 105.

61 Bertolt Brecht, *Edward II: A Chronicle Play*, English version and introduction by Eric Bentley (New York, 1966), pp. 87–88; Brecht, 1, pp. 287ff., especially 290: "Gut war Regen, Nichtessen sättigte. Aber / Das Beste war die Finsternis. Alle / Waren unschlüssig,

zurückhaltend viele, aber / Die Besten waren, die mich verrieten. Darum / Wer dunkel ist, bleibe dunkel, wer / Unrein ist, unrein. Lobet / Mangel, lobet Mißhandlung, lobet / Die Finsternis."

62 Brecht, *Edward II*, pp. 87–88 et passim.

63 Brecht, 8, p. 216.

64 Ibid., 16, p. 700.

65 Ibid., 9, p. 588.

66 Compare my remarks and those of Peter Heller in *Studi tedeschi* 18/3 (1975): 147–61.

67 See, for instance, my article, "Brechts Rad der Fortuna," *German Quarterly* 46 (1973): 549–65; cf. also my volume, *Brecht und Nietzsche*.

68 Camus, *Myth of Sisyphus*, p. 96; cf. Camus, *Mythe de Sisyphe*, p. 168: "Les dieux avaient condamné Sisyphe à rouler sans cesse un rocher jusqu'au sommet d'une montagne d'où la pierre retombait par son propre poids. Ils avaient pensé avec quelque raison qu'il n'est pas de punition plus terrible que le travail inutile et sans espoir."

69 Brecht, 5, pp. 1968, 1994.

70 Camus, *Myth of Sisyphus*, p. 96; cf. Camus, *Mythe de Sisyphe*, p. 168.

71 Ibid.: "L'homme absurde dit oui et son effort n'aura plus de cesse."

72 Brecht, 5, pp. 1968, 1993–94.

73 Camus, *Myth of Sisyphus*, p. 96; cf. Camus, *Mythe de Sisyphe*, p. 168.

74 Brecht, 12, p. 461.

75 Ibid., p. 542.

76 See n. 67 above.

77 A first attempt was provided by Norbert Kohlhase's *Dichtung und politische Moral: Eine Gegenüberstellung von Brecht und Camus* (München, 1965); as to Nietzsche and Camus, see Bianca Rosenthal, *Die Idee des Absurden: Eine Gegenüberstellung von Friedrich Nietzsche und Albert Camus* (Bonn, 1977).

78 Brecht, *Edward II*, p. 69; cf. Brecht, 1, p. 268: "Hochziehend eine kleine Last aus / Verjährtem Teichschlamm, muß ich / Im Fleisch obschon matter, hängen sehn an ihr / Menschliche Algen. Mehr und mehr. / Hochwindend mich, spür ich stets neues / Gewicht. / Und um die Knie des Letzten einen neuen / Letzten. Menschliche Stricke. / Und an dem Treibrad dieses Flaschenzugs / Menschlicher Stricke, atemlos, sie schleppend alle / Ich."

79 Compare Christopher Marlowe, *Edward II*, ed. H. B. Charlton and R. D. Waller (London, 1933).

80 Brecht, 1, pp. 265, 270.

81 Benn, p. 167.

82 See, however, Henry J. Schmidt's *Satire, Caricature, and Perspectivism in the Works of Georg Büchner* (The Hague and Paris, 1970).

83 Compare the commentary in Iwan Goll, *Methusalem oder Der ewige Bürger: Ein satirisches Drama*, text and material for interpretation procured by Reinhold Grimm and Viktor Žmegač (Berlin, 1966).

84 Cf. Alfred Jarry, *Tout Ubu*, edition established by Maurice Saillet (Paris, 1966), p. 493.

85 CCW 254; cf. *HA* 2, 425–26.

86 See chapter 5.
87 Brecht, 1, p. 257.
88 Nietzsche, 5/2, p. 250.
89 Compare again my volume, *Brecht und Nietzsche*.
90 Brecht, 9, p. 614: "Ein weißer Gischt sprang aus verschlammter Woge!"
91 *CCW* 253; cf. *HA* 2, 440.
92 See *HA* 2, 447.
93 See Benn, p. 262.
94 See Ernst Toller, *Prosa, Briefe, Dramen, Gedichte*, foreword by Kurt Hiller (Reinbek, 1961), p. 229: "Dem Starken nimmt es nichts von seinem leidenschaftlichen Wollen, wenn er wissend wird. Not tun uns heute . . . Menschen, die . . . wollen—obwohl sie wissen."
95 Compare the source adduced by John M. Spalek, *Ernst Toller and His Critics: A Bibliography* (Charlottesville, 1968), p. 25.
96 See Toller, pp. 216, 221.
97 See, for instance, my survey article, "Zwischen Expressionismus und Faschismus: Bemerkungen zum Drama der Zwanziger Jahre," in *Die sogenannten Zwanziger Jahre*, ed. Reinhold Grimm and Jost Hermand (Bad Homburg, Berlin, and Zürich, 1970), pp. 15–45.
98 Brecht, 10, p. 966: "Traue nicht deinen Augen / Traue deinen Ohren nicht / Du siehst Dunkel / Vielleicht ist es Licht."
99 See Nietzsche, 6/1, p. 243 and 6/3, p. 60 ("Sprüche und Pfeile," no. 44), respectively.
100 Toller, p. 216.
101 Hans Mayer, *Georg Büchner und seine Zeit* (Frankfurt, 1972), pp. 23, 380.
102 Heiner Müller, *Geschichten aus der Produktion 1: Stücke, Prosa, Gedichte, Protokolle* (Berlin, 1975), p. 83: "ODER BÜCHNER, der in Zürich starb / 100 Jahre vor deiner Geburt / Alt 23, aus Mangel an Hoffnung."
103 Ibid.: "Majakowski, warum / der bleierne Schlußpunkt? / Herzweh, Wladimir? / 'Hat sich / Eine Dame / Ihm verschlossen / Oder / Einem andern / Aufgetan?' / Nehmt / Mein Bajonett / Aus den Zähnen / Genossen! / *Die Mauern stehn / Sprachlos und kalt / Im Winde / Klirren die Fahnen.*" Translated by Felix Pollak and the author.
104 *Selected Poems of Friedrich Hölderlin*, trans. with introduction and notes by J. B. Leishman, 2d rev. ed. (London, 1954), p. 79 (slightly altered).
105 For a different, indeed totally pessimistic, reading of this poem, see Helen Fehervary, *Hölderlin and the Left: The Search for a Dialectic of Art and Life* (Heidelberg, 1977), pp. 162ff.: "private . . . and political breakdown"; "the acknowledgement of impasse," etc. However, it was precisely in his suicide note quoted by Fehervary that Mayakovsky stated: "Do not blame anyone for my death and please do not gossip. The deceased terribly disliked this sort of thing. Mama, sisters, and comrades, forgive me—this is not a way out (I do not recommend it to others), but I have none other. . . . Comrades . . . do

not think me weak-spirited." Cf. Vladimir Mayakovsky, *The Bedbug and Selected Poetry*, ed. Patricia Blake (Cleveland and New York, 1960), p. 47. In addition, compare Müller's "Der Schrecken, die erste Erscheinung des Neuen: Zu einer Diskussion über Postmodernismus in New York," *Theater Heute*, no. 3 (1979): 1.

106 Müller, *Geschichten aus der Produktion 1*, p. 143: "Es gibt da kein privates, unverbindliches, kein Rentner- und Konsumentenglück mehr."

107 Ibid.: "Ein Fehler im Stück: der neue Glücksbegriff wird vorausgesetzt, nicht formuliert." But compare Müller's attempt at an adaptation of Brecht's fragment, "Die Reisen des Glücksgotts" ("The Journeys of the God of Happiness"), in Heiner Müller, *Theater-Arbeit* (Berlin, 1975), pp. 7–18. Schulz in her fine study even goes so far as to attribute "ein dionysisches Jasagen" to Müller; cf. Genia Schulz [with contributions by Hans-Thies Lehmann], *Heiner Müller* (Stuttgart, 1980), p. 4.

108 Müller, *Geschichten aus der Produktion 1*, p. 143: "Das muß korrigiert werden."

109 See Fehervary, in *New German Critique* 2 (Spring 1974): 105.

110 Brecht and Dessau, *Lieder und Gesänge*, new expanded edition (Berlin, 1963), p. 20: "Das Glück ist der Kommunismus."

111 Brecht, 4, p. 1553: "Keinen verderben zu lassen, auch nicht sich selber / Jeden mit Glück zu erfüllen, auch sich, das / Ist gut."

112 See ibid., pp. 1531ff.

113 Ibid., 9, p. 724: "Der Liebe pflegte ich achtlos / Und die Natur sah ich ohne Geduld."

114 See *Über die irdische Liebe und andere gewisse Welträtsel in Liedern und Balladen von Bertolt Brecht*, selection and foreword by Günter Kunert (Frankfurt, 1972).

115 For details, see Klaus Völker's somewhat gossipy biography, *Bertolt Brecht* (München, 1976 [English translation: *Brecht: A Biography*; New York, 1978]), as well as Aija Kuplis's "The Image of Woman in Bertolt Brecht's Poetry" (diss., University of Wisconsin, 1976). Also, compare my "Discours de la méthode," in *Frankfurter Anthologie: Gedichte und Interpretationen*, ed. with afterword by Marcel Reich-Ranicki, 6 (Frankfurt, 1982), pp. 197–200.

116 See Keith A. Dickson, "Brecht's Doctrine of Nature," *Brecht heute/ Brecht today* 3 (1973): 106–121. In addition, see my *Brecht und Nietzsche*, pp. 11ff.

117 Brecht, 9, p. 722: "Wirklich, ich lebe in finsteren Zeiten!"

118 Müller, *Geschichten aus der Produktion 1*, p. 82: "Wirklich, er lebte in finsteren Zeiten. / Die Zeiten sind heller geworden. / Die Zeiten sind finstrer geworden. / Wenn die Helle sagt, ich bin die Finsternis / Hat sie die Wahrheit gesagt. / Wenn die Finsternis sagt, ich bin / Die Helle, lügt sie nicht." Unfortunately, the poem receives short shrift by G. Schulz (cf. p. 168). Although she expressly refers to Max Horkheimer's and Theodor W. Adorno's *Dialektik der Aufklä-*

rung (1947) she fails to recognize the subtle and complex dialectic of Müller's lines.
119 Brecht, 16, p. 700: "als Unterhaltung."
120 Ibid., 7, pp. 2771–91.
121 Bertolt Brecht, *Galileo*, English version by Charles Laughton, ed. with introduction by Eric Bentley (New York, 1966), p. 125; cf. Brecht, 3, p. 1342: "GALILEO: Wie ist die Nacht? / VIRGINIA: Hell."
122 See Müller, *Geschichten aus der Produktion 1*, pp. 81–82.
123 Bertolt Brecht, *Poems*, ed. John Willett and Ralph Manheim with the cooperation of Erich Fried (London, 1976), p. 319; cf. Brecht, 9, p. 724: "Das Ziel / Lag in großer Ferne / Es war deutlich sichtbar, wenn auch für mich / Kaum zu erreichen."
124 Brecht, *Galileo*, p. 124.
125 Quoted by Käthe Rülicke, "*Leben des Galilei:* Bemerkungen zur Schlußszene," in *Sinn und Form: Zweites Sonderheft Bertolt Brecht* (Berlin, 1957), p. 273.
126 Ibid.: "Der Einbruch des Lichts erfolgt in die allertiefste Dunkelheit."
127 Müller, *Geschichten aus der Produktion 1*, p. 82: "Oder der mißverstandene Bertolt Brecht / Mit großer Zähigkeit und etwas Hoffnung / *Mehr als den Bogen spannen konnte auch er nicht* / Wieviele Strohköpfe überlebten ihn. / Sein Leben lang suchte er eine Möglichkeit / Den Nächsten nicht zu töten. Gegen Ende / Hatte er sie von weitem gesehn / Halb verdeckt von einem blutigen Nebel. / . . . / Für uns die Spanne zwischen Nichts und Wenig." Translated by Felix Pollak and the author.
128 Ibid., p. 134: "Ich bin der Ponton zwischen Eiszeit und Kommune."
129 As we have seen, the metaphors of bow and arrow in Müller's poem point to a typical Nietzschean imagery, but their immediate source is, most likely, Camus. Compare the ending of his *The Rebel*: "At this moment, when each of us must fit an arrow to his bow and enter the lists anew, to reconquer, within history and in spite of it, that which he owns already, the thin yield of his fields, the brief love of this earth, at this moment when at last a man is born, it is time to forsake our age and its adolescent furies. The bow bends; the wood complains. At the moment of supreme tension, there will leap into flight an unswerving arrow, a shaft that is inflexible and free" (*A cette heure où chacun d'entre nous doit tendre l'arc pour refaire ses preuves, conquérir, dans et contre l'histoire, ce qu'il possède déjà, la maigre moisson de ses champs, le bref amour de cette terre, à l'heure où naît enfin un homme, il faut laisser l'époque et ses fureurs adolescentes. L'arc se tord, le bois crie. Au sommet de la plus haute tension va jaillir l'élan d'une droite flèche, du trait le plus dur et le plus libre*). In the same paragraph Nietzsche is invoked by Camus and, as it were, redeemed—along with Marx and Lenin. See Camus, *The Rebel*, p. 306; cf. Camus, *L'Homme révolté*, p. 378.
130 Thus Fehervary (cf. n. 109 above), p. 104.
131 Heiner Müller, *Geschichten aus der Produktion 2* (Berlin, 1974), p. 21:

"Immer den gleichen Stein den immer gleichen Berg hinaufwälzen. Das Gewicht des Steins zunehmend, die Arbeitskraft abnehmend mit der Steigung. Patt vor dem Gipfel. Wettlauf mit dem Stein, der vielmal schneller den Berg herabrollt als der Arbeitende ihn den Berg hinaufgewälzt hat. Das Gewicht des Steins relativ zunehmend, die Arbeitskraft relativ abnehmend mit der Steigung. Das Gewicht des Steins absolut abnehmend mit jeder Bergaufbewegung, schneller mit jeder Bergabbewegung. Die Arbeitskraft absolut zunehmend mit jedem Arbeitsgang (den Stein bergauf wälzen, vor neben hinter dem Stein her bergab laufen). Hoffnung und Enttäuschung. Rundung des Steins. Gegenseitige Abnutzung von Mann Stein Berg. Bis zu dem geträumten Höhepunkt: Entlassung des Steins vom erreichten Gipfel in den jenseitigen Abgrund. Oder bis zum gefürchteten Endpunkt der Kraft vor dem nicht mehr erreichbaren Gipfel. Oder bis zu dem denkbaren Nullpunkt: niemand bewegt auf einer Fläche nichts. STEIN SCHERE PAPIER. STEIN SCHLEIFT SCHERE SCHERE SCHNEIDET PAPIER PAPIER SCHLÄGT STEIN." Translated by Felix Pollak and the author.

132 This is the position of Fehervary in her article "Enlightenment or Entanglement: History and Aesthetics in Bertolt Brecht and Heiner Müller," *New German Critique* 8 (Spring 1976): 80–109; see especially p. 87. Contrarily, it has been observed with regard to "Tractor": "[Müller] liquidiert nicht den Mythos zugunsten der Geschichte, sondern läßt sich auf das Spiel zwischen beiden ein." See G. Schulz, p. 125.

133 See Heiner Müller, *Die Umsiedlerin oder Das Leben auf dem Lande* (Berlin, 1975), pp. 7–16, and *Germania Tod in Berlin* (Berlin, 1977), pp. 35–78, respectively.

134 Other such plays are "Leben Gundlings Friedrich von Preußen Lessings Schlaf Traum Schrei: Ein Greuelmärchen" ("Life of Gundling Frederick of Prussia Lessing's Sleep Dream Cry: A Tale of Horrors") and "Hamletmaschine" ("Hamlet Machine"); see *Spectaculum* 26 (Frankfurt, 1977): pp. 149–67 and Heiner Müller, *Mauser* (Berlin, 1978), pp. 89–97, respectively. For Müller's relationship to Camus and, specifically, *Le Mythe de Sisyphe*, see also Schulz, pp. 171, 175, who rightly adduces Müller's poem, "Bilder" ("Images"), from his *Geschichten aus der Produktion 2*, p. 7.

135 Thus Wilhelm Girnus in the aforementioned "Gespräch mit Heiner Müller"; cf. Müller, *Geschichten aus der Produktion 1*, p. 143.

136 Müller, *Geschichten aus der Produktion 2*, p. 24: "Wir hatten Schnaps, der Leutnant war bei Laune / Er sagte: sagt dem Bolschewiken, weil mir / Sein Bart gefällt, erlaub ich ihm, daß er / Sein letztes Loch auf seinem eignen Feld schippt." Translated by Felix Pollak and the author.

137 Ibid.: "Wir fragten, wo sein Feld ist. Sagt der Alte: / Hierallesmein-Feld. Wir: wo sein Feld war / Eh alles kollektiv war. Der zeigt bloß / Wie ein Großgrundbesitzer ins Gelände / Wo kilometerbreit brusthoch der Mais stand. / Der hatte wo sein Feld war glatt vergessen." Translated by Felix Pollak and the author.

138 Ibid.: "UND ALS VERLOREN WAR DIE SCHLACHT / SIE GINGEN HEIM DAS

SCHLACHTFELD IN DER BRUST / UND WURDE MANCHER NOCH ZU FALL
GEBRACHT / SICH SELBER WAFFE UND SICH SELBER FEIND. / UND SIEGTE
MANCHER DER SCHON NICHT MEHR WAR / WIE GRAS WÄCHST AUS DEN
TOTEN FRÜH IM JAHR." Translated by Felix Pollak and the author.

139 Jean Genet, *Le Balcon*, stand. ed. (Décines, 1966), p. 7.

140 Compare his expectorations, "Ich erlaube mir die Revolte," *Die Zeit*
(Overseas Edition) 8, Feb. 20, 1976. Actually, they constitute an interview with the provocative German novelist, Hubert Fichte.

141 What I have in mind is the dialectic of play and reality in revolutionary theater; see my "Spiel und Wirklichkeit in einigen Revolutionsdramen," in Grimm, *Nach dem Naturalismus*.

142 Marlies Menge, "Pfarrer für die Heiden: Eine Begegnung mit dem
DDR-Schriftsteller Reiner Kunze," *Die Zeit* (Overseas Edition) 48,
Nov. 26, 1976.

143 Ibid.: "Auge in Auge mit dem Nichts zu leben und im Bewußtsein
der Absurdität dieses Daseins Mensch sein zu wollen, sich als
Mensch zu erweisen."

144 See Volker Braun, *Es genügt nicht die einfache Wahrheit: Notate* (Frankfurt, 1976), pp. 19–20; but compare also his "Büchners Briefe" cited
in the introduction, n. 76.

145 See Wolfgang Schievelbusch's article of the same title, *New German
Critique* 2 (Spring 1974): 105–13.

146 This is not to belittle the historical role which has to be attributed to
Eugène Ionesco; see, for instance, the volume by various hands,
Sinn oder Unsinn? Das Groteske im modernen Drama, ed. Reinhold
Grimm et al. (Basel and Stuttgart, 1962). Significantly, a Czech ver-
sion appeared under the same title: *Smysl nebo nesmysl? Groteskno v
moderním dramatu* (Praha, 1966).

147 "Faksimile einer Notiz von Heiner Müller zu Antonin Artaud," in
Stücke der Zwanziger Jahre, ed. Wolfgang Storch (Frankfurt, 1977),
p. 132: "Artaud, die Sprache der Qual. Schreiben aus der Erfahrung,
daß die Meisterwerke Komplicen [*sic*] der Macht sind. Denken am
Ende der Aufklärung, das mit dem Tod Gottes begonnen hat, sie
der Sarg, in dem er begraben wurde, faulend mit dem Leichnam.
Leben, eingesperrt in diesen Sarg. / DAS DENKEN GEHÖRT ZU DEN
GRÖSSTEN VERGNÜGUNGEN DER MENSCHLICHEN RASSE läßt Brecht
Galilei sagen, bevor man ihm die Instrumente zeigt. Der Blitz, der
das Bewußtsein Artauds gespalten hat, war Nietzsches Erfahrung,
es könnte die letzte sein. Artaud ist der Ernstfall. Er hat die Literatur der Polizei entrissen, das Theater der Medizin. Unter der Sonne
der Folter, die alle Kontinente des Planeten gleichzeitig bescheint,
blühen seine Texte. Auf den Trümmern Europas gelesen, werden
sie klassisch sein." Translated by Felix Pollak and the author.

148 Compare especially Müller's "Hamletmaschine" as well as the hasty
and elaborate commentaries in *Die Hamletmaschine, Heiner Müllers
Endspiel*, ed. Theo Girshausen (Köln, 1978). For some objections,
see my article, "Eiszeit und Untergang: Zu einem Motiv in der
deutschen Gegenwartsliteratur," *Monatshefte* 73 (1981): 155–86. On

the other hand, it should be noted that Müller's "Hamletmaschine" appeared side by side, as it were, with his most radical formulation of the paradox of revolution and history in *dramatic* terms, "Mauser" (cf. Müller, *Mauser*, pp. 55–69). Also, compare his most recent play, *Der Auftrag: Erinnerung an eine Revolution* ("The Mission: Remembrance of a Revolution") of 1978, as well as Georg Wieghaus, *Heiner Müller* (München, 1981), pp. 7–8 et passim and G. Schulz, pp. 159–66 et passim. (Müller's paradox is mentioned repeatedly by the latter, as are his connections with Büchner; unfortunately, she still subsumes the revolutionary from Hesse under the undifferentiated heading, "nihilism" [cf. ibid., p. 47].) Above all, compare Müller's stunning variation on Gramsci's formula, "pessimism of the intellect, optimism of the will": "constructive defeatism" (*konstruktiver Defätismus*). It is, paradoxically, contained in his radical volume, *Mauser* (cf. ibid., p. 85).

149 Hans Magnus Enzensberger, *Mausoleum: Siebenunddreißig Balladen aus der Geschichte des Fortschritts* ("Mausoleum: Thirty-Seven Ballads from the History of Progress") (München, 1975), p. 117: "Der Text bricht ab, und ruhig rotten die Antworten fort." This is the concluding line, not only of the ballad devoted to Ché Guevara but of Enzensberger's entire volume which is, in effect, centered exclusively on the dialectics of enlightenment and the paradox of progress. For an evaluation of his position in general, see my various contributions, especially "Bildnis Hans Magnus Enzensberger: Struktur, Ideologie und Vorgeschichte eines Gesellschaftskritikers," *Basis* 4 (1973 [*recte* 1974]): 131–74; "Poetic Anarchism? The Case of Hans Magnus Enzensberger," *Modern Language Notes* 97 (1982): 745–58; "Das Messer im Rücken: Utopisch-dystopische Bildlichkeit bei Hans Magnus Enzensberger," in *Literarische Utopie-Entwürfe*, ed. Hiltrud Gnüg (Frankfurt, 1982), pp. 291–310. Compare also my introduction to Hans Magnus Enzensberger, *Critical Essays*, ed. Reinhold Grimm and Bruce Armstrong (New York, 1982), pp. xi–xvi. All these contributions have now been collected in my volume *Texturen: Essays und anderes zu Hans Magnus Enzensberger* (New York, Bern, and Frankfurt, 1984).

Chapter 2

1 *CCW* 48; cf. *HA* 35.

2 See Werner Schlick, *Das Georg-Büchner-Schrifttum bis 1965: Eine internationale Bibliographie* (Hildesheim, 1968) and Klaus-Dietrich Petersen, "Georg-Büchner-Bibliographie," *Philobiblon* 17 (1973): 89–115. Compare also Hinderer's *Büchner-Kommentar zum dichterischen Werk* (München, 1977), as well as Gerhard P. Knapp, *Georg Büchner* (Stuttgart, 1977).

3 Erwin Theodor [Rosenthal], "Büchners Grundgedanke: Sehnsucht nach Liebe," *Revista de Letras* 3 (1962): 201–13.

4 See Gonthier Louis-Fink, "Volkslied und Verseinlage in den Dramen Büchners," in Martens, pp. 442–87.

5 A few of them are quite useful. Particularly noteworthy, although by no means equal to each other in quality, are Bo Ullmann's chapter, "Marie und die Preisgabe der erotischen Utopie," in his *Die sozialkritische Problematik im Werke Georg Büchners und ihre Entfaltung im "Woyzeck": Mit einigen Bemerkungen zu der Oper Alban Bergs* (Stockholm, 1972), pp. 62ff. and 160ff., and Wolfgang Martens, "Zum Menschenbild Georg Büchners: 'Woyzeck' und die Marionszene in 'Dantons Tod,'" in Martens, pp. 373–85, as well as the studies of Swales and Reddick mentioned in the introduction, n. 86. I was unable to consult Ursula Segebrecht-Paulus, "Genuß und Leid im Werk Georg Büchners" (diss., München, 1969).

6 *CCW* 17; cf. *HA* 1, 9: "Sieh die hübsche Dame, wie artig sie die Karten dreht! ja wahrhaftig sie versteht's, man sagt sie halte ihrem Manne immer das cœur und andern Leuten das carreau hin. Ihr könntet einen noch in die Lüge verliebt machen."

7 Herbert Anton, *Büchners Dramen: Topographien der Freiheit* (Paderborn, 1975), p. 17—which means, as has been caustically noted, that the female lap (*Schoß*) is presented as a stage the masks of which conceal the "indestructible muttonhead" (*unverwüstlicher Schaafskopf*) of the masked god Dionysus (cf. Hinderer, p. 90).

8 *CCW* 18; cf. *HA* 1, 10: "Ich würde meine Tochter dergleichen nicht spielen lassen, die Herren und Damen fallen so unanständig übereinander und die Buben kommen gleich hinten nach."

9 Cf. *HA* 1, 41: "lieb Herz."

10 *CCW* 20; cf. *HA* 1, 11: "die gliederlösende, böse Liebe"; "nackte Götter, Bachantinnen [*sic*]"; "die Venus mit dem schönen Hintern." For the latter passage, see Hinderer, p. 93.

11 Ibid.: "Thürsteher der Republik."

12 Cf. *CCW* 124 and *HA* 1, 92–93: "Glückseligkeit"; "ruhig"; "Schicksal"; "centnerschwer auf dem Herzen."

13 *CCW* 125–26; cf. *HA* 1, 93: "fixe Idee"; "mit allem Jammer der Verzweiflung"; "Stehe auf und wandle!"

14 In one of the scattered fragments of *Leonce and Lena*, one finds the line: "Arise in your white dress and glide through the night and say to the corpse arise and walk!" (*Steh auf in deinem weißen Kleid u. schwebe durch die Nacht u. sprich zur Leiche steh auf und wandle!*) *HA* 1, 141.

15 *HA* 2, 423–24: "Ich bin allein, wie im Grabe; wann erweckt mich deine Hand? . . . Sie sagen, ich sei verrückt, weil ich gesagt habe, in sechs Wochen würde ich auferstehen, zuerst aber Himmelfahrt halten, in der Diligence nämlich."

16 *CCW* 117; cf. *HA* 1, 84–85: "Jetzt, ein anderes Seyn, göttliche, zuckende Lippen bückten sich über ihm nieder, und sogen sich an seine Lippen; er ging auf sein einsames Zimmer. Er war allein, allein! Da rauschte die Quelle, Ströme brachen aus seinen Augen, er krümmte sich in sich, es zuckten seine Glieder, es war ihm als müsse er sich auflösen, er konnte kein Ende finden der Wollust."

17 See *CCW* 160–61; cf. *HA* 1, 125.

18 *HA* 2, 426: "Ich glühte, das Fieber bedeckte mich mit Küssen und

umschlang mich wie der Arm der Geliebten. Die Finsterniß wogte über mir, mein Herz schwoll in unendlicher Sehnsucht, es drangen Sterne durch das Dunkel, und Hände und Lippen bückten sich nieder."

19 See Knapp, *Georg Büchner*, pp. 75ff., who provides further bibliographical references.

20 In this regard, a particularly prominent role is being played by Wolfgang Wittkowski, who has launched a full-scale campaign to "Christianize" Büchner; see his contributions listed in chapter 5, n. 26. The weakness of Wittkowski's approach is revealed specifically with regard to *Lenz* in an article by Heinrich Anz (see chapter 3, n. 37).

21 *CCW* 126; cf. *HA* 1, 93: "daß Gott ein Zeichen an ihm thue, und das Kind beleben möge." Once again, *Leonce and Lena* provides a corresponding text; *CCW* 160 and *HA* 1, 124:

> LENA. . . . The moon is like a sleeping child, its golden locks have fallen over its dear face.—Oh, its sleep is death. Look how the dead angel rests its dark pillow and the stars burn around it like candles. Poor child, are the bogeymen coming to get you soon? Where is your mother? Doesn't she want to kiss you once more? Ah, it's sad, dead, and so alone.
>
> LEONCE. Arise in your white dress and follow the corpse through the night and sing its requiem.
>
> (LENA. . . . *Der Mond ist wie ein schlafendes Kind, die goldnen Locken sind ihm im Schlaf über das liebe Gesicht heruntergefallen.—O sein Schlaf ist Tod. Wie der todte Engel auf seinem dunkeln Kissen ruht und die Sterne gleich Kerzen um ihn brennen. Armes Kind, kommen die schwarzen Männer bald dich holen? Wo ist deine Mutter? Will sie dich nicht noch einmal küssen? Ach es ist traurig, todt und so allein.*
>
> LEONCE. *Steh auf in deinem weißen Kleide und wandle hinter der Leiche durch die Nacht und singe ihr das Todtenlied.*)

Thus the final version. But originally Leonce continued in a manner reminiscent of Lenz (cf. *HA* 1, 141).

22 See the summary provided by Hermann Bräuning-Oktavio, *Georg Büchner: Gedanken über Leben, Werk und Tod* (Bonn, 1976), pp. 41ff.; the following two quotes are also taken from this book.

23 See Hinderer, p. 172.

24 See Bräuning-Oktavio, p. 42.

25 Gaston Salvatore, *Büchners Tod* (Frankfurt, 1972), pp. 75ff.; for a "generic" background of sorts, see my survey essay, "Dichter-Helden: 'Tasso,' 'Empedokles' und die Folgen," *Basis* 7 (1977): 7–25.

26 See, for instance, *Brechts Tui-Kritik*, ed. Wolfgang Fritz Haug (Karlsruhe, 1976). "Tui" is a playful *chinoiserie* of Brecht's, derived from "tellect-*uel*-in" = "*in*tellect*uel*."

27 The famous epithet, "the divine one," which has already been mentioned, also stems from Ariosto; see Peter Stafford's introduction to Pietro Aretino, *The Ragionamenti* (London, 1970), p. v.

28 See ibid., p. ix.

29 *CCW* 64; cf. *HA* 1, 49: "Dogge mit Taubenflügeln."

30 It appears that Büchner worked on his Aretino play in the summer or fall of 1836; see Knapp, *Georg Büchner*, p. 26 (who mistakenly writes "1837").

31 Bräuning-Oktavio, pp. 42, 46.

32 See *CCW* 31–32 and *HA* 1, 21–22; compare Aretino's declaration in Antonino Foschini, *L'Aretino* (Milano, 1951), p. 137: "E tu mi fai lagrimar di piacere solo a pensarti."

33 See ibid., p. 139: "O Iddio, salva Perina, ché io l'ho amata, l'amo e l'amerò sempre, finché la sentenza del dí novissimo giudicherà le vanità nostre." Although those quotes are taken from a biographical essay which is strongly novelistic, their content and, to some extent, their wording are based on Aretino's letters.

34 Stafford, p. viii. It appears that the Englishman knows nothing of Büchner and has never heard of the interesting as well as shocking if, admittedly, less significant "cinquecento drama" by Oskar Panizza, *Das Liebeskonzil* (*The Council of Love*), which first appeared in 1895.

35 There is a certain irony in the fact that, instead of Büchner's own work, we have his translation of a play which the same English critic judges to be "probably the worst drama" dealing with this period: Victor Hugo's *Lucrèce Borgia*; cf. ibid. and compare *HA* 1, 193ff.

36 See *CCW* 16; cf. *HA* 1, 8 and Benn, p. 135.

37 As to *Woyzeck*, compare in particular Klotz, *Geschlossene und offene Form im Drama*, p. 110 and Wilhelm Emrich, "Von Georg Büchner zu Samuel Beckett: Zum Problem einer literarischen Formidee," in *Aspekte des Expressionismus: Periodisierung · Stil · Gedankenwelt*, ed. Wolfgang Paulsen (Heidelberg, 1968), pp. 11–32. Both emphasize the circularity, the carrousel, the "world-wheel" (*Weltrad*) in the structure of *Danton's Death*. There are others, however, who reject this view or at least wish to modify it; see especially Benn, p. 254: "It has occasionally been suggested that the action of the play is circular, that the end is implicit in the beginning. This is evidently not so. The action has rather the form of a spiral ascending to an acme of tragic suffering." But he also states with regard to *Leonce and Lena*: "At the end of the play the situation—politically, psychologically, metaphysically—is still essentially the same as at the beginning" (ibid., p. 169). The same thesis is advanced by Richards, *Georg Büchner and the Birth of Modern Drama*, p. 114.

38 As for *Danton's Death*, there is a rather general reference to a "circular structure" (*struttura circolare*) in Giorgio Dolfini, *Il teatro di Georg Büchner* (Milano, 1961), p. 52. It is interesting to note that a similar structure can be detected in Heiner Müller's play *Germania Tod in Berlin*; see Schulz, p. 137.

39 See *CCW* 18, 95–96; cf. *HA* 1, 9, 75:

> DANTON. Nein Julie, ich liebe dich wie das Grab. . . . Die Leute
> sagen im Grab sey Ruhe und Grab und Ruhe seyen
> eins. Wenn das ist, lieg' ich in deinem Schooß schon
> unter der Erde. Du süßes Grab, deine Lippen sind Tod-
> tenglocken, deine Stimme ist mein Grabgeläute, deine
> Brust mein Grabhügel und dein Herz mein Sarg.
>
> LUCILE. (*tritt auf und setzt sich auf die Stufen der Guillotine*) Ich
> setze mich auf deinen Schooß, du stiller Todesengel. . . .
> Du liebe Wiege, die du meinen Camille in Schlaf gelullt,
> ihn unter deinen Rosen erstickt hast. / Du Todtenglocke,
> die du ihn mit deiner süßen Zunge zu Grabe sangst.

40 *CCW* 19; cf. *HA* 1, 11: "Särge zur Wiege haben."
41 Norman O. Brown, *Love's Body* (New York, 1966), p. 47; see also
   p. 42.
42 *CCW* 92; cf. *HA* 1, 72.
43 *CCW* 73; cf. *HA* 1, 73: "Schlafe, schlafe"; "Schlummer."
44 *CCW* 17; *HA* 1, 9: "wir sind sehr einsam."
45 *CCW* 55–56; cf. *HA* 1, 41.
46 It has been correctly pointed out that Danton's fears are "entirely
   inconsistent with his rational assumptions about death and what
   follows it" (cf. Richards, p. 55). When the same critic—in the same
   sentence, moreover—perceives in this an "essentially religious feeling," he errs grievously.
47 *CCW* 78–79; cf. *HA* 1, 61: "O Julie! Wenn ich *allein* ginge! Wenn sie
   mich einsam ließe! . . . Und wenn ich ganz zerfiele, mich ganz
   auflöste—ich wäre eine Handvoll gemarterten Staubes, jedes meiner
   Atome könnte nur Ruhe finden bey ihr. . . . Ich kann nicht sterben,
   nein, ich kann nicht sterben."
48 *CCW* 82; cf. *HA* 1, 64: "Da, bring ihm das und sag' ihm er würde
   nicht allein gehn. Er versteht mich schon und dann schnell zurück,
   ich will seine Blicke aus deinen Augen lesen."
49 *CCW* 85; *HA* 1, 67: "Ich werde nicht allein gehn, ich danke dir
   Julie."
50 See Hinderer, p. 90.
51 Ibid., p. 106; also, compare Josef Jansen, ed., *Erläuterungen und
   Dokumente [zu] Georg Büchner[s] 'Dantons Tod'* (Stuttgart, 1969),
   p. 10.
52 Benn, p. 138.
53 Ibid., p. 139.
54 *CCW* 96; cf. *HA* 1, 75:

> EIN BÜRGER. He werda?
> LUCILE. Es lebe der König!
> BÜRGER. Im Namen der Republik! (*Sie wird von der Wache um-
> ringt und weggeführt.*)

55 *CCW* 94; cf. *HA* 1, 74: "auf dem Boden des Korbes küssen."
56 See especially Helmut Koopmann, "Dantons Tod und die antike Welt: Zur Geschichtsphilosophie Georg Büchners," *Zeitschrift für deutsche Philologie* 84 (special issue, 1965): 22–41.
57 Clearly, the notions of a circular movement of history and a cyclical recurrence of that which has already been were not entirely foreign to the playwright. Not only the death of God and the rise of European nihilism, but also other elements of Nietzsche's thought were indisputably anticipated by Büchner. Yet can one proceed to read the "eternal recurrence of the same" (*ewige Wiederkehr des Gleichen*) into his works—especially since even Nietzsche's own use of the concept is far more complex than is commonly realized? It seems to me that one must be much more careful here and, in any event, differentiate with greater care, not only in regard to Büchner but also in regard to Heinrich Heine and Ludwig Börne, who are likewise forced into Koopmann's scheme.
58 *CCW* 306; cf. *HA* 2, 425–26.
59 Gramsci's *pessimismo dell'intelligenza, ottimismo della volontà* is also invoked—the text in question was first published in 1970—by Hans Magnus Enzensberger, *Palaver: Politische Überlegungen (1967–1973)* (*"Palaver: Political Considerations"*) (Frankfurt, 1974), p. 129. It would seem to be no accident that, five years earlier, this same critic had edited the radical pamphlet, *The Hessian Messenger*.
60 See *HA* 1, 141: ". . . Leben u. Liebe eins seyn lassen, daß die Liebe das Leben ist, und das Leben die Liebe."
61 They constitute a response by Leonce to Valerio's ironic question, "Marry?" (*Heirathen?*) Büchner apparently realized that this was too serious, too weighty for a comedy for he later struck the words. However, the fact that they express one of his basic concerns is established by the ensuing line, which was not struck, but only slightly altered: "Do you know, Valerio, that even the most insignificant human being is so great that life is far too short to love him?" (*Weißt du auch, Valerio, daß selbst der Geringste unter den Menschen so groß ist, daß das Leben noch viel zu kurz ist, um ihn lieben zu können?*) In the initial draft, this passage read: "Do you know, Valerio, that even he who is most insignificant is so great that human life is far too short to love him?" (*Weißt du auch Valerio, daß auch der Geringste so groß ist, daß das menschliche Leben viel zu kurz ist um ihn lieben zu können?*) See *CCW* 162 and *HA* 1, 126, 142.
62 See especially Martens, "Zum Menschenbild Georg Büchners"; however, Benn has also adopted this view to a large extent. Its inversion, a nonmoralistic judgment which simultaneously stresses the notion of eternal recurrence à la Koopmann, was provided early on by Walter Höllerer, "Büchner: Dantons Tod," in *Das deutsche Drama: Vom Barock bis zur Gegenwart. Interpretationen*, ed. Benno von Wiese (Düsseldorf, 1958), 2, pp. 65–88; here, p. 73.
63 *CCW* 32; cf. *HA* 1, 22: "das Einzige."

64 See Martens, p. 375.
65 See, for example, *HA* 2, 451–52.
66 See especially Karl Gutzkow, *Wally, die Zweiflerin*; Theodor Mundt, *Madonna, oder: Unterhaltungen mit einer Heiligen* (both published in 1835).
67 See *HA* 2, 444: "Marionetten mit himmelblauen Nasen und affectirtem Pathos"; "sogenannte Idealdichter" (from a letter to his family of July 28, 1835).
68 See Martens, p. 376; this is also the source of the ensuing quotation. At the same time, Martens fully realizes that it is mistaken to speak of a "Young German sensualism" (*jungdeutscher Sensualismus*) in regard to Büchner and his works (ibid., p. 380).
69 *CCW* 31; cf. *HA* 1, 21: "Meine Mutter war eine kluge Frau, sie sagte mir immer die Keuschheit sey eine schöne Tugend, wenn Leute in's Haus kamen und von manchen Dingen zu sprechen anfingen, hieß sie mich aus dem Zimmer gehn; frug ich was die Leute gewollt hätten so sagte sie mir ich solle mich schämen; gab sie mir ein Buch zu lesen so mußt ich fast immer einige Seiten überschlagen."
70 *CCW* 31–32; cf. *HA* 1, 21–22: "Ich gerieth in eine eigne Atmosphäre, sie erstickte mich fast. . . . Ein junger Mensch kam zu der Zeit in's Haus, er war hübsch und sprach oft tolles Zeug. . . . Endlich sahen wir nicht ein, warum wir nicht eben so gut zwischen zwei Bettüchern bei einander liegen, als auf zwei Stühlen neben einander sitzen durften. . . . Aber ich wurde wie ein Meer, was Alles verschlang und sich tiefer und tiefer wühlte. Es war für mich nur ein Gegensatz da, alle Männer verschmolzen in einen Leib. Meine Natur war einmal so, war kann da drüber hinaus?"
71 *CCW* 32; cf. *HA* 1, 22: "Er kam eines Morgens und küßte mich, als wollte er mich ersticken, seine Arme schnürten sich um meinen Hals, ich war in unsäglicher Angst. . . . Das war der einzige Bruch in meinem Wesen."
72 Ibid.: "Die andern Leute haben Sonn- und Werktage, sie arbeiten sechs Tage und beten am siebenten, sie sind jedes Jahr auf ihren Geburtstag einmal gerührt und denken jedes Jahr auf Neujahr einmal nach. Ich begreife nichts davon. Ich kenne keinen Absatz, keine Veränderung. Ich bin immer nur Eins. Ein ununterbrochnes Sehnen und Fassen, eine Gluth, ein Strom. . . . Es läuft auf eins hinaus, an was man seine Freude hat, an Leibern, Christusbildern, Blumen oder Kinderspielsachen, es ist das nemliche Gefühl, wer am Meisten genießt, betet am Meisten."
73 *CCW* 32–33; cf. *HA* 1, 22:

> DANTON. Warum kann ich deine Schönheit nicht ganz in mich fassen, sie nicht ganz umschließen?
> MARION. Danton, deine Lippen haben Augen.
> DANTON. Ich möchte ein Theil des Aethers seyn, um dich in meiner Fluth zu baden, um mich auf jeder Welle deines schönen Leibes zu brechen.

74 Ibid., pp. 21ff.

75 See Ullmann's study cited in n. 5 above.

76 Benn, p. 137. Even the charge of soullessness, which in this context is thoroughly odd, is flung at Marion by the otherwise perceptive critic (cf. ibid.): "But [Marion] has no soul." Many additional examples of this view could be adduced.

77 This is perhaps the place to state emphatically that my exacting and provocative criticism of the existing secondary literature on Büchner is not intended to obscure or denigrate its many significant accomplishments. I readily admit that I am indebted to other critics in various respects. However, a theme as complex and important as the one at hand must be pursued with complete freedom, indeed audacity, "wherever it may lead" (Benn, p. 3).

78 See Wolfgang Wittkowski, "Georg Büchner, die Philosophen und der Pietismus," *Jahrbuch des Freien Deutschen Hochstifts 1976* (Tübingen, 1976), p. 371: "Die Triebkraft des Unbewußten und die Begrenztheit des Erkennens fanden wir . . . bei Büchner. . . . Darüber hinaus praktizierte er letztere gegenüber Schopenhauer selbst (falls er ihn las)." Or ibid., p. 399: "In seiner Dissertation—leider [!] erst in der 2. Auflage nach Büchners Tod—kritisierte Schopenhauer . . ." —whereupon, as in the first instance, our critic blithely concludes that "perhaps here, too" (*vielleicht auch hier*) Büchner is speaking ironically from Schopenhauer's position. What speaks volumes is the use of "unfortunately" in regard to a text which was not even available "until . . . after Büchner's death" (assuming the latter 'failed' to find some way of reading it in spite of this).

79 Peter Weiss, *Dramen I* (Frankfurt, 1968), p. 244: "Denn was wäre schon diese Revolution / ohne eine allgemeine Kopulation." For the English version, see Peter Weiss, *Marat/Sade*, trans. Geoffrey Skelton, verse adaptation by Adrian Mitchell (New York, 1966), p. 92.

80 See Ullmann, pp. 64–65.

81 See Georg Büchner, *Dantons Tod and Woyzeck*, ed. with introduction and notes by Margaret Jacobs (Manchester, 1968), p. 119; the ensuing quotation is taken from the same source.

82 Regarding this and what follows, see Ullmann, pp. 64ff.

83 See especially the essay by Martens, "Zum Menschenbild Georg Büchners."

84 I should like to remind the reader that the relevant chapter in Ullmann's book is entitled, "Marie and the Abandonment of the Erotic Utopia"—as if the impossibility of realizing a utopia in the proletarian milieu of Woyzeck and Marie, that is to say, in the midst of the most extreme poverty and exploitation, could in any way refute this utopia!

85 *CCW* 32; cf. *HA* 1, 22: "Meine Mutter ist vor Gram gestorben, die Leute weisen mit Fingern auf mich. Das ist dumm."

86 *CCW* 161; cf. *HA* 1, 125: "Lieutenantsromantik."

87 *CCW* 32; cf. *HA* 1, 22: "ein dummer Streich." Büchner, however,

does not apply the term to the young man's suicide, but rather to his impulse, fed by passion and jealousy, to murder Marion, an impulse which he very nearly satisfies. Here again the "comic" parallel to *Woyzeck* is unmistakable.

88 See Friedrich Nietzsche, *Werke in drei Bänden*, ed. Karl Schlechta (München, 1954–56), 3, p. 739 (to which I have to resort in this case). Obviously, mine is a rather free, perhaps even daring, application of Nietzsche, who so conspicuously ignored Büchner. Nevertheless, I do not feel that this is unjustified. The two writers have far more in common than is generally supposed.

89 See *CCW* 21, 37, 45; cf. *HA* 1, 12, 25–26, 33: "Mühe"; "Arbeit"; "Handeln."

90 *CCW* 20; cf. *HA* 1, 12: "sie reiben mich mit ihrer Politik noch auf."

91 *CCW* 37; cf. *HA* 1, 26: "Deine Lippen sind kalt geworden, deine Worte haben deine Küsse erstickt." The image of suffocation is also employed by Lucile (cf. *CCW* 96 and *HA* 1, 75). It would be very useful to have detailed investigations of such clusters of words and images; see, for example, William Bruce Armstrong, "'Arbeit' und 'Muße' in den Werken Georg Büchners," in *GB III*, pp. 63–98.

92 For an opposing view, see Helmut Krapp, *Der Dialog bei Georg Büchner* (München, 1968), p. 141.

93 See Höllerer, p. 83 and, in a similar vein, Krapp, p. 141.

94 Hinderer, p. 98.

95 See Brown, p. 249.

96 Thus Krapp, *Georg Büchner*, p. 141; he is to be commended for having accurately recognized this aspect.

97 For the ensuing quotes, see Brown, pp. 307, 308.

98 *CCW* 51; cf. *HA* 1, 38: "Trägheit."

99 See Norman O. Brown, *Life Against Death: The Psychoanalytical Meaning of History* (Middletown, Conn., 1970), p. 322. The book was first published in 1959.

100 See Brown, *Love's Body*, p. 318.

101 First published in 1955. A brief report on Brown, Reich, and Marcuse as well as a massive condensation of their thought is contained in Jost Hermand, *Pop International: Eine kritische Analyse* (Frankfurt, 1971), pp. 72ff. Yet there are Marxist critics who take these trends very seriously; see, for example, the important study by the Czech theoretician Robert Kalidova, "Marx und Freud," in *Weiterentwicklungen des Marxismus*, ed. Willy Oelmüller (Darmstadt, 1977), pp. 130–89.

102 Simon, in his introduction to Georg Büchner, *Danton's Death*, p. 17.

103 *CCW* 20, 32; cf. *HA* 1, 12, 22: "Meine Natur war einmal so"; "Mein Naturell ist einmal so."

104 Richard Schechner, in his introduction to Georg Büchner, *Woyzeck*, p. 20.

105 See Ullmann, p. 70.

106 See ibid., pp. 75–76.

107 See Gonthier-Louis Fink, "Leonce und Lena: Komödie und Realis-

mus bei Georg Büchner," in Martens, pp. 488–506; here, pp. 495, 500, 505–6. Compare also Fink, "Volkslied und Verseinlage in den Dramen Büchners," p. 482: "failure of love" (*Versagen der Liebe*).
108 See Rosenthal, pp. 205–6. As for that contact with Julie, it has occurred long before the opening scene.
109 Even Martens is more cautious here. See his "Büchner: Leonce und Lena," in *Die deutsche Komödie: Vom Mittelalter bis zur Gegenwart*, ed. Walter Hinck (Düsseldorf, 1977), pp. 145–59; here, p. 156. Others, however, simply parrot the view to which I have referred.
110 See Fink, "Leonce und Lena," p. 500.
111 See Hinderer, p. 69.
112 Ibid., pp. 53, 60–61. Although I wonder if it is really necessary to regard Danton as the "negative counterpart" of his friend, Camille.
113 *CCW* 171; cf. *HA* 1, 133–34: "*Lena lehnt sich an ihn. . . .*"
114 *CCW* 145; cf. *HA* 1, 112: "Mein Gott, wieviel Weiber hat man nöthig, um die Scala der Liebe auf und ab zu singen? Kaum daß Eine einen Ton ausfüllt. Warum ist der Dunst über unsrer Erde ein Prisma, das den weißen Gluthstrahl der Liebe in einen Regenbogen bricht?"
115 It seems that primary responsibility for this must be assigned to the speculations advanced by the editor of the Insel edition of the *Woyzeck* fragment; see Georg Büchner, *Woyzeck: Texte und Dokumente*, ed. Egon Krause (Frankfurt, 1969).
116 *CCW* 182; cf. *HA* 1, 170: "vergeistert."
117 *CCW* 210; cf. *HA* 1, 148: "Aber Andres, sie war doch ein einzig Mädel."
118 *CCW* 194; cf. *HA* 1, 178.
119 *CCW* 200; cf. *HA* 1, 152: "Was du heiße Lippen hast! (heiß, heiß Hurenathem) und doch möcht' ich den Himmel geben sie noch eimal zu küssen. . . ."
120 Marie, referring to Woyzeck, goes on to draw the logical conclusion: "He'll go crazy with those thoughts of his." (*Er schnappt noch über mit den Gedanken*—see *CCW* 182 and *HA* 1, 170).
121 It must be admitted that the dead child whom Lenz wishes to bring back to life is never directly identified as being a girl; the suggestive name Friederike was added by the editor on the basis of Büchner's source material. At the same time, the transition from Lenz's memories to his mad deed is clearly underscored by the author in the line: "Meanwhile his *religious* torments continued." (*Unterdessen ging es fort mit seinen* religiösen *Quälereien*) (*CCW* 125 and *HA* 1, 92; my emphasis). Yet the close connection between this religiosity and the theme of love is established shortly thereafter when, in the midst of a spiritual conversation with Oberlin, Lenz suddenly begins to speak of Friederike (*CCW* 127 and *HA* 1, 94): "Lenz raised his head, wrung his hands and said: 'Ah! Ah! Divine consolation.' Then he suddenly asked affably how the lady was. Oberlin said he knew nothing about this, yet he would help and advise him in all things, but he must tell him the place, circumstances, and the name. He answered only in broken words: 'Ah, she's dead! Is she

still alive? You angel, she loved me—I loved her, she was worthy of it, oh, you angel. Damned jealousy, I sacrificed her—she still loved another—I loved her, she was worthy of it—oh, good mother, she loved me too. I'm a murderer." (*Lenz erhob das Haupt, rang die Hände, und sagte: 'Ach! ach! göttlicher Trost.' Dann frug er plötzlich freundlich, was das Frauenzimmer mache. Oberlin sagte, er wisse von nichts, er wolle ihm aber in Allem helfen und rathen, er müsse ihm aber Ort, Umstände und Person angeben. Er antwortete nichts wie gebrochene Worte: 'Ach sie ist todt! Lebt sie noch? du Engel, sie liebte mich—ich liebte sie, sie war's würdig, o du Engel. Verfluchte Eifersucht, ich habe sie aufgeopfert— sie liebte noch einen andern—ich liebte sie, sie war's würdig—o gute Mutter, auch die liebte mich. Ich bin ein Mörder.'*) It is clear that this self-accusation does not refer to his mother only, but also—and above all—to Friederike; see Roy C. Cowen, "Identity and Conscience in Büchner's Works," *Germanic Review* 43 (1968): 258–66; here, p. 261 ("his supposed murder of Friederike and his mother"). If this is the case, then we have an additional (albeit very subtle) connection to Lenz's attempt to raise the dead child; also, the objection that the child's name and sex are never revealed loses much of its impact. As for Woyzeck, we must consider whether his strange and meaningless epithet, *Zickwölfin* (which he uses to refer to Marie; *CCW* 195 and *HA* 1, 178), should not be read as *Fickwölfin* (literally, "fuck[she]wolf"), especially since the female wolf has traditionally been regarded as a symbol of lasciviousness. For the above objection as well as the ensuing reference, I am indebted to Peter Jansen (Chicago).

122 *CCW* 56; cf. *HA* 1, 41: "zu Bette."

123 The phrase, *das große, weiße, breite Bett*, is found at the end of Bertolt Brecht's play, *Trommeln in der Nacht* (*Drums in the Night*); see Brecht, 1, p. 123.

124 The question needs to be raised whether Danton really "betrays" Julie in the accepted sense of the word or whether she is not fully aware of her husband's "conduct." The impression conveyed by the play in its entirety seems to support the latter interpretation. Viewed from this perspective, Julie's "dear heart" would take on yet another dimension of meaning.

125 *CCW* 41; cf. *HA* 1, 29: "ein ausgemachter Spitzbube."

126 See n. 72 above.

127 See *CCW* 17, 31; cf. *HA* 1, 9, 21: "auf einem Schemel zu den Füßen von Julie"; "zu [seinen] Füßen."

128 See Herbert Kolb, "Das Melker Marienlied," in *Interpretationen mittelhochdeutscher Lyrik*, ed. Günther Jungbluth (Bad Homburg, 1969), pp. 47–82; Walter Johannes Schröder, *Die Soltane-Erzählung in Wolframs Parzival: Studien zur Darstellung und Bedeutung der Lebensstufen Parzivals* (Heidelberg, 1963), pp. 63ff.

129 See Egon Friedell, *Kulturgeschichte der Neuzeit: Die Krisis der europäischen Seele von der Schwarzen Pest bis zum Ersten Weltkrieg* (München, n.d.), 1, p. 128.

130 Mundt's novel cannot be equated with what Büchner has accomplished. True, it does attempt—with pedantic obtrusiveness—something similar. But here we see with particular clarity the difference, already alluded to, between Marion and marionettes, that is to say, between droning on and on about an idea, and giving it poetic form. Unlike Mundt, Büchner did not churn out hundreds of pages of "conversations" with a modern bluestocking. Instead, in the space of a page and a half, he provided an unforgettable *presentation* of the "holiness" of a "whore."

131 See Hinderer, p. 93.

132 Cf. *HA* 2, 464: "ich muß mich bald wieder an Deiner inneren Glückseligkeit stärken und Deiner göttlichen Unbefangenheit und Deinem lieben Leichtsinn und all Deinen bösen Eigenschaften, böses Mädchen. Adio [*sic*] piccola mia!"

133 For a discussion of all the relevant passages of this letter, including their parallels in *Danton's Death*, see chapters 1 and 5.

134 Compare *CCW* 171–72; cf. *HA* 1, 133–34.

135 *CCW* 8; cf. *HA* 2, 44–45: "Der Fürstenmantel ist der Teppich, auf dem sich die Herren und Damen vom Adel und Hofe in ihrer Geilheit übereinander wälzen. . . . Die Töchter des Volks sind ihre Mägde und Huren."

136 *CCW* 76; cf. *HA* 1, 59: "der Tugendhafte."

137 *CCW* 112, 117, 130, 134; cf. *HA* 1, 80, 85, 98, 101: "Leere"; "entsetzlich einsam"; "allein, allein"; "ganz allein."

138 *CCW* 151–52; cf. *HA* 1, 117: "Man geht ja so einsam und tastet nach einer Hand, die einen hielte, bis die Leichenfrau die Hände auseinandernähme und sie Jedem über der Brust faltete."

139 *CCW* 199; cf. *HA* 1, 151: "Es war eimal ein arm Kind und hat kei Vater und kei Mutter war Alles todt und war Niemand mehr auf der Welt. Alles todt, und es ist hingangen und hat greint Tag und Nacht. Und weil auf der Erd Niemand mehr war, wollt's in Himmel gehn, und der Mond guckt es so freundlich an und wie's endlich zum Mond kam, war's ein Stück faul Holz und da ist es zur Sonn gangen und wie's zur Sonn kam, war's ein verwelkt Sonneblum und wie's zu den Sterne kam, warens klei golde Mück, die waren angesteckt wie der Neuntödter sie auf die Schlehe steckt und wie's wieder auf die Erd wollt, war die Erd ein umgestürzter Hafen und war ganz allein und da hat sich's hingesetzt und geweint und da sitzt es noch und ist ganz allein."

140 See also the laconic couplet sung by a maid in *Lenz*; *CCW* 124 and *HA* 1, 92: "In all this world no joy for me, / I have a love, far off is he." Significantly, it has a strong effect on Lenz: "This crushed him, he almost dissolved from the sound." (*Auf dieser Welt hab' ich kein' Freud', / Ich hab' mein Schatz und der ist weit. / Das fiel auf ihn, er verging fast unter den Tönen.*)

141 *CCW* 33; cf. *HA* 1, 23.

142 Compare *CCW* 48 and *HA* 1, 35.

143 Compare *CCW* 194 and *HA* 1, 178.

144 *CCW* 86; cf. *HA* 1, 178.
145 *CCW* 168; cf. *HA* 1, 131: "Nichts als Kunst und Mechanismus, nichts als Pappendeckel und Uhrfedern."
146 Ibid.: "ein feines sittliches Gefühl"; "gar kein Wort für den Begriff Beinkleider."
147 Ibid.: "Mitglieder der menschlichen Gesellschaft"; "sehr edel"; "sehr moralisch."
148 Ibid.: "Geben Sie Acht, meine Herren und Damen, sie sind jetzt in einem interessanten Stadium, der Mechanismus der Liebe fängt an sich zu äußern, der Herr hat der Dame schon einige Mal den Shawl getragen, die Dame hat schon einige Mal die Augen verdreht und gen Himmel geblickt. Beide haben schon mehrmals geflüstert: Glaube, Liebe, Hoffnung! beide sehen bereits ganz accordirt aus, es fehlt nur noch das winzige Wörtchen: Amen."
149 *Heinrich Heines Sämtliche Werke*, ed. Ernst Elster (Leipzig and Wien, n.d.), 1, p. 233: "Sie schmachten gelinde / Und seufzen von Liebe, Hoffnung und Glauben." See also Jost Hermand, "Erotik im Juste Milieu: Heines 'Verschiedene,'" in *Heinrich Heine: Artistik und Engagement*, ed. Wolfgang Kuttenkeuler (Stuttgart, 1977), pp. 86–104.
150 *CCW* 31; cf. *HA* 1, 20–21: "Er sucht . . . die mediceische Venus stückweise bey allen Grisetten des palais royal zusammen, er macht Mosaik, wie er sagt."
151 See n. 70 above.
152 *CCW* 31; cf. *HA* 1, 21: "stückweise"; "zerstückelt."
153 As has been pointed out, Marion, according to a manuscript variant, comes "from a good family" (*aus guter Familie*) and was given "a careful upbringing" (*eine sorgfältige Erziehung*); see Martens, pp. 383–84, n. 21.
154 *CCW* 23; cf. *HA* 1, 14: "Ihr Hunger hurt und bettelt."
155 Ibid.: "mit den Töchtern des Volkes huren."
156 Lacroix concludes by urging: "Let's go to the Palais Royal" (*Gehn wir ins palais royal*) (*CCW* 31 and *HA* 1, 21).
157 *CCW* 29; cf. *HA* 1, 19: "dieße Marquis und Grafen der Revolution"; "reiche Weiber heirathen, üppige Gastmähler geben, spielen, Diener halten und kostbare Kleider tragen."
158 *CCW* 28; cf. *HA* 1, 19: "das Cainszeichen des Aristocratismus."
159 *CCW* 76; cf. *HA* 1, 59: "ein impotenter Mahomet."
160 See *CCW* 29, 76; cf. *HA* 1, 19, 59.
161 See Brecht, 5, p. 2148.
162 *CCW* 33; cf. *HA* 1, 22–23:

> (*Lacroix, Adelaide, Rosalie treten ein.*)
> LACROIX. (*Bleibt in der Thür stehn*) Ich muß lachen, ich muß lachen.
> DANTON. (*unwillig*) Nun?
> LACROIX. Die Gasse fällt mir ein.
> DANTON. Und?
> LACROIX. Auf der Gasse waren Hunde, eine Dogge und ein Bologneser Schooßhündlein, die quälten sich.

DANTON. Was soll das?
LACROIX. Das fiel mir nun grade so ein und da mußt' ich
    lachen.

163 In addition to Lehmann's edition, compare Georg Büchner, *Werke
    und Briefe: Gesamtausgabe*, ed. Fritz Bergemann (Frankfurt, 1953),
    p. 499; Hans Mayer, *Georg Büchner: Woyzeck* (Frankfurt and Berlin,
    1963), p. 42; Krause's edition of *Woyzeck*, p. 127.
164 Cf. *HA* 1, 348: "Ich hatt' en Hundele [und] das schnuffelt' an eim
    großen *Hut* u. konnt' nicht drauf und da hab' ich's ihm aus Gut-
    müthigkeit erleichtert und hab' ihn drauf gesezt. Und da standen
    die Leut herum und [remainder illegible]" (my emphasis).
165 Since the first publication of this conjecture in *GB I/II*, both a me-
    ticulous facsimile edition of the manuscripts and, based on them,
    a "reconstruction" of the play have been published: see Georg
    Büchner, *Woyzeck*, ed. Gerhard Schmid (Wiesbaden, 1981) and
    Georg Büchner, *Woyzeck*, ed. Henri Poschmann (Leipzig, 1984).
    Schmid as well as Poschmann (see pp. 11 and 53, respectively) ad-
    here to the standard reading "Hut"; hence I feel that it is all the
    more mandatory to propound my emendation, especially since
    Poschmann continues: "Und da stande die Bube [*lads*] herum und
    die Madeln [*lassies*]." For T. M. Mayer's endorsement of my conjec-
    ture, see the postface.

Chapter 3

1 Landau's essay was first published in 1909; a portion of it has been
    reprinted in Martens, pp. 16–81.
2 See especially Dietmar Goltschnigg, ed., *Materialien zur Rezeptions-
    und Wirkungsgeschichte Georg Büchners* (Kronberg, 1974), as well as
    Goltschnigg's monograph, *Rezeptions- und Wirkungsgeschichte Georg
    Büchners* (Kronberg, 1975).
3 See Georg Heym, *Dichtungen und Schriften: Gesamtausgabe*, ed. Karl
    Ludwig Schneider (Hamburg, 1960–64), 3, pp. 118, 124: "Büchner
    (den ich wenig kenne)"; "Georg Büchner erhalten und einen neuen
    Gott . . . auf den Altar gestellt."
4 Robert Walser, "Büchners Flucht," *Die Schaubühne* 8 (1912): 174.
5 See Edschmid's "Vorspiel," in his *Das rasende Leben* (Leipzig, 1915):
    "Ich widme dies Buch [meinem sehr großen toten Bruder Georg
    Büchner und] seinem . . . Andenken."
6 See Rilke, *Briefe*, 2, p. 26: "ein Schauspiel ohnegleichen"; "eine un-
    geheure Sache."
7 See Robert Musil, *Prosa, Dramen, späte Briefe*, ed. Adolf Frisé (Ham-
    burg, 1957), p. 604: "dichterische Vision."
8 Compare Cynthia Walk, *Hofmannsthals "Großes Welttheater": Drama
    und Theater* (Heidelberg, 1980), especially pp. 146ff.
9 Franz Theodor Csokor, *Gesellschaft der Menschenrechte: Stück um
    Georg Büchner* (Berlin, Wien, and Leipzig, 1929); Arnold Zweig,
    Lessing, Kleist, Büchner: Drei Versuche (Berlin, 1925).

10 Thus Knapp, *Georg Büchner*, p. 105.

11 Georg Büchner and Ludwig Weidig, *Der Hessische Landbote: Texte, Briefe, Prozeßakten*, with commentary by Hans Magnus Enzensberger (Frankfurt, 1965), p. 162.

12 Peter Schneider, *Lenz: Eine Erzählung* (Berlin, 1973); Volker Braun, *Unvollendete Geschichte* (Frankfurt, 1977) and "Büchners Briefe," in *GB III*, pp. 5–14. For more names and titles, see the listing in *Georg Büchner Jahrbuch* 1 (1981): 345.

13 Heiner Müller, "Der Auftrag: Erinnerung an eine Revolution," *Sinn und Form* 31 (1979): 1244–63.

14 Müller, *Geschichten aus der Produktion 1*, p. 83.

15 Cf. *HA* 2, 440, 442.

16 See Wilhelm Schulz's review-essay of 1851, reprinted in Grab, *Ein Mann, der Marx Ideen gab*; as for Adamov, see his *Ici et maintenant* (Paris, 1964), pp. 188, 217.

17 See Arthur Adamov, *L'Homme et l'enfant* (Paris, 1968), p. 130; also, compare his *Ici et maintenant*, p. 217.

18 Artaud, *Œuvres complètes*, 4, p. 119.

19 See Virmaux, *Antonin Artaud et le théâtre*, p. 111.

20 See Artaud, 3, pp. 229, 257; 5, pp. 33, 331–32.

21 See Virmaux, p. 111; in addition, compare Eric Sellin, *The Dramatic Concepts of Antonin Artaud* (Chicago and London, 1975), pp. 54ff.

22 Like myself, Guy Scarpetta is convinced that Brecht and Artaud "jouent ce rôle de pôles majeurs de la réflexion actuelle sur le théâtre" (p. 61), and Henri Gouhier even refers to them as the "deux maîtres" (p. 191). See also chapter 1, n. 20.

23 See Leo Gilson Ribeiro, *Cronistas do absurdo: Kafka, Büchner, Brecht* (Rio de Janeiro, 1964).

24 See chapter 1, nn. 21, 147.

25 See Heinz Wetzel, "Revolution and the Intellectual: Büchner's Danton and Koestler's Rubashov," *Mosaic* 10/4 (1977): 23–33.

26 Mayer, *Georg Büchner und seine Zeit*, p. 492.

27 Peter von Becker, "Die Trauerarbeit im Schönen: "Dantons Tod"—Notizen zu einem neu gelesenen Stück," in *Georg Büchner, Dantons Tod: Die Trauerarbeit im Schönen. Ein Theaterlesebuch* (Frankfurt, 1980), pp. 75–90; here, p. 76.

28 *CCW* 8; cf. *HA* 2, 44–45.

29 Ernst Johann, "Der Georg-Büchner-Preis 1923–1951," in *Der Georg-Büchner-Preis 1951–1978: Eine Ausstellung des Deutschen Literaturarchivs und der Deutschen Akademie für Sprache und Dichtung* (Darmstadt and Marbach, 1978), pp. 13–38; here, p. 17.

30 Peter Weiss, letter to me of 9 March 1982: "Seit Mitte der sechziger Jahre ist der Büchner-Preis tatsächlich immer in meiner Nähe gewesen und mir aus politischen Gründen entzogen worden. Ich weiß gar nicht, ob ich ihn heute überhaupt noch annehmen könnte."

31 Karl Viëtor, *Georg Büchner: Politik · Dichtung · Wissenschaft* (Bern, 1949).

32 See Mayer, *Georg Büchner und seine Zeit*, pp. 11, 443, 447.

33 Richard Thieberger, *Georges* [sic] *Büchner: La Mort de Danton,* published with the text of the sources and of the manuscript corrections of the author (Paris, 1953); Jean Auger-Duvignaud, *Georg Büchner, dramaturge* (Paris, 1954).

34 Ullmann, *Die sozialkritische Problematik im Werk Georg Büchners . . .* (cf. chapter 2, n. 5).

35 Dolfini, *Il teatro di Georg Büchner* (Milano, 1961).

36 *Studi tedeschi* 19/2 (1976).

37 Heinrich Anz, "'Leiden sey all mein Gewinnst': Zur Aufnahme und Kritik christlicher Leidenstheologie bei Georg Büchner," *Text und Kontext* 4, no. 3 (1976): 57–72.

38 See Benn.

39 See my review in *Educational Theatre Journal* 29 (1977): 126–27; also, compare the remarks by Knapp and Thomas Michael Mayer, in *GB I/II*, pp. 338, 441.

40 A. H. J. Knight, *Georg Büchner* (Oxford, 1951).

41 See Lindenberger's *Georg Büchner;* "*Danton's Death* and the Conventions of Historical Drama," *Comparative Drama* 3 (1969): 99–109, and *Historical Drama: The Relation of Literature and Reality* (Chicago and London, 1975).

42 Benjamin Bennett, *Modern Drama and German Classicism: Renaissance from Lessing to Brecht* (Ithaca and London, 1979), especially pp. 156ff.

43 *GB I/II.*

44 Rolf Michaelis, "Die Wahrheit unter dem Rock," *Die Zeit* no. 29 (July 20, 1979), p. 16.

45 Heinz Wetzel, in an offprint of his article, "Die Entwicklung Woyzecks in Büchners Entwürfen," *Euphorion* 74 (1980): 375–96: "Übrigens habe ich im Weimar nachgesehen. Es war ein *Hut,* ganz eindeutig. Ein Veterinär-Psychiater sagte mir, Hunde, vor allem kleine, seien oft Filz-Fetischisten." See my review of Georg Büchner, *Woyzeck,* ed. Schmid, in *Monatshefte* 74 (1982): 360–64; also, compare introduction, n. 86.

46 See *GB I/II*, pp. 299–326; also, compare the remarks of T. M. Mayer, ibid., p. 11. Thus when in a monograph on *Danton's Death* (which explicitly refers to the aforementioned volume) one encounters the contention that heretofore the appearance of women in this play, and the meaning they possess, has neither been discussed nor even mentioned, one can only conclude that the authors are deliberately misinforming their readers; see Alfred Behrmann and Joachim Wohlleben, *Büchner: Dantons Tod. Eine Dramenanalyse* (Stuttgart, 1980), pp. 166–67 n. 137.

47 T. M. Mayer, in *GB I/II*, p. 134.

48 H. Mayer, p. 476.

49 See Georg Jancke, *Georg Büchner: Genese und Aktualität seines Werkes* (Kronberg, 1975), p. 286; Erwin Kobel, *Georg Büchner: Das dichterische Werk* (Berlin and New York, 1974), pp. 3, 317.

50 See Kobel, p. 2; Wolfgang Wittkowski, *Georg Büchner: Persönlichkeit · Weltbild · Werk* (Heidelberg, 1978), p. 73 n. 3.

51 See Kobel, p. 2.
52 Ibid., p. 3; Wittkowski, p. 8.
53 See *GB I/II*, p. 390.
54 Hans-Thies Lehmann, "Dramatische Form und Revolution: Überlegungen zur Korrespondenz zweier Theatertexte. Georg Büchners *Dantons Tod* und Heiner Müllers *Der Auftrag*," in *Die Trauerarbeit im Schönen*, pp. 106–21; here, p. 121 n. 23.
55 See Georg Lukács, "Der faschistisch verfälschte und der wirkliche Georg Büchner," in Martens, pp. 197–224; here, p. 203. Also, compare Jancke, p. 120.
56 Kobel, p. 325.
57 See Lehmann, p. 117; as for Camille's words, compare *CCW* 50 and *HA* 1, 37.
58 See *GB I/II*, pp. 330–31.
59 See n. 44 above.
60 See T. M. Mayer, in *GB I/II*, p. 354.
61 Lehmann, p. 117.
62 See Hans Magnus Enzensberger, "Bescheidener Vorschlag zum Schutze der Jugend vor den Erzeugnissen der Poesie," *German Quarterly* 49 (1976): 425–37.
63 *HA* 2, 236.
64 See n. 16 above.
65 For a first survey and summary, see his "Büchner und Weidig," in *GB I/II*, pp. 16–298.
66 Ivan Nagel, "Verheißungen des Terrors: Vom Ursprung der Rede des Saint-Just in *Dantons Tod*," *Frankfurter Allgemeine Zeitung*, no. 296 (December 20, 1980), supplement.
67 The book in question is the anthology, *Die Trauerarbeit im Schönen* (cf. n. 27 above). Also included in it is the first part of Karl Marx's famous essay, "Der Achtzehnte Brumaire des Louis Bonaparte" ("The Eighteenth Brumaire of Louis Bonaparte"). However, the connection between this essay and Büchner's character, Simon the prompter, as well as the play's emphasis on the themes of theater and role playing is recognized neither here nor in the fine essay by Janis L. Solomon, "Büchner's *Dantons Tod*: History as Theater," *Germanic Review* 54 (1979): 9–19. See the essay on "Spiel und Wirklichkeit in einigen Revolutionsdramen" in my volume, *Nach dem Naturalismus* (cf. chapter 1, n. 20), pp. 141–84.
68 The most recent outgrowth of this kind of reception is Frederik Hetmann's narrative, *Georg B. oder Büchner lief zweimal von Gießen nach Offenbach und wieder zurück* ("Georg B. or Büchner Hurried Twice from Gießen to Offenbach and Back"). Hetmann, whose real name is Hans Christian Kirsch, states explicitly that his story was "decisively influenced" (*entscheidend beeinflußt*) by recent Büchner scholarship; cf. Frederik Hetmann, *Georg B. oder Büchner lief zweimal von Gießen nach Offenbach und wieder zurück: Zeit- und Lebensbild. Erzählung mit Dokumenten* (Weinheim and Basel, 1981), p. 156.
69 See, for instance, Becker, in *Die Trauerarbeit im Schönen*; but compare

also Dolf Oehler, "Liberté, Liberté, Chérie: Männerphantasien über die Freiheit—Zur Problematik der erotischen Freiheitsallegorie," ibid., pp. 91–105.

70 Becker, p. 81.

71 See Lehmann, p. 120.

72 H. Mayer, p. 477.

73 See Schulz as quoted in Grab's monograph, pp. 151ff. In order to guard against any misunderstanding, let me once again emphasize that it was not my intention to provide anything even remotely resembling an exhaustive analysis of the critical literature on Büchner. Thus the fact that I do not mention certain important works (for example, Walter Hinderer's *Büchner-Kommentar zum dichterischen Werk* [München, 1977]) should not be viewed as a value judgment on my part. For additional information, see Gerhard P. Knapp, *Georg Büchner: Eine kritische Einführung in die Forschung* (Frankfurt, 1975) and "Kommentierte Bibliographie zu Georg Büchner," in *GB I/II*, pp. 426–55; Thomas Michael Mayer, "Zu einigen neueren Tendenzen der Büchner-Forschung," in ibid., pp. 327–56 and "Zu einigen neueren Tendenzen der Büchner-Forschung: Ein kritischer Literaturbericht (Teil II: Editionen)," in *GB III*, pp. 265–311; Heinz Wetzel, "Ein Büchnerbild der siebziger Jahre: Zu Thomas Michael Mayer: 'Büchner und Weidig—Frühkommunismus und revolutionäre Demokratie,'" ibid., pp. 247–64.

Chapter 4

1 *CCW* 111; cf. *HA* 1, 79: "Den 20. ging *Lenz* durch's Gebirg" (my emphasis).

2 *Goethes Werke*, Hamburg edition in 14 vols., ed. Erich Trunz (Hamburg, 1948), 6, p. 65: "Nicht *einen* Augenblick der Fülle des Herzens, nicht *eine* selige Stunde! nichts! nichts! Ich stehe wie vor einem Raritätenkasten und sehe die Männchen und Gäulchen vor mir herumrücken, und frage mich oft, ob es nicht optischer Betrug ist. Ich spiele mit, vielmehr, ich werde gespielt wie eine Marionette und fasse manchmal meinen Nachbar an der hölzernen Hand und schaudere zurück. . . . Ich weiß nicht recht, warum ich aufstehe, warum ich schlafen gehe." For the English version, see Johann Wolfgang von Goethe, *The Sorrows of Young Werther and Selected Writings*, trans. Catherine Hutter (New York, 1962), p. 74.

3 Goethe, *Werther*, p. 63; cf. *Goethes Werke*, 6, p. 53: "Und so taumle ich beängstigt. Himmel und Erde und ihre webenden Kräfte um mich her: ich sehe nichts als ein ewig verschlingendes, ewig wiederkäuendes Ungeheuer."

4 Goethe, *Werther*, p. 92; cf. *Goethes Werke*, 6, p. 84: "Ich habe so viel, und . . . ohne sie wird mir alles zu Nichts."

5 Goethe, *Werther*, pp. 120–21; cf. *Goethes Werke*, 6, pp. 116–17: "Nein, Lotte, nein—Wie kann ich vergehen? Wir *sind* ja! . . . Ich träume nicht, ich wähne nicht! Nahe am Grab wird mir es heller.

Wir werden sein! wir werden uns wieder sehen!" The two ensuing quotes (*Vater* and *des Unendlichen*) are taken from the same passage.
6 See *CCW* 82, 85; cf. *HA* 1, 64, 67. Regarding "chaos" (*Chaos*) and "nothingness" (*Nichts*), see *CCW* 91 and *HA* 1, 72.
7 *Goethes Werke*, 6, pp. 533–34: "Wenn das *taedium vitae* den Menschen ergreift, so ist er nur zu bedauern, nicht zu schelten. Daß alle Symptome dieser wunderlichen, so natürlichen als unnatürlichen Krankheit auch einmal mein Innerstes durchrast haben, daran läßt *Werther* wohl niemand zweifeln. Ich weiß recht gut, was es mich für Entschlüsse und Anstrengungen kostete, damals den Wellen des Todes zu entkommen, so wie ich mich aus manchem spätern Schiffbruch auch mühsam rettete und mühselig erholte. . . . Ich getraute mir, einen neuen *Werther* zu schreiben, über den dem Volke die Haare noch mehr zu Berge stehn sollten als über den ersten."
8 See Hinderer, *Büchner-Kommentar*, passim.
9 Thus Anz in *Georg Büchner Jahrbuch* 1 (1981): 160–68; here, p. 163.
10 See Brecht, 5, p. 2*.
11 See Gerhard Schaub, *Georg Büchner und die Schulrhetorik: Untersuchungen und Quellen zu seinen Schülerarbeiten* (Bern and Frankfurt, 1975), pp. 65–66.
12 See T. M. Mayer, "Büchner und Weidig," p. 76.
13 Bräuning-Oktavio (cf. chapter 2, n. 22), p. 36.
14 See *HA* 2, 444.
15 See T. M. Mayer, p. 80. I should like to take this opportunity to express my gratitude to Dr. Mayer for the bibliographical information he so generously provided.
16 Hideo Nakamura, "Goethe und Büchner," *Gête Nenkan* 5 (1963): 141–50. The author kindly sent me the German summary of his article, which might be translated as follows: "In the literary generation of the 1830's, we encounter a consciousness of the 'end of the Goethean art-period' [*Ende der Goetheschen Kunstperiode*], indeed even a sort of insurrection against Goethe. Georg Büchner thought highly of Goethe, and in this respect he stands alone. The author seeks to elucidate the 'elective affinity' that existed between these two writers, as well as the differences which separate their concepts of art, history, and nature." Neither this summary nor the accompanying letter points to a treatment of our theme.
17 Hans Mayer, *Zur deutschen Klassik und Romantik* (Pfullingen, 1963), p. 309.
18 See Bräuning-Oktavio, pp. 36ff. and, more specifically, Otto Döhner, "Georg Büchners Naturauffassung" (diss., Marburg, 1967).
19 Hans-Jürgen Schings, *Der mitleidigste Mensch ist der beste Mensch: Poetik des Mitleids von Lessing bis Büchner* (München, 1980), pp. 68ff.
20 Most particularly in Jansen (cf. chapter 2, n. 51), pp. 94ff.
21 Wittkowski, *Georg Büchner*, pp. 234–35, n. 22.
22 See Johann Wolfgang von Goethe, "Egmont: A Tragedy," English version by Michael Hamburger, in *The Classic Theater*, ed. Eric Bent-

ley (Garden City, N.Y., 1959), 2, pp. 1–91; here p. 56. See *Goethes Werke*, 4, p. 420: "langfüßige, schmalleibige"; "dünne Fäden"; "Kreuzspinne." Compare *CCW* 41 and *HA* 1, 30: "dünne, auf der Tribüne herumzuckende Finger."

23 Bennett, *Modern Drama and German Classicism*, p. 158; the following quote is taken from the same page.

24 Hartmut Reinhardt, "Egmont," in *Goethes Dramen: Neue Interpretationen*, ed. Walter Hinderer (Stuttgart, 1980), pp. 122–43.

25 See my essay, "Spiel und Wirklichkeit in einigen Revolutionsdramen," which was first published in *Basis* 1 (1970): 49–93. This study has been stubbornly ignored by Büchner scholars, in spite of Hinderer's hint in his *Büchner Kommentar*, p. 90. But compare, at long last, Volker Bohn's essay, " 'Bei diesem genialen Cynismus wird dem Leser zuletzt ganz krankhaft pestartig zu Muthe': Überlegungen zur Früh- und Spätrezeption von 'Dantons Tod,'" in *GB III*, pp. 104–30; here, pp. 122, 130.

26 Bennett, p. 156; the ensuing quote is taken from the same page.

27 Ibid., p. 157 (the page numbers in the quote refer to volume 8 of the *Weimarer Ausgabe* of Goethe's works and to *HA* 1).

28 See Bennett, p. 158.

29 Ibid., p. 159.

30 See ibid., pp. 156, 158–59.

31 Goethe, "Egmont," p. 28; cf. *Goethes Werke*, 4, pp. 393–94.

> (*Egmont tritt auf mit Begleitung.*)
> EGMONT. Ruhig! Ruhig, Leute! Was gibt's? Ruhe! Bringt sie auseinander!
> ZIMMERMEISTER. Gnädiger Herr, Ihr kommt wie ein Engel des Himmels. Stille! seht ihr nichts? Graf Egmont! Dem Grafen Egmont Reverenz!

32 *CCW* 24–25; cf. *HA* 1, 15:

> (*Robespierre tritt auf, begleitet von Weibern und Ohnehosen.*)
> ROBESPIERRE. Was giebt's da Bürger? . . . Im Namen des Gesetzes! / . . .
> EIN WEIB. Hört den Messias, der gesandt ist zu wählen und zu richten . . . Seine Augen sind die Augen der Wahl, seine Hände sind die Hände des Gerichts!

33 Goethe, "Egmont," pp. 29–30; cf. *Goethes Werke*, 4, p. 395:

> JETTER. Hast du das Kleid gesehen? Das war nach der neuesten Art, nach spanischem Schnitt.
> ZIMMERMEISTER. Ein schöner Herr!
> JETTER. Sein Hals wäre ein rechtes Fressen für einen Scharfrichter.
> SOEST. Bist du toll? was kommt dir ein?

JETTER. Dumm genug, daß einem so etwas einfällt.—Es ist mir nun so. Wenn ich einen schönen langen Hals sehe, muß ich gleich wider Willen denken: Der ist gut köpfen,—Die verfluchten Exekutionen! man kriegt sie nicht aus dem Sinne.

34 *CCW* 41; cf. *HA* 1, 29: "Ein schöner Kopf. / . . . Er war der schöngemalte Anfangsbuchstaben der Constitutionsacte, wir haben dergleichen Zierrath nicht mehr nöthig, er wird ausgewischt."
35 *CCW* 95; cf. *HA* 1, 74–75:

ERSTES WEIB. Ein hübscher Mann, der Hérault.
ZWEITES WEIB. Wie er beym Constitutionsfest so am Triumphbogen stand da dacht' ich so, der muß sich gut auf der Guillotine ausnehmen, dacht' ich. Das war so ne Ahnung.
DRITTES WEIB. Ja man muß die Leute in allen Verhältnissen sehen, es ist recht gut, daß das Sterben so öffentlich wird.

36 See *CCW* 93; cf. *HA* 1, 73: "*Männer und Weiber singen und tanzen die Carmagnole*"; "Platz! Platz! Die Kinder schreien, sie haben Hunger. Ich muß sie zusehen machen, daß sie still sind. Platz!"
37 *CCW* 80; cf. *HA* 1, 63: "Ihr wollt Brod und sie werfen euch Köpfe hin. Ihr durstet und sie machen euch das Blut von den Stufen der Guillotine lecken."
38 Goethe, "Egmont," p. 61; cf. *Goethes Werke*, 4, p. 425: "ALBA. Aus dir spricht mein böser Genius."
39 *CCW* 64; cf. *HA* 1, 49: "MERCIER. (*zu Payne*) . . . Er ist der böse Genius der Revolution."
40 Goethe, "Egmont," pp. 38–39; cf. *Goethes Werke*, 4, p. 404: "Wer sollte wagen, Hand an uns zu legen? . . . Nein, sie wagen nicht, das Panier der Tyrannei so hoch aufzustecken. . . . Ich glaub's nicht."
41 *CCW* 45, 53; cf. *HA* 1, 33, 39: ". . . sie werden's nicht wagen. (*Zu Camille.*) Komm mein Junge, ich sage dir sie werden's nicht wagen. . . . Das ist leerer Lärm, man will mich schrecken, sie werden's nicht wagen."
42 *CCW* 45; cf. *HA* 1, 33:

PHILIPPEAU. Da geht er hin.
LACROIX. Und glaubt kein Wort von dem was er gesagt hat.

43 See Goethe, "Egmont," pp. 58–59; cf. *Goethes Werke*, 4, p. 423: "ALBA. Drum rasch . . ." Compare *CCW* 42; cf. *HA* 1, 30: "ROBESPIERRE. Dann rasch . . . !"
44 Goethe, "Egmont," p. 66; cf. *Goethes Werke*, 4, p. 429: "einzuengen, daß man sie wie Kinder halten, wie Kinder zu ihrem Besten leiten

kann"; "ein Volk wird nicht alt, nicht klug; ein Volk bleibt immer kindisch."

45 CCW 36; cf. HA 1, 25: "das Volk ist wie ein Kind, es muß Alles zerbrechen, um zu sehen was darin steckt."

46 See Goethe, "Egmont," p. 31; cf. Goethes Werke, 4, p. 397: "Ich bin des Hängens müde"; "wie die andern soll hängen lassen." Compare CCW 44; cf. HA 1, 32: "Ich hab es satt"; "lieber guillotinirt werden, als guillotiniren lassen"; ". . . wozu sollen wir Menschen miteinander kämpfen? Wir sollten uns nebeneinander setzen und Ruhe haben. Es wurde ein Fehler gemacht, wie wir geschaffen wurden, es fehlt uns etwas, ich habe keinen Namen dafür, wir werden es einander nicht aus den Eingeweiden herauswühlen, was sollen wir uns drum die Leiber aufbrechen? Geht, wir sind elende Alchymisten."

47 Goethes Werke, 3, p. 110; the following quotation (Schall und Rauch) is taken from the same page.

48 Goethe, "Egmont," p. 11; cf. Goethes Werke, 4, p. 377: "O was sind wir Großen auf der Woge der Menschheit? Wir glauben sie zu beherrschen, und sie treibt uns auf und nieder, hin und her."

49 See CCW 254; cf. HA 2, 425–26.

50 CCW 44; cf. HA 1, 32: "Du bist ein starkes Echo."

51 Goethe's Regent and Büchner's prostitute are, dramaturgically speaking, peripheral figures; indeed the former, although she is allowed to appear a second time, is even more isolated than the latter.

52 In connection with Klärchen, we also find the motif of the lover at the beloved's feet, a motif which Büchner utilized, as we have seen, in Danton's Death. Compare Goethe, "Egmont," p. 50; cf. Goethe's Werke, 4, p. 414.

53 See Goethes Werke, 11, p. 432: "Begriff der Volkommenheit des Geliebten"; "Entzücken"; "Genuß des Unbegreiflichen, daß dieser Mann ihr gehört."

54 CCW 51; cf. HA 1, 37–38:

CAMILLE. Was sagst du Lucile?
LUCILE. Nichts, ich seh dich so gern sprechen.
CAMILLE. Hörst mich auch?
LUCILE. Ey freilich.
CAMILLE. Hab ich Recht, weißt du auch, was ich gesagt habe?
LUCILE. Nein wahrhaftig nicht.

55 Goethe, "Egmont," p. 73; cf. Goethes Werke, 4, p. 436: "Meinst du, ich sei ein Kind, oder wahnsinnig?"

56 CCW 52; cf. HA 1, 38: "Mein Camille! das ist Unsinn, gelt, ich bin wahnsinnig?"

57 CCW 90; cf. HA 1, 70: "Was sie an dem Wahnsinn ein reizendes Kind geboren hat. Warum muß ich jezt fort? Wir hätten zusammen mit ihm gelacht, es gewiegt und geküßt."

58 Along with the rest of the Flemish nobility—who are referred to but never actually appear on stage.

59 See *Goethes Werke,* 12, p. 303: "bretterhafter."

60 See Goethe, "Egmont," pp. 51–52, 75; cf. *Goethes Werke,* 4, pp. 416, 438: "als wäre der Himmel mit einem schwarzen Flor überzogen und hinge so tief herunter, daß man sich bücken müsse, um nicht dran zu stoßen"; "des Grabes Vorbild"; "zwischen düstern Wänden eines Saals"; "die Balken der Decke"; "erdrückten."

61 See *CCW* 78, 85; cf. *HA* 1, 61, 66: "lebendig begraben"; "fünfzig Jahre lang am Sargdeckel"; "Will denn die Uhr nicht ruhen? Mit jedem Picken schiebt sie die Wände enger um mich, bis sie so eng sind wie ein Sarg. / Ich las einmal als Kind so n'e Geschichte, die Haare standen mir zu Berg."

62 *CCW* 85–86; cf. *HA* 1, 67:

> CAMILLE. Oh! (*Er hat sich aufgerichtet und tastet nach der Decke.*)
> DANTON. Was hast du Camille?
> CAMILLE. Oh, oh!
> DANTON. (*Schüttelt ihn.*) Willst du die Decke herunterkratzen?
> CAMILLE. Ach du, du, o halt mich, sprich, du!
> DANTON. Du bebst an allen Gliedern, der Schweiß steht dir auf der Stirne.
> CAMILLE. Das bist du, das ich, so! Das ist meine Hand! ja jezt besinn' ich mich. O Danton, das war entsezlich.
> DANTON. Was denn?
> CAMILLE. Ich lag so zwischen Traum und Wachen. Da schwand die Decke und der Mond sank herein, ganz nahe, ganz dicht, mein Arm erfaßt' ihn. Die Himmelsdecke mit ihren Lichtern hatte sich gesenkt, ich stieß daran, ich betastete die Sterne, ich taumelte wie ein Ertrinkender unter der Eisdecke. Das war entsezlich Danton.

63 See *Goethes Werke,* 10, p. 187.

64 Goethe, "Egmont," p. 35; cf. *Goethes Werke,* 4, pp. 400–401: "EG-MONT. . . . Wie von unsichtbaren Geistern gepeitscht, gehen die Sonnenpferde der Zeit mit unsers Schicksals leichtem Wagen durch; und uns bleibt nichts, als mutig gefaßt die Zügel festzuhalten, und bald rechts, bald links, vom Steine hier, vom Sturze da, die Räder wegzulenken. Wohin es geht, wer weiß es? Erinnert er sich doch kaum, woher er kam."

65 *CCW* 54–55; cf. *HA* 1, 40–41:

> JULIE. Du träumtest Danton. Faß dich.
> DANTON. Träumtest? ja ich träumte, doch das war anders, ich will dir es gleich sagen, mein armer Kopf ist schwach, gleich! so jezt hab ich's! Unter mir keuchte die Erdkugel in ihrem Schwung, ich hatte sie wie ein wildes Roß gepackt, mit riesigen Gliedern wühlt' ich in ihrer Mähne

und preßt' ich ihre Rippen, das Haupt abwärts gebückt,
die Haare flatternd über dem Abgrund. So ward ich ge-
schleift. Da schrie ich in der Angst, und ich erwachte.

66 Regarding this category, see especially Wolfgang Kayser, *Das Groteske: Seine Gestaltung in Malerei und Dichtung* (Oldenburg, 1957).
67 See *CCW* 55; cf. *HA* 1, 41.
68 Reinhardt, p. 131.
69 Goethe, "Egmont," p. 34; cf. *Goethes Werke*, 4, p. 399: "EGMONT.
Und doch berührt er immer diese Saite. Er weiß von alters her, wie
verhaßt mir diese Ermahnungen sind; sie machen nur irre, sie
helfen nichts. Und wenn ich ein Nachtwandler wäre und auf dem
gefährlichen Gipfel eines Hauses spazierte, ist es freundschaftlich,
mich beim Namen zu rufen und mich zu warnen, zu wecken und
zu töten? Laßt jeden seines Pfades gehn."
70 *CCW* 39–40; cf. *HA* 1, 28: "ROBESPIERRE. (*allein*) . . . Die Nacht
schnarcht über der Erde und wälzt sich im wüsten Traum. Gedanken, Wünsche kaum geahnt, wirr und gestaltlos, die scheu sich vor
des Tages Licht verkrochen, empfangen jezt Form und Gewand
und stehlen sich in das stille Haus des Traums. Sie öffnen die
Thüren, sie sehen aus den Fenstern, sie werden halbwegs Fleisch,
die Glieder strecken sich im Schlaf, die Lippen murmeln.—Und ist
nicht unser Wachen ein hellerer Traum, sind wir nicht Nachtwandler, ist nicht unser Handeln, wie das im Traum, nur deutlicher, be-
stimmter, durchgeführter? Wer will uns darum schelten?"
71 Reinhardt, p. 131. It must be added, however, that Reinhardt is mistaken when he limits this "fatalistic valence" to Robespierre's use of
the image of sleepwalking (ibid., p. 140, n. 61).
72 *CCW* 42; cf. *HA* 1, 30: "Blutmessias."
73 See Brecht, 15, pp. 105–6.
74 See once again Brecht, 5, p. 2*.
75 See Dieter Borchmeyer, "*Altes Recht* und Revolution: Schillers 'Wilhelm Tell,'" in *Friedrich Schiller: Kunst, Humanität und Politik in der
späten Aufklärung. Ein Symposium*, ed. Wolfgang Wittkowski (Tübingen, 1982), pp. 69–113; here, especially p. 72.
76 *CCW* 60–61; cf. *HA* 1, 46: "Die Revolution ist wie die Töchter des
Pelias; sie zerstückt die Menschheit um sie zu verjüngen. Die
Menschheit wird aus dem Blutkessel wie die Erde aus den Wellen
der Sündfluth mit urkräftigen Gliedern sich erheben, als wäre sie
zum Erstenmale geschaffen. (*Langer, anhaltender Beyfall. Einige Mitglieder erheben sich im Enthusiasmus.*) / Alle geheimen Feinde der Tyrannei, welche in Europa und auf dem ganzen Erdkreise den Dolch
des Brutus unter ihren Gewändern tragen, fordern wir auf dießen
erhabenen Augenblick mit uns zu theilen. (*Die Zuhörer und die De-
putirten stimmen die Marseillaise an.*)"
77 Goethe, "Egmont," pp. 99–100; cf. *Goethes Werke*, 4, pp. 453–54:
"für die Freiheit"; "Braves Volk! Die Siegesgöttin führt dich an! Und
wie das Meer durch eure Dämme bricht, so brecht, so reißt den

Wall der Tyrannei zusammen und schwemmt ersäufend sie von ihrem Grunde, den sie sich anmaßt, weg! . . . Es blinken Schwerter—Freunde, höhren Mut! Im Rücken habt ihr Eltern, Weiber, Kinder! (*Auf die Wache zeigend.*) Und diese treibt ein hohles Wort des Herrschers, nicht ihr Gemüt. Schützt eure Güter! Und euer Liebstes zu erretten, fallt freudig, wie ich euch ein Beispiel gebe. (*Trommeln. Wie er auf die Wache los und auf die Hintertür zu geht, fällt der Vorhang; die Musik fällt ein und schließt mit einer Siegessymphonie das Stück.*)"

78 CCW 96; cf. *HA* 1, 75.

79 Ibid.: "Es ist ein Schnitter, der heißt Tod, / Hat Gewalt vom höchsten Gott. / . . . Viel hunderttausend ungezählt / Was nur unter die Sichel fällt."

80 Goethe, "Egmont," p. 90; cf. *Goethes Werke*, 4, p. 454: "rings umgeben vom drohenden Tod"; "das mutige Leben nur doppelt rasch zu fühlen."

81 Friedrich Schiller, *Sämtliche Werke*, based on the original printing, ed. Gerhard Fricke and Herbert G. Göpfert (München, 1958), 5, p. 942: "Salto mortale in eine Opernwelt."

82 As to the imaginary title, "Egmont's Death," see also Jürgen Schröder, "Poetische Erlösung der Geschichte—Goethes *Egmont*," in *Geschichte als Schauspiel: Deutsche Geschichtsdramen. Interpretationen*, ed. Walter Hinck (Frankfurt, 1981), pp. 101–15; here, p. 110.

83 See especially chapter 2.

84 I Corinthians 15:55.

85 Goethe, "Egmont," p. 90; cf. *Goethes Werke*, 4, p. 453: "leidend opfre."

86 Ibid., p. 76; cf. *Goethes Werke*, 4, p. 439: "Geschick"; "Glück."

87 Ibid., p. 77; cf. *Goethes Werke*, 4, p. 440: "Unzuverlässigkeit"; "Welt"; "Wankelmut."

88 Letter of May 14, 1778; quoted in *Goethes Werke*, 4, p. 562: "wie die Großen mit den Menschen und die Götter mit den Großen *spielen*" (my emphasis).

89 Constraints of space prevent me from offering a detailed discussion of these connections; even a study limiting itself to a comparison of Gryphius's *Carolus Stuardus* and *Egmont* would prove to be most instructive.

90 See chapter 3, n. 13; also, compare Lehmann's "Dramatische Form und Revolution" (chapter 3, n. 54) as well as the supplementary remarks to my "Georg Büchner und der moderne Begriff der Revolte," *Georg Büchner Jahrbuch* 1 (1981): 22–67; here, p. 67.

91 See Borchmeyer, who also provides valuable insights regarding *Egmont*.

92 See *Goethes Werke*, 1, p. 47.

93 Goethe, "Egmont," p. 89; cf. *Goethes Werke*, 4, p. 452: "ungehindert fließt der Kreis der inneren Harmonien."

94 Schings, pp. 71–72 (my emphasis).

95 *CCW* 126; cf. *HA* 1, 94: "Lenz mußte laut lachen, und mit dem Lachen griff der *Atheismus* in ihn und faßte ihn ganz sicher und ruhig und fest" (my emphasis).
96 *CCW* 130; cf. *HA* 1, 98: "Er hatte *Nichts.*"
97 *CCW* 61; *HA* 1, 47: "*Es giebt keinen Gott.*"
98 *CCW* 75; cf. *HA* 1, 58: "Perioden."
99 The complete text of Philippeau's speech reads as follows: "My friends, one needn't stand very far above the earth to see nothing more of all this confused vacillation and flickering and to have one's eyes filled with a small number of great, divine forms. There is an ear for which cacophony and deafening outcries are a *stream of harmonies.*" (*Meine Freunde man braucht gerade nicht hoch über der Erde zu stehen um von all dem wirren Schwanken und Flimmern nichts mehr zu sehen und die Augen von einigen großen, göttlichen Linien erfüllt zu haben. Es giebt ein Ohr für welches das Ineinanderschreien und der Zeter, die uns betäuben, ein* Strom von Harmonien *sind.*) *CCW* 91 and *HA* 1, 71 (my emphasis). Clearly, my little montage accurately reflects the meaning of the passage and is therefore permissible.
100 *CCW* 91; cf. *HA* 1, 71–72:

> DANTON. Aber wir sind die armen Musicanten und unsere Körper die Instrumente. Sind die häßlichen Töne, welche auf ihnen herausgepfuscht werden nur da um höher und höher dringend und endlich leise verhallend wie ein wollüstiger Hauch in himmlischen Ohren zu sterben?
>
> HÉRAULT. Sind wir wie Ferkel, die man für fürstliche Tafeln mit Ruthen todtpeitscht, damit ihr Fleisch schmackhafter werde?
>
> DANTON. Sind wir Kinder, die in den glühenden Molochsarmen dießer Welt gebraten und mit Lichtstrahlen gekitzelt werden, damit die Götter sich über ihr Lachen freuen?
>
> CAMILLE. Ist denn der Aether mit seinen Goldaugen eine Schüssel mit Goldkarpfen, die am Tisch der seeligen Götter steht und die seeligen Götter lachen ewig und die Fische sterben ewig und die Götter erfreuen sich ewig am Farbenspiel des Todeskampfes?

101 *CCW* 91; cf. *HA* 1, 72: "Die Welt ist das *Chaos.* Das *Nichts* ist der zu gebärende Weltgott" (my emphasis).
102 Nietzsche, *Werke,* 5/2, p. 255: "Das größte neuere Ereigniß—daß 'Gott todt ist' . . .—beginnt bereits seine ersten Schatten über Europa zu werfen." For the English version, see Friedrich Nietzsche, *The Gay Science,* trans. with commentary by Walter Kaufmann (New York, 1974), p. 279.
103 Ibid., p. 181; cf. Nietzsche, *Werke,* 5/2, p. 159 ("Der tolle Mensch"):

"Wir haben ihn getödtet,—ihr und ich! Wir Alle sind seine Mörder! Aber wie haben wir dieß gemacht? Wie vermochten wir das Meer auszutrinken? Wer gab uns den Schwamm, um den ganzen Horizont wegzuwischen? Was thaten wir, als wir diese Erde von ihrer Sonne losketteten? Wohin bewegt sie sich nun? Wohin bewegen wir uns? Fort von allen Sonnen? Stürzen wir nicht fortwährend? Und rückwärts, seitwärts, vorwärts, nach allen Seiten? Giebt es noch ein Oben und ein Unten? Irren wir nicht wie durch ein unendliches *Nichts?* Haucht uns nicht der leere Raum an? Ist es nicht kälter geworden? Kommt nicht immerfort die Nacht und mehr Nacht? Müssen nicht Laternen am Vormittage angezündet werden?" (The first emphasis occurs in the original, the second is mine.)

104 See the overview offered by Bernhard Böschenstein, "Umrisse zu drei Kapiteln einer Wirkungsgeschichte Jean Pauls: Büchner— George—Celan," *Jahrbuch der Jean-Paul-Gesellschaft* 10 (1975): 187– 204. For a modern, even modernistic, reading of Jean Paul's "Speech of the Dead Christ," see Alice A. Kuzniar, "The Bounds of the Infinite: Self-Reflection in Jean Paul's 'Rede des todten Christus,'" *German Quarterly* 57 (1984): 183–96; Kuzniar does not discuss, however, its relationship to Büchner.

105 For the most part, even specialists are familiar only with §99 of *Menschliches, Allzumenschliches II: Der Wanderer und sein Schatten* (*Human, All-Too-Human: The Wanderer and His Shadow*) in which Jean Paul is summarily—and caustically—described as a "fatality in a morning-gown" (*Verhängniß im Schlafrock*); see Nietzsche, *Werke,* 4/3, p. 235. There is, however, an early autobiographical note in which Nietzsche admits that Jean Paul's life quite attracted him. "The fragments of his works that I have read," he goes on to declare, "strongly attract me with their lush, effusive descriptions, delicate thoughts, and satirical wit. I believe that at some point when I am more mature Jean Paul will become my favorite [!] author." (*Die Bruchstücke seines Werkes, die ich gelesen habe, ziehen mich ungemein durch die blühende, überschwengliche Schilderung, die zarten Gedanken und den satirischen Witz an. Ich glaube, Jean Paul wird einmal bei reiferen Jahren mein Lieblingsschriftsteller.*) See Nietzsche, *Werke in drei Bänden,* 3, pp. 63–64. Additional comments made by Nietzsche in "more mature" years (comments which, by the way, are mostly positive in tone) also attest to a detailed knowledge of Jean Paul and his work; see Nietzsche, *Werke* 3/2, p. 327; 4/3, pp. 446, 471; 6/2, p. 192.

106 This is also true of the first aphorism I quoted (n. 102 above).

107 *Jean Pauls Sämtliche Werke,* historical–critical edition, ed. Preußische Akademie der Wissenschaften (Weimar, since 1927), 1. Abteilung, 6, p. 247: "[das] ganze geistige Universum"; "durch die Hand des Atheismus zersprengt und zerschlagen in zahllose quecksilberne Punkte von Ichs, welche blinken, rinnen, irren, zusammen und auseinander fliehen, ohne Einheit und Bestand."

108 Ibid., p. 248: "dieselbe Nothwendigkeit, die in diesem Leben meinen

lichten Thautropfen von Ich in einen Blumenkelch und unter eine
Sonne warf, kann es ja im zweiten wiederholen:—ja noch leichter
kann sie mich zum zweiten male verkörpern als zum ersten male."
109 "Das größte Schwergewicht"; see Nietzsche, *Werke*, 5/2, p. 250.
110 "Was es mit unserer *Heiterkeit* auf sich hat" (cf. n. 102 above; my
emphasis).
111 See, for example, *Ecce homo* ("Der Fall Wagner," §4): "amor fati ist
meine innerste Natur" (Nietzsche, *Werke*, 6/3, p. 361); also, cf. ibid.,
p. 434.
112 Thus Uwe Schweikert, *Jean Paul* (Stuttgart, 1970), p. 21.
113 Jean Paul, 6, p. 249:

> Ich . . . erwachte auf dem Gottesacker [und] suchte im ausge-
> leerten Nachthimmel die Sonne, weil ich glaubte, eine Son-
> nenfinsternis verhülle sie mit dem Mond. Alle Gräber waren
> aufgethan, und die eisernen Thüren des Gebeinhauses gin-
> gen unter unsichtbaren Händen auf und zu. An den Mauern
> flogen Schatten, die niemand warf, und andere Schatten gin-
> gen aufrecht in der bloßen Luft. In den offenen Särgen schlief
> nichts mehr als die Kinder. Am Himmel hing in großen Falten
> blos ein grauer schwüler Nebel, den ein Riesenschatte wie ein
> Netz immer näher, enger und heißer herein zog. Ueber mir
> hört' ich den fernen Fall der Lauwinen, unter mir den ersten
> Tritt eines unermeßlichen Erdbebens. Die Kirche schwankte
> auf und nieder von zwei unaufhörlichen Mistönen, die in ihr
> miteinander kämpften und vergeblich zu einem Wohllaut zu-
> sammenfließen wollten. Zuweilen hüpfte an ihren Fenstern
> ein grauer Schimmer hinan, und unter dem Schimmer lief
> das Blei und Eisen zerschmolzen nieder.

"Alle Schatten"; "um den Altar"; "statt des Herzens die Brust";
"Zifferblatt der *Ewigkeit*."
114 Jean Paul, 6, p. 250:

> Jetzo sank eine hohe edle Gestalt mit einem unvergäng-
> lichen Schmerz aus der Höhe auf den Altar hernieder, und
> alle Todten riefen: "Christus! ist kein Gott?"
> Er antwortete: "es ist keiner."
> Der ganze Schatten jedes Todten erbebte, nicht blos die
> Brust allein, und einer um den andern wurde durch das Zit-
> tern zertrennt.
> Christus fuhr fort: "ich ging durch die Welten, ich stieg in
> die Sonnen und flog mit den Milchstraßen durch die Wüsten
> des Himmels; aber es ist kein Gott. Ich stieg herab, so weit
> das Sein seine Schatten wirft, und schauete in den Abgrund
> und rief: "Vater, wo bist du?" aber ich hörte nur den ewigen
> Sturm, den niemand regiert, und der schimmernde Regen-
> bogen aus Wesen stand ohne eine Sonne, die ihn schuf, über

dem Abgrunde und tropfte hinunter. Und als ich aufblickte zur unermeßlichen Welt nach dem göttlichen *Auge*, starrte sie mich mit einer leeren bodenlosen *Augenhöle* an; und die Ewigkeit lag auf dem Chaos und zernagte es und wieder- käuete sich.—Schreiet fort, Mistöne, zerschreiet die Schat- ten; denn Er ist nicht!"

Die entfärbten Schatten zerflatterten, wie weißer Dunst, den der Frost gestaltet, im warmen Hauche zerrinnt; und alles wurde leer. Da kamen, schrecklich für das Herz, die ge- storbenen Kinder, die im Gottesacker erwacht waren, in den Tempel und warfen sich vor die hohe Gestalt am Altare und sagten: "Jesus! haben wir keinen Vater?"—Und er antwortete mit strömenden Thränen: "wir sind alle Waisen, ich und ihr, wir sind ohne Vater."

Da kreischten die Mistöne heftiger—die zitternden Tempel- mauern rückten auseinander—und der Tempel und die Kin- der sanken unter—und die ganze Erde und die Sonne sanken nach—und das ganze Weltgebäude sank mit seiner Uner- meßlichkeit vor uns vorbei—und oben am Gipfel der uner- meßlichen Natur stand Christus und schauete in das mit tau- send Sonnen durchbrochne Weltgebäude herab, gleichsam in das in die ewige Nacht gewühlte Bergwerk, in dem die Son- nen wie Grubenlichter und die Milchstraßen wie Silberadern gehen.

115 Jean Paul, 6, 251: "groß wie der höchste Endliche"; "die Augen empor gegen das *Nichts* und die leere Unermeßlichkeit"; "Starres, stummes *Nichts*! Kalte, ewige Nothwendigkeit! Wahnsinniger Zu- fall! . . . Wann zerschlagt ihr das Gebäude und mich?"
116 Ibid.: "Wie ist jeder so *allein* in der weiten Leichengruft des Alls!" (my emphasis).
117 Ibid., p. 252:

Und als ich niederfiel und ins leuchtende Weltgebäude blickte, sah ich die emporgehobenen Ringe der Riesenschlange der Ewigkeit, die sich um das Welten-All gelagert hatte—und die Ringe fielen nieder, und sie umfaßte das All doppelt—dann wand sie sich tausendfach um die Natur—und quetschte die Welten aneinander—und drückte zermalmend den unend- lichen Tempel zu einer Gottesacker-Kirche zusammen—und alles wurde eng, düster, bang—und ein unermeßlich ausge- dehnter Glockenhammer sollte die letzte Stunde der Zeit schlagen und das Weltgebäude zersplittern. . . . als ich erwachte.

Meine Seele weinte vor Freude, daß sie wieder Gott an- beten konnte—und die Freude und das Weinen und der Glaube an ihn waren das Gebet. Und als ich aufstand, glimmte die Sonne tief hinter den vollen purpurnen Kornähren und warf friedlich den Wiederschein ihres Abendrothes dem kleinen Monde zu, der ohne eine Aurora im Morgen aufstieg; und zwischen dem Himmel und der Erde streckte eine frohe vergängliche Welt ihre kurzen Flügel aus und lebte, wie ich, vor dem unendlichen Vater; und von der ganzen Natur um mich flossen friedliche Töne aus, wie von fernen Abendglocken.

118 Ibid., p. 247: "Das Ziel dieser Dichtung ist die Entschuldigung ihrer Kühnheit."

119 Ibid.: "Wenn einmal mein Herz so unglücklich und ausgestorben wäre, daß in ihm alle Gefühle, die das Dasein Gottes bejahen, zerstöret wären: so würd' ich mich mit diesem meinem Aufsatz erschüttern und—er würde mich heilen und mir meine Gefühle wiedergeben."

120 CCW 199; cf. HA 1, 151: "arm Kind."

121 For the complete text, see chapter 2, and n. 139.

122 "Des todten Shakespears [sic] Klage unter todten Zuhörern in der Kirche, daß kein Gott sei"; see Kurt Schreinert's introduction to Jean Paul, 4; here, p. l.

123 I have lifted this phrase in a free—though by no means inappropriate—manner from Nietzsche's aphorism, "The Meaning of Our Cheerfulness" (see n. 102 above). The "parallelism" between the "intellectual [geistig] revolution in Germany" and the "material revolution in France" was first perceived—or, at least, first pronounced—by Büchner's contemporary, Heinrich Heine. His Zur Geschichte der Religion und Philosophie in Deutschland ("On the History of Religion and Philosophy in Germany"), which dates from 1834–35, contains a famous passage dealing with the death of God. In it, one encounters the following lines: "On both sides of the Rhine, we see the same break with the past; all respect for tradition has been withdrawn. Here in France, every law must justify its existence, and the same holds true in Germany for every idea; here, the monarchy, the keystone of the old social order, is collapsing, while in Germany the same thing is happening to deism, the keystone of the old intellectual order." (Auf beiden Seiten des Rheines sehen wir denselben Bruch mit der Vergangenheit, der Tradition wird alle Ehrfurcht aufgekündigt; wie hier in Frankreich jedes Recht, so muß dort in Deutschland jeder Gedanke sich justifizieren, und wie hier das Königtum, der Schlußstein der alten sozialen Ordnung, so stürzt dort der Deismus, der Schlußstein des alten geistigen Regimes.) See Heines Sämtliche Werke, ed. Elster, 4, p. 245.

124 "Wie von einer neuen Morgenröthe angestrahlt"; "Verdüsterung und Sonnenfinsterniß"; "deren Gleichen es wahrscheinlich noch nicht auf Erden gegeben hat" (see n. 102 above).

125 Goethe, "Egmont," p. 90; cf. Goethes Werke, 4, p. 453: "göttlich."

126 "Vorausverkünder . . . dieser ungeheuren Logik von Schrecken" (see n. 102 above).

127 CCW 62; cf. HA 1, 48: "Verstand consequent zu gebrauchen weiß

[und] wagt"; Nietzsche, *Werke*, 5/2, p. 256: "daß der 'alte Gott todt' ist."

128 *CCW* 63; cf. *HA* 1, 48: "warum leide ich? Das ist der Fels des Atheismus. Das leiseste Zucken des Schmerzes und rege es sich nur in einem Atom, macht einen Riß in der Schöpfung von oben bis unten."

Chapter 5

1 *CCW* 199. For the German text, see chapter 2, n. 139.
2 See Benn, pp. 234, 260–61.
3 Ibid., pp. 244–45.
4 See ibid., p. 239.
5 *CCW* 186–87; cf. *HA* 1, 1, 172: "Unseins ist doch einmal unseelig in der und der andern Welt, ich glaub' wenn wir in Himmel kämen so müßten wir donnern helfen."
6 *CCW* 224; cf. *HA* 1, 164: "Sehn sie so ein schön, festen groben Himmel, man könnte Lust bekomm, ein Kloben hineinzuschlagen und sich daran zu hänge."
7 See Knapp (chapter 3, n. 73), p. 118.
8 See Schweikert, p. 32, who even calls it "die vermutlich erste dichterische Gestaltung des Nihilismus in der europäischen Literatur."
9 Benn, p. 233.
10 Ibid.
11 Gottfried Benn, *Gesammelte Werke in vier Bänden*, 3, p. 68: "Theogonien— / von den Dingen der Welt / ziehn Melancholien / an der Sterne Zelt, / weben Götter und Drachen, / singen Brände und Baal, / sinnvoll zu machen / Knechtschaft und Qual." Translated by Felix Pollak and the author.
12 For more details, see the commentary in Friedrich Wilhelm Wodtke's edition of Gottfried Benn, *Selected Poems* (Oxford, 1970), pp. 135–36, to which I am indebted here.
13 Gottfried Benn, *Gesammelte Werke*, 3, pp. 68–69: "Wie mußten sie alle leiden, / um so zum Traum zu fliehn, / und sein des Kummers Weiden / wie hier die Algonkin! / Auch anderen Tieren, Steinen / vertrauten sie ihren Tod / und gingen hin zu weinen / die Völker, weiß und rot." Translated by Felix Pollak and the author.
14 See Wodtke, pp. 135–36.
15 Benn, pp. 233–34.
16 Compare ibid., p. 14 et passim.
17 For a critical discussion of this position, see my article, "Bewußtsein als Verhängnis: Über Gottfried Benns Weg in die Kunst," in *Die Kunst im Schatten des Gottes: Für und wider Gottfried Benn*, ed. Wolf-Dieter Marsch and Reinhold Grimm (Göttingen, 1962), pp. 40–84.
18 See Gottfried Benn, *Gesammelte Werke*, 3, p. 135: "Wer allein ist—."
19 In particular, compare Benn's commemorative speech, "Nietzsche—nach fünfzig Jahren," in his *Gesammelte Werke*, 1, pp. 482–93. As to Nietzsche, see, for example, *Werke*, 5/2, p. 20.

20 *CCW* 85; cf. *HA* 1, 67: "Wie schimmernde Thränen sind die Sterne durch die Nacht gesprengt, es muß ein großer Jammer in dem Aug seyn, von dem sie abträufelten."
21 See Knapp (chapter 3, n. 73), pp. 161–62.
22 Büchner, *Werke und Briefe* (chapter 2, n. 163), pp. 297–98: "Wir haben der Schmerzen nicht zu viel, wir haben ihrer zu wenig, denn durch den Schmerz gehen wir zu Gott ein!—Wir sind Tod, Staub, Asche, wie dürften wir klagen?" For the English version, see Benn, p. 72.
23 Büchner, *Werke und Briefe*, pp. 297–98.
24 See Benn, pp. 72–73.
25 See ibid., pp. 69–74.
26 Compare, for instance, Wolfgang Wittkowski's impassioned contributions, "Georg Büchners Ärgernis," *Jahrbuch der deutschen Schillergesellschaft* 17 (1973): 362–83; "Georg Büchner, die Philosophen und der Pietismus: Umrisse eines neuen Büchnerbildes," *Jahrbuch des Freien Deutschen Hochstifts 1976* (Tübingen, 1976), pp. 352–419; *Georg Büchner: Persönlichkeit · Weltbild · Werk* (Heidelberg, 1978). For a brief critical assessment of the latter, see my review in *German Studies* [Section III], 16 (1983): 43–45.
27 *CCW* 42; cf. *HA* 1, 31: "Wahrlich des Menschensohn [*sic*] wird in uns Allen gekreuzigt, wir ringen Alle im Gethsemanegarten im blutigen Schweiß, aber es erlöst Keiner den Andern mit seinen Wunden."
28 *CCW* 78; cf. *HA* 1, 61: "Das Nichts hat sich ermordet, die Schöpfung ist seine Wunde, wir sind seine Blutstropfen, die Welt ist das Grab worin es fault."
29 Ibid.: "Das lautet verrückt, es ist aber doch was Wahres daran."
30 Compare especially chapter 4. One could, for instance, supplement Büchner's "last words" with what might be called Danton's "last philosophical statement": "The world is chaos. Nothingness is the world-god yet to be born." (*Die Welt ist das Chaos. Das Nichts ist der zu gebärende Weltgott.*) As a consequence, not only would all creation, the life of mankind as well as the world as such, become a mere chaos of suffering, death, dust, and ashes, but God Himself would in fact, even in Büchner's pronouncement, be equated with nothingness. Actually, what the dying man wanted to say would simply amount to the insight: 'Through pain we enter into nothingness.' Which doesn't "sound crazy" at all, for in a previous utterance Danton, Büchner's *alter ego* in this regard, had expressly confessed that he yearned for "peace . . . in nothingness" (*Ruhe / . . . Im Nichts*). "Try to immerse yourself in something more peaceful than nothingness," he had told Philippeau, "and if God is the greatest peace, isn't nothingness God" (*Versenke dich in was Ruhigers, als das Nichts und wenn die höchste Ruhe Gott ist, ist nicht das Nichts Gott*)? These words are addressed to the proponent of Christianity or, at least, a kind of Christian deism—a belief decidedly *not* shared by Danton. He immediately continues: "But I'm an atheist" (*Aber ich*

bin ein Atheist). Shortly thereafter, he pronounces that sequence about nothingness having killed itself, from which we departed. Cf. *CCW* 78, 91; cf. *HA* 1, 61, 72.

31 Primarily, perhaps exclusively, Benn drew upon Camus's theoretical and historical work, *L'Homme révolté* of 1951, while ignoring Camus's earlier philosophical treatise, *Le Mythe de Sisyphe* of 1942 which, significantly, bears the additional title, *Essai sur l'absurde*. See chapter 1.

32 *CCW* 119–20; cf. *HA* 1, 87.

33 *CCW* 50; cf. *HA* 1, 37.

34 *CCW* 48; cf. *HA* 1, 35. As to the preceding quote, see *CCW* 49 and *HA* 1, 36: "Muthe mir nur nichts Ernsthaftes zu."

35 *CCW* 199; cf. *HA* 1, 151. Contrary to the editor, however, I still find *verwelkt* more convincing (and actually more in keeping with the general tone of the fairy tale) than *verreckt*. The former reading is also supported by the facsimile edition cited in chapter 2, n. 165 (see p. 6).

36 *CCW* 48; cf. *HA* 35: "Ich wittre was in der Athmosphäre [*sic*], es ist als brüte die Sonne Unzucht aus. / Möchte man nicht drunter springen, sich die Hosen vom Leibe reißen und sich über den Hintern begatten wie die Hunde auf der Gasse?"

37 *CCW* 49; cf. *HA* 1, 36: "Ich begreife nicht warum die Leute nicht auf der Gasse stehen bleiben und einander in's Gesicht lachen. Ich meine sie müßten zu den Fenstern und zu den Gräbern heraus lachen und der Himmel müsse bersten und die Erde müsse sich wälzen vor Lachen."

38 *CCW* 194; cf. *HA* 1, 178: "Warum bläßt Gott nicht die Sonn aus, daß Alles in Unzucht sich übernanderwälzt, Mann und Weib, Mensch und Vieh. Thut's am hellen Tag, thut's einem auf den Händen, wie die Mücken."

39 Ibid.: "Das Weib ist heiß, heiß!—Immer zu, immer zu. . . . Der Kerl! Wie er an ihr herumtappt, an ihrem Leib, er, *er hat sie wie ich zu Anfang*" (my emphasis).

40 Compare also what Lacroix says about the "girls," i.e., prostitutes, who "sit in the sun" and thus invite "the flies [to] do it on their hands" (*Die Mädel guckten aus den Fenstern, man sollte vorsichtig seyn und sie nicht einmal in der Sonne sitzen lassen, die Mücken treiben's ihnen sonst auf den Händen, das macht Gedanken*). As we have seen, similar "food for thought" is provided—in the same scene, incidentally— by that other remark of Lacroix's: "There were dogs on the street, a Great Dane and an Italian lapdog—they were trying to have a go at it." Not only is this remark reminiscent of Danton's words about "copulating . . . like dogs in the street," but it is in fact connected by Lacroix, shrewdly yet unmistakably, to the love-making between Danton and Marion. Compare *CCW* 33; cf. *HA* 1, 22–23.

41 See ibid.

42 Or, to be more precise, Büchner's "religion of pleasure" (*Genußreligion*). See Heinz Lipmann, *Georg Büchner und die Romantik* (Mün-

chen, 1923), but compare also Martens, especially p. 380. That Martens categorically rejects Lipmann's one-sided view while advocating, in equally one-sided manner, the very opposite thereof is quite indicative, both of the prevailing methods and of certain ideologies.

43 Between these two sentences, Marion merely interjects, "Danton, your lips have eyes." For a detailed discussion of this enigmatic image, see chapter 2.

44 Or, to be more precise, "theology of pain" (*Leidenstheologie*), even "religion of the Cross" (*Religion des Kreuzes*). See, for instance, the Wittkowskian contributions cited above, but compare also the objections raised by Anz in his excellent little article of 1976 (cf. chapter 3, n. 37) so conspicuously ignored in Wittkowski's book of 1978.

45 *CCW* 86; cf. *HA* 1, 67: "[Das Leben] ist eine Hure, es treibt mit der ganzen Welt Unzucht."

46 The phrasing, as will be remembered, is Norman O. Brown's.

47 *CCW* 32; cf. *HA* 1, 22: "Da kam ein Haufe die Straße herab, die Kinder liefen voraus, die Weiber sahen aus den Fenstern. Ich sah hinunter, sie trugen ihn in einem Korb vorbei, der Mond schien auf seine bleiche Stirn, seine Locken waren feucht, er hatte sich ersäuft."

48 *CCW* 92; cf. *HA* 1, 72–73: "Komm liebster Priester, dessen Amen uns zu Bette gehn macht. / (*Sie tritt ans Fenster.*) Es ist so hübsch Abschied zu nehmen, ich habe die Thüre nur noch hinter mir zuzuziehen. (*Sie trinkt.*) / Man möchte immer so stehn. Die Sonne ist hinunter. Der Erde Züge waren so scharf in ihrem Licht, doch jezt ist ihr Gesicht so still und ernst wie einer Sterbenden. Wie schön das Abendlicht ihr um Stirn und Wangen spielt. / Stets bleicher und bleicher wird sie, wie eine Leiche treibt sie abwärts in der Fluth des Aethers; will denn kein Arm sie bey den goldnen Locken fassen und aus dem Strom sie ziehen und sie begraben? / Ich gehe leise. Ich küsse sie nicht, daß kein Hauch, kein Seufzer sie aus dem Schlummer wecke. / Schlafe, schlafe. (*Sie stirbt.*)"

49 Compare especially the motif and/or imagery of drowning in both cases.

50 Similarly, the light plays just as lovingly on the sun's "forehead and cheeks" as Danton wishes tenderly to caress Marion.

51 "Le ciel est triste et beau comme un grand reposoir; / Le soleil s'est noyé dans son sang qui se fige." Baudelaire's poem, "Harmonie du soir," bears the number xlvii in his famous collection; for the English version quoted see Charles Baudelaire, *The Flowers of Evil*, trans. William Aggeler (Fresno, 1954), p. 165. However, we must not overlook that *reposoir* also denotes a "sofa" or "couch," (i.e., a "resting-place"). It is obvious that Baudelaire was playing on this ambiguity.

52 See the first stanza of Hölderlin's great elegy, "Brod und Wein" ("Bread and Wine"), and compare in particular the following lines: ". . . then high-fantastical Night comes, / Crowned with stars, and

(it seems) little regardful of us, / Lost in her wondering gaze, among mankind but a stranger, / Over the mountain peaks sadly and splendidly shines." (. . . *die Schwärmerische, die Nacht kommt,* / *Voll mit Sternen, und wohl wenig bekümmert um uns* / *Glänzt die Erstaunende dort, die Fremdlingin unter den Menschen* / *Über Gebirgeshöhn traurig und prächtig herauf.*) *Selected Poems of Friedrich Hölderlin* (cf. chapter 1, n. 104), p. 93. Once more a conscious ambiguity is at work here; for *die Erstaunende* is also to be understood as *die Staunen Erregende,* the one that "makes us wonder." See Friedrich Hölderlin, *Sämtliche Gedichte: Studienausgabe in zwei Bänden,* ed. with commentary by Detlev Lüders (Bad Homburg, 1970), 2, p. 251.

53 In addition, see the essay on "Georg Trakls Sonne" in my volume, *Strukturen: Essays zur deutschen Literatur* (Göttingen, 1963), pp. 146–71.

54 See Benn, pp. 14, 17ff., et passim. But though Benn speaks of Büchner's "most extraordinary paradox" he does not really expand it beyond the realm of history and revolution. As has been shown, Büchner's fourth dimension remained, for the most part, alien and inaccessible to him.

55 CCW 50; cf. HA 1, 37: "um und in [uns]."

56 But compare also n. 30 above. A similar digression could be provided, *mutatis mutandis,* on Marion's prayers and her evaluation of *Christusbilder* ("icons"). They are as remote from blasphemy in a traditional sense as is Büchner's "God" from any such piety.

57 Only the author from Chile writing in German, Gaston Salvatore, appears to have realized at least some of this interchangeability; see his *Büchners Tod,* especially pp. 63ff., 75, where Minna, Büchner's fiancée, turns into Imperia, the most famous courtesan of her time.

58 Compare, for instance, Camille's reference to "God's creatures" (*Gottes Geschöpfe*) (see CCW 50 and HA 1, 37).

59 For these as well as the following quotations, see CCW 211; cf. HA 1, 149: "Was ist der Mensch? Knochen! Staub, Sand, Dreck. Was ist die Natur? Staub, Sand, Dreck. Aber die dummen Menschen, die dummen Menschen. Wir müssen Freunde seyn. . . . Was ist das? Bein, Arm, Fleisch, Knochen, Adern? Was ist das? Dreck? Was steckt's im Dreck? Laß ich den Arm so abschneide? nein. Der Mensch is egoistisch, aber haut, schießt, sticht, hurt. (*Er schluchzt.*) Wir müssen. Freunde ich bin gerührt. Seht ich wollte unsre Nasen wärn zwei Bouteillen und wir könnten sie uns einander in den Hals gießen. Ach was die Welt schön ist! Freund! ein Freund! Die Welt! (*Gerührt.*) Seht die Sonn kommt zwischen de Wolke hervor, als würd e potchambre ausgeschütt. (*Er weint.*)" Schmid in his facsimile edition suggests a number of different readings, notably *hi-[nein]* for *hurt* (cf. p. 4).

60 Henry J. Schmidt has: "When will it be dirt?" Whether he tacitly emended the text (*wann* instead of *was*) or not, his rendering is hardly convincing. Granted, the *Woyzeck* manuscripts are ex-

tremely difficult to decipher. But if indeed one feels that an emendation is necessary, I should rather suggest to insert a comma: *Was[,] steckt's im Dreck?* However, there is no need for that. When compared with other passages in *Woyzeck* and, in particular, with the usage of *was* in Hessian dialect (cf. the barber's *Ach was die Welt schön ist*), then this sentence makes perfectly good sense. It might perhaps be paraphrased by something like: *Wie, steckt's im Dreck?* As to *steckt's*, Büchner himself offers the clue (cf. *CCW* 161): . . . *da steckt's! da!* Schmidt has rendered these words quite correctly: "There—that's where it is." The reading in the facsimile edition (p. 4: "Wo[rin] steckts, im Dreck?") amounts to the same basic meaning as does my own conjecture.

61 The atmospheric phenomenon behind the barber's image is what in English is called—or so I am told—"the sun's eyelashes." In German, the term is *Wasserziehen*, or more often, *die Sonne zieht Wasser.*

62 Compare *CCW* 206 and *HA* 1, 146 (the announcer) as well as *CCW* 218 and *HA* 1, 177 (the apprentices).

63 *CCW* 254; cf. *HA* 2, 425–26: "Ich studirte die Geschichte der Revolution. Ich fühlte mich wie zernichtet unter dem gräßlichen Fatalismus der Geschichte. Ich finde in der Menschennatur eine entsetzliche Gleichheit, in den menschlichen Verhältnissen eine unabwendbare Gewalt, Allen und Keinem verliehen. Der Einzelne nur Schaum auf der Welle, die Größe ein bloßer Zufall, die Herrschaft des Genies ein Puppenspiel, ein lächerliches Ringen gegen ein ehernes Gesetz, es zu erkennen das Höchste, es zu beherrschen unmöglich. Es fällt mir nicht mehr ein, vor den Paradegäulen und Eckstehern der Geschichte mich zu bücken. Ich gewöhnte mein Auge ans Blut. Aber ich bin kein Guillotinenmesser. Das *muß* ist eins von den Verdammungsworten, womit der Mensch getauft worden. Der Ausspruch: es muß ja Aergerniß kommen, aber wehe dem, durch den es kommt,—ist schauderhaft. Was ist das, was in uns lügt, mordet, stiehlt? Ich mag dem Gedanken nicht weiter nachgehen." Note that an *Eck[en]steher* (lit., "one standing at a corner") was a witty idler occupying some street corner, and commenting on the daily events, whereas "cornerstone(s)" would be *Eckstein(e)* in German. However, since Büchner is clearly satirizing the great figures of history by ironically likening them to such idlers, Schmidt's translation of an otherwise untranslatable term is quite justified.

64 Compare, for instance, Schmidt's remarks in *CCW* 254.

65 Compare also Luke 17:1.

66 *CCW* 55; cf. *HA* 1, 41: "Der Mann am Kreuze hat sich's bequem gemacht: es muß ja Aergerniß kommen, doch wehe dem, durch welchen Aergerniß kommt. / Es muß, das war dieß Muß. Wer will der Hand fluchen, auf der der Fluch des Muß gefallen? Wer hat das *Muß* gesprochen, wer? Was ist das, was in uns hurt, lügt, stiehlt und mordet? / Puppen sind wir von unbekannten Gewalten am

Draht gezogen; nichts, nichts wir selbst! Die Schwerter, mit denen Geister kämpfen, man sieht nur die Hände nicht, wie im Mährchen."

67 Cf. *HA* 2, 426. Deceptively enough, this fantasy is couched in the language of mysticism—a language largely erotic, anyhow. See also chapter 2.

68 *CCW* 55–56; cf. *HA* 1, 41: "Jetzt bin ich ruhig."—"Ganz ruhig, lieb Herz?"—"Ja, Julie, komm, zu Bette!"

69 See my essay on "Spiel und Wirklichkeit in einigen Revolutionsdramen." A short English version entitled "The Play within a Play in Revolutionary Theatre" is contained in *Mosaic* 9/1 (1975): 41–52.

70 *CCW* 225 and *HA* 1, 165.

71 *CCW* 210; *HA* 1, 148: "Was kann der liebe Gott nicht, was? Das Geschehene ungeschehn machen. Hä hä hä!—Aber es ist eimal so, und es ist gut, daß es so ist. Aber besser ist besser."

72 Cf. Genesis 1, 10ff.

73 Cf. *HA* 2, 463.

74 Compare, for instance, the role of children in *Woyzeck*, especially where they appear together with an "idiot" or "fool" (cf. *CCW* 227–28, 197; cf. *HA* 1, 167, 180).

75 *CCW* 30; cf. *HA* 1, 20: "Narren, Kinder und—nun?—Betrunkne sagen die Wahrheit."

76 Compare, above all, what he says in a letter to Karl Gutzkow (see *HA* 2, 449).

77 As mentioned in the introduction, Büchner's French contemporary, Victor Hugo, propounded his revolutionary theory of such a mixture (*mêler . . . le grotesque au sublime*) only a few years before the German started to write. However, I venture to say that solely Büchner, for many decades to come, accomplished that which Hugo postulated, although the latter specified that even the vulgar and trivial sphere must receive due emphasis, for "nothing must be neglected" (*Le vulgaire et le trivial même doit avoir un accent. Rien [!] ne doit être abandonné*). See Victor Hugo, *Hernani. Édition classique avec les Extraits de la Préface de Cromwell*, review and critical notes by Maurice Levaillant (Paris, 1933), pp. 13, 23. Both the famous *Préface de Cromwell* (1827) and the *Préface d'Hernani* are important in this context.

78 Enzensberger, "Bescheidener Vorschlag zum Schutze der Jugend vor den Erzeugnissen der Poesie" (see chapter 3, n. 62), p. 432: "Die Lektüre ist ein anarchischer Akt." Enzensberger's polemic seems to have been prompted by the questionable attacks in the writings of Susan Sontag, particularly in her *Against Interpretation and Other Essays* of 1967, from which he quotes profusely. Of course, I am fully aware of the laws of rhetoric, especially as they apply to polemical style, and I am also willing to grant Enzensberger that most of his points, not just the one I cite approvingly, are well taken. Nevertheless, we must not go from one extreme to the other.

79 See Wittkowski, "Georg Büchner, die Philosophen und der Pietismus," pp. 417–18: "Der Kunst empfahl er [i.e. Schopenhauer]
das ethische Verfahren, mit dessen Hilfe ich z.b. den angeblichen
Atheisten Büchner als einen der religiösesten Dichter ausweisen
konnte."

80 See Anz, pp. 63–64: "Deutungsmöglichkeiten christlicher oder
metaphysischer Tradition werden [bei Büchner] hinfällig, *ohne daß
doch*, wie häufig behauptet, eine nihilistische Position eingenom-
men wird" (my emphasis).

81 For a more detailed discussion, see chapter 1.

82 Compare the following passage from his notes on Spinoza: "*Gott
oder die aus unendlichen Attributen, deren jedes eine ewige und unendliche Wesenheit ausdrückt, bestehende Substanz existirt nothwendiger-
weise. /* I. Beweis. *Wer es läugnet, begreife, wenn es möglich ist, wie Gott
nicht existiren kann. Sein Wesen involvirt alsdann nicht Daseyn, was
widersinnig ist. /* Anmerkung. Dießer Beweis läuft ziemlich auf den
hinaus, daß Gott nicht anders als seyend gedacht werden könne.
Was zwingt uns aber ein Wesen zu denken, was nicht anders als
seyend gedacht werden kann? Wir sind durch die Lehre von dem,
was in sich oder in etwas Anderm ist freilich gezwungen auf etwas
zu kommen, was nicht anders als seyend gedacht werden kann;
was berechtigt uns aber deßwegen aus dießem Wesen das absolut
Vollkommne, Gott, zu machen? / Wenn man auf die Definition von
Gott eingeht, so muß man auch das Daseyn Gottes zugeben. Was
berechtigt uns aber, dieße Definition zu machen?" He then continues: "*Der Verstand? /* Er kennt das Unvollkommne. / *Das Gefühl? /*
Es kennt den Schmerz." Cf. *HA* 2, 236–37; roughly, this might be
rendered as follows: "*God or the substance consisting of infinite attributes, each of which bespeaks an eternal and infinite entity, must needs exist. /* I. Demonstration. *He who denies this may comprehend, if possible,
how God can not exist. For His essence then does not involve existence,
which is absurd. /* Corollary. More or less, this demonstration boils
down to the one according to which God cannot be conceived of
other than as being. But what forces us to conceive of an entity that
cannot be conceived of other than as being? Granted that we are
forced by the doctrine of that which is in itself, or in something
else, to arrive at something which cannot be conceived of other
than as being. But what, on such grounds, entitles us to make of
this entity that which is absolutely perfect, God? / If one agrees to
the definition of God, then one must also admit of God's existence.
But what entitles us to make this definition? / *Reason? /* It knows
what is imperfect. / *Feeling? /* It knows pain."

83 As is well known, these are the last words of John Millington
Synge's moving one-act play, *Riders to the Sea*, a work that is but a
long and mournful dirge, full of pain and without any trace whatsoever of a paean. And yet, oddly enough, these same words evoke
pleasure as well. As I am putting them down, looking back at what I

have said on the preceding pages, I have the distinct feeling that my fragmentary remarks do make up something coherent, consistent, and, perhaps, even plausible—though, to be sure, far from perfect. But this supreme irony is unavoidable.

Index

Except for *Danton's Death*, *The Hessian Messenger*, *Lenz*, *Leonce and Lena*, *Pietro Aretino*, and *Woyzeck*, Büchner's writings are listed under his name.

Adamov, Arthur, 41, 120–121; mentioned, 125
Adorno, Theodor W., 218n.118
Anz, Heinrich, 199, 224n.20, 255n.44
Apollonian, 39. *See also* Nietzsche, Friedrich
Aretino, Pietro, 85, 105, 225nn.27, 30, 32–33. *See also* Pietro Aretino
Ariosto, Lodovico, 84, 225n.27
Aristotle, 29
Arp, Hans, 98
Artaud, Antonin, 39–42, 46–52, 55–56, 75, 77, 120–123, 213n.21, 215n.58, 221n.147, 236n.22; mentioned, 30, 44, 51, 57, 72, 125
Auger-Duvignaud, Jean, 125

Balladic elements in drama, 21, 45–47
Baudelaire, Charles, 191, 255n.51
Beckett, Samuel, 26–27
Behrmann, Alfred, 237n.46
Benn, Gottfried, 24, 124, 178–180, 182, 197–198
Benn, Maurice B., 35–37, 39, 56, 59–60, 126, 177–178, 180, 183, 199, 225n.37, 227n.62, 229nn.76–77, 254n.31, 256n.54; mentioned, 56, 88, 93

Bennett, Benjamin, 127, 142–145, 147, 152, 154; mentioned, 149
Bentley, Eric, 26–27, 50–51
Berg, Alban. *See Wozzeck*
Bible, references to, 82–83, 104–105, 162, 164, 182, 194, 196–197
Bismarck, Otto von, 18
Bloch, Ernst, 37
Blok, Alexander, 63
Bohn, Volker, 241n.25
Börne, Ludwig, 227n.57
Braun, Volker, 27, 65, 75–76, 119
Bräuning-Octavio, Hermann, 84
Brecht, Bertolt, 19–21, 38–47, 50–55, 57–58, 60, 65–70, 76–78, 120–123, 159–160, 207nn.36, 43, 208n.45, 210n.83, 213n.21, 214n.40, 218n.107, 219n.127, 221n.147, 224n.36, 232n.123, 236n.22; mentioned, 47, 61–63, 71, 75, 84, 115, 118, 127, 141
Brecht, Stefan S. (son of Bertolt Brecht), 213n.24
Brown, Norman O., 87, 98–99, 230n.101
Büchner, Alexander (brother), 12
Büchner, Ernst Karl (father), 11

Büchner, Georg
—biographical information: birth, 11;
correspondence, 14, 28, 141 (*see also*
"Fatalism letter"); death, 18; doctorate received, 8; early schooling,
13; fatal illness, 8; in Darmstadt,
3, 11–16; in Gießen, 14–16; in
Strasbourg, 4, 13–15, 17–18; in
Zurich, 8–10, 18; last years of life,
17–18; revolutionary activities,
15–17; studies in philosophy, 8,
16–18, 259 n.82; as university student, 13–14
—writings and lectures: course on
Comparative Anatomy of the Fish
and the Amphibians, 8, 18; course
on Comparative Anatomy of the
Vertebrates, 18; edition, 201; lecture
"On Cranial Nerves," 8; *Lucretia
Borgia* (translation of Hugo's *Lucrèce
Borgia*), 8, 17; *Maria Tudor* (translation of Hugo's *Marie Tudor*), 8, 17;
*Mémoire sur le système nerveux du
barbeau* (*Cyprinus barbus L.*), 8,
17–18; treatise on nervous system
of barbel, 8, 17–18; "Über Schädel-
nerven," 8; Vergleichende Ana-
tomie der Fische und Amphibien,
8, 18; Vergleichende Anatomie der
Wirbelthiere, 18
Büchner, Karl (brother), 13
Büchner, Karoline Louise (née Reuß)
(mother), 11
Büchner, Ludwig (brother), 12, 18,
207 n.38
Büchner, Luise (sister), 12
Büchner, Mathilde (sister), 13
Büchner, Wilhelm (brother), 13
Büchner Prize, 21–22, 123–124
Burroughs, William, 24

Calderón de la Barca, Pedro, 117
Camus, Albert, 36–38, 49, 52–
55, 59–60, 70, 75–76, 216 n.77,
219 n.129, 220 n.134, 254 n.31;
mentioned, 57, 61, 64, 93, 183
Canetti, Elias, 21–22, 26–27
Carlyle, Thomas, 211 n.87
Castañeda, Belén, 211 n.85
Castri, Massimo, 38–40, 213 n.18
Classicism, 46–47
Comedy, 29, 210 n.83
Corneille, Pierre, 46

Crowd scene, 43, 146, 154
Csokor, Franz Theodor, 117

Dadaism, 10, 210 n.85
Danton's Death, 4–5, 14–19, 21, 25,
27, 29, 37–39, 42–45, 47, 50, 61,
79–81, 83, 85–101, 103, 105–111,
130–131, 133–135, 141–167,
171, 173–175, 181–195, 206 n.25,
207 n.43, 225 nn.37–38, 231 n.108,
231 n.112, 232 n.124, 237 n.46,
238 n.67, 243 nn.51–52, 245 n.71,
247 n.99, 253 n.30, 254 n.40,
255 nn.49–50, 256 n.56; mentioned, 12, 36, 62, 84, 118–119,
122–123, 129, 132, 176
Dantons Tod. See Danton's Death
Dessau, Paul, 65
Dionysian. *See* Artaud, Antonin;
Nietzsche, Friedrich; Theater of
cruelty
Documentary theater, 29, 40, 50, 55
Dolfini, Giorgio, 126
Dostoevsky, Fyodor, 22
Dürrenmatt, Friedrich, 210 n.85

Edschmid, Kasimir, 117–118
Eichendorff, Joseph von, 115
Einem, Gottfried von, 21
Emrich, Wilhelm, 25–26, 225 n.37
Engel, Erich, 68, 207 n.43
Engels, Friedrich, 54
Enlightenment, 10–11, 174–175
Enzensberger, Hans Magnus, 118,
124, 134, 198, 222 n.149, 258 n.78;
mentioned, 132
Epic theater, 21, 29, 39, 41, 46, 50, 55,
121–122, 210 n.84. *See also* Brecht,
Bertolt; Theater of alienation
Ernst, Max, 209 n.78
Euripides, 41, 46, 213 n.24
Expressionism, 19, 40, 42–43, 116,
183, 210 n.85

"Fatalism letter," 14, 56, 58, 83, 105,
152, 193–194, 233 n.133, 257 n.63,
258 n.67
Fehervary, Helen, 217 n.105, 220 n.132
Feuerbach, Ludwig, 179
Fichte, Hubert, 221 n.140
Fink, Gonthier-Louis, 101, 109
Franzos, Karl Emil, 116–117, 208 n.46
French classicism, 46–47

Freud, Sigmund, 99
Frisch, Max, 118

Galois, Evariste, 208n.45
García Lorca, Federico, 210n.85
Geerdts, Hans Jürgen, 119–120
Genet, Jean, 75
Georg Büchner Gesellschaft, 115
Georg Büchner Society, 115
Georgi, Konrad, 16
Gesellschaft der Menschenrechte. See
Society for Human Rights
Gilman, Richard, 26–27
Gladkov, Fyodor V., 71
Goethe, Johann Wolfgang, 5, 6, 13,
43, 115, 123, 140–143, 240n.1;
Egmont, 30, 134, 141–166; 168,
171, 173–175, 243n.51, 244n.58,
246nn.89, 91; Faust, 46, 142, 151;
Götz von Berlichingen, 20, 142; Italian
Journey (Italienische Reise), 152;
Poetry and Truth (Dichtung und
Wahrheit), 156; The Sorrows of Young
Werther (Die Leiden des jungen
Werthers), 139–141, 152, 165, 171;
Urfaust, 41, 45; works, Büchner's
familiarity with, 141, 151, 159
Gogol, Nikolai V., 210n.85
Goll, Iwan [Yvan], 56, 210n.85
Görres, Johann Joseph von, 115
Gouhier, Henri, 213n.21, 215n.5,
236n.22
Grab, Walter, 133
Grabbe, Christian Dietrich, 12, 56,
85, 115, 206n.25
Gramsci, Antonio, 37–38, 56, 59–61,
76, 90, 202, 222n.148, 227n.59
Grass, Günter, 124
Grotesque, 29, 258n.77
Grotowski, Jerzy, 38
Gryphius, Andreas, 164, 246n.89
Guevara, Ché, 222n.149
Gutzkow, Karl, 4–5, 11, 17, 116,
210n.85, 258n.76

Hacks, Peter, 65
Hamburger, Michael, 35
Hartwig, Gilbert Frederick, 23
Hašek, Jaroslav, 53
Hauptmann, Gerhart, 27, 116, 210n.83
Hebbel, Friedrich, 12, 115
Heine, Heinrich, 11, 17, 104,
108–109, 227n.57, 251n.123

Herder, Johann Gottfried, 105
Hesiod, 179
Hessian Messenger, The, 9, 15–16, 44,
62, 90, 106, 110, 118, 123, 193,
227n.59
Hessische Landbote, Der. See Hessian
Messenger, The
Hetmann, Frederik, 238n.68
Heym, Georg, 116–117
Hildesheimer, Wolfgang, 27
Hinderer, Walter, 84, 98, 241n.25
Hitler, Adolf, 50, 73–74
Hoffmann, E. T. A., 115
Hofmannsthal, Hugo von, 117
Hölderlin, Friedrich, 63–64, 66, 191,
255n.52
Höllerer, Walter, 98, 227n.62
Horkheimer, Max, 218n.118
Hugo, Victor, 8, 210n.85, 225n.35,
258n.77

Infeld, Leopold, 208n.45
Ionesco, Eugène, 55–56, 76, 122,
221n.146

Jacobs, Margaret, 94
Jaeglé, Wilhelmine (Minna), 14–15,
82, 105, 197, 256n.57
Jansen, Peter, 232n.121
Jarry, Alfred, 56, 210n.85
Jean Paul, 115, 168–173, 175, 178, 180,
182, 248nn.104–105
Jouvet, Louis, 121
Jungdeutsche. See Young Germans

Kafka, Franz, 28, 212n.9
Kalidova, Robert, 230n.101
Keyserling, Hermann, 207n.38
Kirsch, Hans Christian, 238n.68
Kleist, Heinrich von, 41, 43, 45–46
Klotz, Volker, 25, 27, 225n.37
Knight, A. H. J., 35, 126
Koestler, Arthur, 123
Koopmann, Helmut, 227nn.57, 62
Krapp, Helmut, 230n.96
Krause, Egon, 231n.115
Kroetz, Franz Xaver, 210n.83
Kuhl, Johann Conrad, 16
Kunze, Reiner, 75–76
Kuzniar, Alice A., 248n.104

Landau, Paul, 116, 235n.1
Lange, Hartmut, 65

Laughton, Charles, 68
Lehmann, Werner R., 127
Lenin, Vladimir I., 10, 219n.129
Lenz, 5–8, 17, 19, 27, 38, 82, 106,
    139–141, 165–166, 183, 185, 187–
    188, 205n.10, 206n.35, 224nn.20–
    21, 231n.121, 233n.140; mentioned,
    28, 36, 44, 50, 128, 192, 196
Lenz, Jakob Michael Reinhold, 4–5,
    82–83, 231n.121
Leonce and Lena, 17, 19, 21, 27, 29, 43,
    56, 79–80, 83, 90, 95, 101–103,
    106, 108–109, 223n.14, 224n.21,
    225n.37, 227n.61; mentioned, 10,
    36, 44, 82, 86, 121, 142, 193, 196
Leonce und Lena. See *Leonce and Lena*
Lessing, Gotthold Ephraim, 43, 127,
    142–143
Lindenberger, Herbert, 29, 35, 126
Lipmann, Heinz, 255n.42
Ludwig, Otto, 12
Lukács, Georg, 39, 131

Mann, Thomas, 214n.40
Marcuse, Herbert, 99, 230n.101
Marlowe, Christopher, 50, 52
Martens, Wolfgang, 228n.68,
    231n.109, 255n.42
Martyr drama, 164–165, 174
Marx, Karl, 9–10, 38, 41, 75, 99,
    208n.45, 219n.129, 238n.67
Massenszene. See Crowd scene
Mayakovsky, Vladimir V., 63–64,
    217n.105
Mayer, Hans, 61–62, 123, 125–126,
    129, 142
Mayer, Thomas Michael, xii, 127,
    130–131, 133, 202, 235n.165,
    240n.15
Metternich, Klemens von, 12, 18
Minnigerode, Karl, 16
Müller, Heiner, 62–78, 118–120, 122,
    134–135, 164, 218n.107, 219n.129,
    220nn.132, 134, 222n.148, 225n.38
Mundt, Theodor, 233n.130
Musil, Robert, 117

Nagel, Ivan, 133–134
Nakamura, Hideo, 141–142, 240n.16
Napoleon Bonaparte, 12, 174
Naturalism, 19, 30, 40, 77, 116
Neue Sachlichkeit. See New Objec-
    tivity

New Left, 38
New Objectivity, 40, 116
Nietzsche, Friedrich, 37–43, 46, 49,
    52, 58, 60–61, 67–68, 70, 77, 122–
    123, 167–169, 171–172, 174, 180,
    183, 211n.89, 213n.21, 215n.58,
    216n.77, 219n.129, 221n.147,
    227n.57, 230n.88, 248n.105; men-
    tioned, 18–19, 30, 45, 50, 56–57,
    64, 96, 99

Oberlin, Jean-Frédéric, 4–5, 231n.121

Pabst, G. W., 209n.78
Panizza, Oskar, 225n.34
Pascal, Blaise, 202
Peixoto, Fernando, 211n.90
Pietro Aretino, 18, 82–84
Piscator, Erwin, 55
Poe, Edgar Allan, 210n.85
Political theater, 38–39
Poschmann, Henri, 235n.165
Price, Victor, 35

Racine, Jean, 46
Reich, Wilhelm, 99, 230n.101
Reinhardt, Hartmut, 143
Reinhardt, Max, 20, 117, 207n.40,
    245n.71
Richards, David G., 28, 225n.37,
    226n.46
Richter, Johann Paul Friedrich. See
    Jean Paul
Rilke, Rainer Maria, 19–20, 117,
    207nn.36, 37
Rimbaud, Arthur, 98
Rolland, Romain, 202
Romano, Giulio, 84
Romanticism, 5
Rosenthal, Erwin Theodor, 80, 101

Sade, Donatien Alphonse François
    de, 83
Saint-Simonians, 90, 103
Salvatore, Gaston, 84–85, 118,
    256n.57
Saporta, Marc, 24, 208n.61
Sappho, 79, 81, 83, 105
Sauerländer, Johann David, 4, 203n.4
Scarpetta, Guy, 236n.22
Schechner, Richard, 213n.24
Schiller, Friedrich, 5, 43, 45–46, 115,
    123, 142, 163, 165, 209n.63

Schings, Hans-Jürgen, 142
Schmid, Gerhard, 235 n.165
Schmidt, Henry J., xii, 35, 256 n.60,
   257 n.63
Schneider, Peter, 27, 119
Schopenhauer, Arthur, 93–94, 198,
   229 n.78
Schulz, Caroline (wife of Wilhelm), 9
Schulz, Genia, 118, 218 n.107,
   222 n.148
Schulz, Wilhelm, 9–10, 116, 120,
   133, 135, 205 n.12, 206 nn.23, 31,
   236 n.16, 239 n.73
Schwaen, Kurt, 21
Seghers, Anna, 28
Shakespeare, William, 20, 26–27,
   42–43, 45–47, 120, 141, 181,
   214 n.45
Shelley, Percy Bysshe, 52
Sisyphus (myth of). See Camus,
   Albert; Müller, Heiner
Society for Human Rights, 15–16, 44,
   59, 90
Socrates, 46
Socratic. See Brecht, Bertolt;
   Nietzsche, Friedrich; Theater of
   alienation
Solomon, Janis L., 238 n.67
Sontag, Susan, 258 n.78
Sophocles, 22, 47
Spinoza, Baruch, 259 n.82
Stafford, Peter, 225 nn.34–35
Stein, Charlotte von, 164
Steinrück, Albert, 20
Storm and Stress, 5
Strindberg, August, 19, 120, 207 n.38
Sturm und Drang, 5
Surrealism, 40, 56, 210 n.85
Synge, John Millington, 259 n.83

Theater of alienation, 30, 56, 121
Theater of cruelty, 30, 39, 41, 48–50,
   72, 120–122
Theater of history, 72. See also epic
   theater, Theater of alienation
Theater of the absurd, 27, 55–56, 121
Theodor, Erwin. See Rosenthal, Erwin
   Theodor
Thieberger, Richard, 125
Thurn und Taxis-Hohenlohe, Marie
   von, 19

Toller, Ernst, 59–61
Tragedy, 29, 39–40, 46, 164, 210 n.83
Tragicomedy, 27

Ullmann, Bo, 93–95, 97, 100, 125,
   229 n.84

Valle-Inclán, Ramón del, 210 n.85
Vattimo, Gianni, 38
Viëtor, Karl, 125–126
Vilar, Jean, 21
Virmaux, Alain, 121, 213 n.21
Vishnevsky, Vsevolod V., 76
Volksszene. See crowd scene
Vormärz, 90, 133

Wagner, Richard, 12, 40
Walser, Martin, 124
Walser, Robert, 117
Wedekind, Frank, 116, 210 n.83
Weidig, Friedrich Ludwig, 9, 15, 106
Weigel, Helene (wife of Bertolt
   Brecht), 207 n.43
Weiss, Peter, 72, 91, 94, 118, 122–124,
   236 n.30
Wiese, Benno von, 100
Willett, John, 20
Wittkowski, Wolfgang, 142–143, 145,
   154, 224 n.20, 229 n.78, 255 n.44;
   mentioned, 149
Wohlleben, Joachim, 237 n.46
Woyzeck, 18–22, 25–27, 29, 41, 43–
   45, 47–48, 50, 79–80, 85, 95, 100–
   103, 106–108, 111, 121, 128, 173,
   176–197, 201–202, 207 nn.38,
   40, 213 n.27, 225 n.37, 229 n.84,
   230 n.87, 231 nn.120–121, 233 n.130,
   234 n.153, 237 n.45, 257 n.61,
   258 n.74; mentioned, 8, 12, 36, 42,
   62, 82, 86, 118, 120, 168
Wozzeck (opera by Alban Berg), 21,
   117, 208 n.46. See also Woyzeck

Young, Edward, 93
Young Germans, 11, 17, 90–91, 103,
   228 n.68

Zuckmayer, Carl, 115
Zweig, Arnold, 117
Zweig, Stefan, 59

COMPOSED BY G&S TYPESETTERS, AUSTIN, TEXAS
MANUFACTURED BY THOMSON-SHORE, INC., DEXTER, MICHIGAN
TEXT AND DISPLAY LINES ARE SET IN PALATINO

Library of Congress Cataloging in Publication Data
Grimm, Reinhold.
Love, lust, and rebellion.
Includes index.
1. Büchner, Georg, 1813–1837.   2. Authors, German—
19th century—Biography.   I. Title.
PT1828.B6G75   1985   832′.7   84-40497
ISBN 0-299-09860-5